CAPTAIN JACK

CAPTAIN JACK WHITE

★★★

IMPERIALISM, ANARCHISM & THE IRISH CITIZEN ARMY

★★★★

LEO KEOHANE

MERRION PRESS

First published in 2014 by Merrion Press
an imprint of Irish Academic Press
8 Chapel Lane
Sallins
Co. Kildare

© 2014 Leo Keohane

British Library Cataloguing in Publication Data
An entry can be found on request

978-1-908928-92-4 (Paper)
978-1-908928-93-1 (Cloth)
978-1-908928-94-8 (PDF)
978-1-908928-71-9 (EPUB)
978-1-908928-72-6 (MOBI)

Library of Congress Cataloging in Publication Data
An entry can be found on request

All rights reserved. Without limiting the rights under copyright reserved alone, no part of this publication may be reproduced, stored in or introduced into a retrieval system, or transmitted, in any form or by any means (electronic, mechanical, photocopying, recording or otherwise) without the prior written permission of both the copyright owner and the above publisher of this book.

Printed in Ireland by SPRINT-print Ltd

Contents

List of Plates   vi
Acknowledgements   viii

Introduction   1
1. Beginnings   8
2. Training for Imperialism   18
3. Awakenings   34
4. Wanderings and Home   50
5. Unionism and Nationalism   65
6. Dublin: The Cast   80
7. The Search for a Role   94
8. James Connolly   109
9. The Irish Citizen Army   123
10. Adventures in the Army   138
11. Departure and Arrival: The National Volunteers   152
12. Plan for Ireland   167
13. 1916 Arrest and Imprisonment   181
14. War of Independence   197
15. Reality, Theory and Jail   212
16. Spain, War and the End   229

Notes   245
Bibliography   268
Index   275

LIST OF PLATES

1. Jack White as a teenager. (*Family photo*)
2. Lady Amy White, Jack White's mother. (*Family painting*)
3. Field Marshal Sir George White, VC. As the 'Hero of Ladysmith' he was a substantial celebrity figure in these islands in 1900. (*Biography of Sir George by Sir Mortimer Durand*)
4. Whitehall, Cooreen, outside Broughshane, Co. Antrim, the White's rather modest family home. (*Family photo*)
5. Sir George, then Governor of Gibraltar, and the Kaiser on his visit to Gibraltar c. 1903. (*Biography of Sir George by Sir Mortimer Durand*)
6. Sir George picnicking in Gibraltar with his wife and daughters, c. 1904. (*Family photo*)
7. Jack White as a subaltern in the Gordon Highlanders. (*Family photo*)
8. Jack White c. 1930. (*from Jonathan Cape's original autobiography*)
9. Jack White on Irish Citizen Army manoeuvres with Francis Sheehy Skeffington. (*1913*)
10. Women stick training under the auspices of the Irish Citizen Army. On the right is Jack White with Constance Markievicz and possibly his wife Dollie. All surrounded by a group of admirers. (*Family photo*)
11. Jack White supervising the women stick training with again a substantial number of observers and advisers. (*Family photo*)
12. Jack White supervising the women stick training. (*Family photo*)
13. The happy stick fighters with Constance Markievicz on the far left with hat and Dollie, Jack's wife, on the far right also in hat. (*Family photo*)
14. A newspaper image of Jack White with his bandaged head accompanied by Francis Sheehy Skeffington, March 1914. This was after the incident at Butt Bridge.

15. Jack White, left, with Colonel Maurice Moore, right, and the redoubtable Commander McGlinchey (the man who almost precipitated a Civil War single-handedly). (*Irish Independent*)
16. Jack White in his sixties. (*Family photo*)
17. Pat English (neé Napier) on her wedding day. Jack White's niece, she was his most frequent correspondent in the last few years of his life. (*Family photo*)

Acknowledgements

Probably the hardest part of a book to write is the acknowledgments section. How can I thank properly all those who were of assistance in putting this together? An elegant quip, a gracious nod, a suggestion of a shared secret joke and a singling out of someone from the collection of names would be delightful. But the strain of putting it all together, indeed the ability even, can be beyond the best. How can I describe the tit bit of information that had the effect of clarifying months of work? What about the late night conversation that gave encouragement to take up the task once more, or the remark that inspired? And what about the forgetfulness?

I've been blessed with a number of friends that engaged with me, that tolerated me and that most of all showed me aspects of this journey that doesn't just end with the publication of a book. There are others, of course, whom I'm either forgetting to mention, or have not been involved with the book. I list the participants, not in any particular order, but just as they come to mind. Some are very close friends, some old friends and some are friends that I've made since I started this project; all have been involved peripherally or otherwise. All are a testimony to the human spirit that refreshes one when the daily outpourings of political and economic grief and military strife sap the spirit –

There are others very dear to me, but these were the ones directly involved with the book: Aengus Daly, Trish Holmes, Ellen McGaley, Joe Hogan, Madeline O'Neill, Joe Chambers, Mark Phelan and Risteard Crimmins.

There are then those that gave me the opportunity to do this. Who gave me refuge, so to speak, and the freedom to research and examine wherever I willed in a spirit of remarkable openness. Nowhere else could one meet such a group as the Centre for Irish Studies, NUI Galway, Louis De Paor, their director and the core of four, Nessa Cronin, Meabh Ni Fhuarthain, Samantha Williams and Verena Commins. The man who introduced me to all this was of course the inimitable Professor Tadhg Foley who has continued to give support with his famed generosity. I would also like to thank two academics who gave me help beyond measure – John Cunningham and Angus Mitchell.

There is also my good friend and editor and erudite conversationalist Maurice Sweeney.

To those who helped me with my research: it is a remarkable testimony to humankind that there is such helpfulness in the promotion of what I hope is some tiny contribution to history. Katy English, Jack White's grand-niece, is the person who stands out above all. She made available to me a vast haul of family papers ranging from the middle of the nineteenth century up to the time of White's death. Only for her there would be very little insight into his life outside the public writings that are available. The rest of the White family are owed my deep gratitude as well. His two sons, Alan and Derrick, provided me with every assistance at their disposal and it is worth remarking that not once was there a suggestion that I should alter matters that might feature unflatteringly – in fact I can say I was positively encouraged to examine warts and all. The remainder of the White family that I met in Edinburgh demonstrated what in Ireland is termed a decency about them and is almost impossible to translate. To Bernice, Ann, Jennifer, Andrew, Eleanor and the others I am so thankful for their hospitality (and thank you again Bernice for those photographs). I was privileged as well to meet Noreen (née Shanahan) White's relations Patricia Wheeler and her brother and sister Laura and David Webster who provided some fascinating background information. Sadly the occasion of this meeting was Derrick's memorial service. He died in September 2007. I can pay him no greater compliment than to say he was his father's son – ar dheis Dé go raibh an anam.

There were others who provided information, again, in this great spirit of co-operation. Rory Campbell had reminiscences from his grandmother and other relations. Jean Rose, Jonathan Cape's chief archivist, provided a find that was completely unknown. Dr Tony Redmond, G.P. and historian from Broughshane supplied me with an absolute trove of documents and accounts of the White family. Other assistance and kindnesses for which mere acknowledgments are so inadequate came from Morine Krissdotir, John Cowper Powys' biographer.

Finally, to my family, to my wife Anna, a woman with a lot to put up with and to Louise, Aoife, Maeve, Li Kai and David.

Introduction

Jack White was born in the very heart of the greatest socio-economic structure the world has ever known. Blessed both physically and intellectually, he enjoyed every privilege, from education at Winchester, England's oldest public school to access to the highest and mightiest of the British Empire. A man both of wit and charm, brave and bold like a knight of old, with a beautiful wife by his side, he projected a glamour that even still emanates from the dusty old manuscripts and letters of the archives.

But, there were extraordinary contrasts in White's life. He was a decorated soldier embroiled at the start of the revolution that eventually expelled the British from Ireland; at one point his every move was followed and reported like a forerunner of the celebrity cult of today. His writings portray a fascinating intellectual insight into the struggles of his day, and he had a considerable grasp of the subtleties of political philosophy.

For all that I met a very eminent local historian, a great admirer of Jack's father, Field Marshal Sir George White VC, who said to me, 'Frankly, I think he was a bit of an eejit.'

White came to blows, literally in some cases, with every single institution and organisation he was involved with, except the anarchists and some extremely radical movements. Similarly he fought with all the law enforcement bodies and was locked up, at various times, by all four jurisdictions on these islands. He ended his life selling vegetables in his local village of Broughshane to support his family and left an estate of just £80.

Although having a vast number of acquaintances, there appears to be little indication of a close friendship with anyone; he enjoyed a long correspondence with the novelist John Cowper Powys who greatly admired White, but there is no evidence of them actually meeting.

An outsider, with an unbending adherence to an idealism that disqualified him from the cynical pragmatism of politics, he had an inherent scepticism of all authority.

His insights into the strategies of illusion employed to buttress hierarchical structures sadly allowed him little or no tolerance for the opposition and earned him a reputation as a fiery and temperamental foe. Influenced by Tolstoy, his eventual recourse was to a transcendent solution for the woes of humankind but untrammelled by the garb of organised religion.

His life and outlook provides, I would suggest, a distinctive alternative to the conventional narratives of early twentieth-century histories, in particular those relating to the whole island of Ireland.

* * *

When I started researching Jack White, his only generally available writings were his autobiography, *Misfit*, and six political pamphlets. These had been collected by Kevin Doyle, the anarchist writer from Cork, and were available online. Phil Meiler of Livewire Publications published a new edition of *Misfit* in 2005 and included most of these pamphlets. Doyle had literally kept White's memory alive for a number of years and he wrote a brief but accurate biography of White, and this is also available online (he also wrote a play on the tragic loss of White's papers). Andrew Boyd wrote a more detailed pamphlet on White's life, which was published in 2001. Apart from Boyd and Doyle I could find little comment on White's actions and no analysis of his thinking.

It is regrettable that White's personal papers are missing. It was generally believed that his family had destroyed the manuscript of a second volume of *Misfit* and other papers after his death. This arose from an account by Randall McDonnell that Noreen Shanahan, Jack White's second wife, decided the manuscript of *Misfit II* was 'too outrageous and defamatory ever to be published and consigned it to the flames'.[1] Not alone have I not found any evidence to support this, I am confident that this has no foundation. In conversation with the family and from the correspondence I have seen, I would surmise that it is quite probable that the papers are mouldering in some solicitor's redundant files.

Since I began my research I made a considerable discovery of documents, including what I have termed the Katy English papers (KE). These include a large tranche of correspondence White had with his niece in the last six years of his life (about 300 pages). Katy English is the daughter of White's correspondent, Pat English, *née* Napier, whose mother Lady Gladys Napier was one of White's sisters. Katy English has very kindly allowed me full access to these papers. These include family records, in particular by Rose, White's older sister, who wrote a history of the White family with great detail on the exploits of her father, Field Marshall Sir George White VC.

Family reminiscences included conversations with White's two sons, Alan and the late Derrick (who sadly died in 2007 RIP), their wives, and children, and Noreen's (White's second wife) nieces and nephew. Rory Campbell supplied reminiscences from his grandparents who knew White socially.

White's story is representative of something outside, and even opposed to, the dominant narrative of Irish history in the early twentieth century. It is nonetheless a valid one which questions robustly the conventional account of a straightforward struggle between indigenous and coloniser. Here was a man who agonised about divided loyalties and courted no popularity in an adherence to a rare integrity. His particular claim to significance can be justified on two bases: firstly, his involvement in the Irish Citizen Army, which included a considerable amount of contact with James Connolly, probably the most important political thinker in Ireland in the early twentieth century. Secondly, White's professed anarchism marks him out as one of the few figures of that period in Ireland associated with that system of beliefs. Although it would be at least twenty years after the revolutionary events in which he was involved that White used the word 'anarchism' at all, I believe that at that late stage he saw it as an explanation of his earlier outlook. Additionally, I would contend that he was far from being an outsider in his thinking at that time; that at least some of the ideas he adopted in 1913 onwards were shared by others, not least Connolly. Consequently, a study of the writings of anarchists like Proudhon, Bakunin and Kropotkin was called for along with subsidiary analysts and commentators like Georges Sorel. Although E.P. Thompson's 'enormous condescension of hindsight' is always a danger, it was also necessary to assess how the position of those people are viewed today, particularly by those of a poststructuralist leaning, that is, thinkers like Todd May and Saul Newman. Todd May in his seminal work on anarchism – *The Political Philosophy of Poststructuralist Anarchism* – argues that the robust scepticism against received wisdom that primarily defines poststructuralism is equivalent to modern anarchist theory and terms it postanarchism. Current commentators on Irish counter-hegemonic theory, David Lloyd and Heather Laird, in particular, proved relevant to the analysis. Finally, wherever power is discussed and the nature of its multiple manifestations reviewed, Michel Foucault's writings cannot be ignored.

Anarchism

An important part of Jack White's claim for remembrance today is that he is regarded as one of the few self-proclaimed anarchists in Ireland. Unfortunately, anarchism has connotations of violence and bloodshed and, even in the most august of journals, is often used interchangeably with chaos. When it does get a sympathetic hearing, the idea that it supports the general abandonment of governance leads to dismay; how can sophisticated structures like the economy, or institutions like education or medicine, be organised without some central authority? Recently lack of regulation has been blamed on the destruction wrought on the world's finances.

Accepting a general resistance to a concept that appears initially to be totally at odds with common sense, this account is not an attempt to persuade the reader to adopt at least some of the tenets of anarchism. Rather, during the course of White's life, it is hoped to demonstrate that there was at least a justification to some of the positions he adopted, and it may surprise to note that these had their roots in anarchist thinking.

Colin Ward, in his book *Anarchy in Action*,[2] attempts to show that quite an amount of anarchistic beliefs are tacitly accepted, and although not appearing to be obviously logical, possess, at least, a resonance of truth. One of his favourite examples is the industrial strike. Nowadays, the more conventional strike by trade unions is not to withhold their members' labour, but instead 'work to rule'. In other words, what they are actually stating is that they are now going to put into practise every one of the regulations laid down by the authorities which were initially drawn up to ensure the smooth running of the operation. Instead, everyone accepts that chaos will ensue.

It is far too complex a topic to address fully in a book of this type. Apart from possibly antagonising the reader, the very nature of the concept does not readily acquiesce with a succinct summary. In fact the various strands can even appear to be opposed politically, and quite often charges of subjectivity can be justly levelled at its various exponents. I actually believe there is a nebulous aspect to it that is absolutely necessary, as there appear to be premises that are not susceptible to conventional intellectual analysis.

But, before this is dismissed as nonsense, I would remind the reader of the cutting edge of science today, the world of quantum physics which Arthur Koestler described as 'Alice in Wonderland'. Here phenomena like the ghostly quark occurs or other extraordinary entities whose behaviour alter as they are being observed. The fabled 'man in the street', with his concept of 'science', would be aghast at this nonsense.

Lao Tse, the ancient Chinese sage, purportedly wrote a book, called the *Tao De Ching*, which is seen as personifying anarchism. This basically consists of a collection of seemingly illogical aphorisms, including statements like 'The sharper the spears the more restive the people'. Although appearing to be irrational and directly opposed to modern state legislation (in effect, it is saying, the more regulation, the less submission) it resonates with a truth beyond logic.

One of the principal thinkers in classical anarchism, Peter Kropotkin, a Russian aristocrat and scientist, argued that it was a fallacy that humankind needed strict control. In his book on evolution, *Mutual Aid (1902)*, he maintained that an innate co-operation existed in all species and that this, more than the notion of 'survival of the fittest', was the primary dynamic of evolution. Oscar Wilde, no supporter of the status quo, was an enthusiastic fan and remarked that he 'wrote like an angel'.

Peter Kropotkin's entry on anarchism in the *Encyclopedia Britannica* begins by describing it as:

> a principle or theory of life and conduct under which society is conceived without government – harmony in such a society being obtained, not by submission to law, or by obedience to any authority, but by free agreements concluded between the various groups, territorial and professional.[3]

The antithesis, that is, a government with an emphasis on law and an authority to enforce it, is questioned by anarchists. In examining Jack White's outlook and actions this book will confine the criteria for a support for anarchism to the two basic tenets arising from the above: one, a considerable caution against the focusing of power because of its fostering of a central authoritarianism; and, two, a scepticism about what post-structuralist theory terms the meta-narrative.

The former, a caveat about power, acknowledges Lord Acton's dictum regarding its corrupting effect, and its role in encouraging excessive regulation and interference by the state (power tends to corrupt, absolute power tends to corrupt absolutely). This can result in oppressive government mechanisms of control leading to political structures ranging from the irritating ineffectiveness of a 'nanny' state to the horrors of a totalitarian regime.

The second tenet is specifically concerned with questioning generally accepted 'truths' that serve oppression of one type or another. Saul Newman defines anarchism as 'fundamentally an *unmasking* of power'.[4] This is similar to Lyotard's definition of post-structuralism as an 'incredulity directed against all grand narratives' and arises from the belief that these are the constructs, or Foucauldian 'discursive formations', that allow, among other manifestations of power, the various dominant parties to buttress their position in a state, institution, or other collective of some sort.

In other words, received wisdom – '-isms' like nationalism, communism, or even Catholicism, as well as general beliefs purveyed as icons of truth – are all to be interrogated. A classic example is the phrase 'Health and Safety'. Two inarguably acceptable conditions but in this phrase they are often employed to enforce what at times are the most asinine of regulations. Anarchists see them as seducing and misleading humankind to acquiesce in inequities and oppression. They are the ingredients of Gramsci's concept of hegemony; they can be the delusions encouraged, or allowed to persist, that lead to the outrages of history.

Jack White displayed an inherent disposition that corresponded with this kind of mindset. His instincts were those of an anarchist and his actions and judgments were consistent with those ideas long before he identified himself as such. At an early age he adopted Tolstoyan beliefs, and, although he committed many apostasies during his lifetime, he remained basically a man who lived by spiritual principles, as he saw them, to the end. It should also be noted that Tolstoy was himself an anarchist in all but name; such was the reputation of nonsensical bloodshed associated with *fin-de-siècle* anarchism that even eminent figures such as he were reluctant to be associated with their principles.

From the very beginning of his life, White related incidents of rejecting any form of authority whether it was received wisdom, tradition, or some edict handed down by his elders. This rebelliousness indicated something more than just incorrigibility; there was a consistency and a rationale to his continual questioning. The aptness of the title *Misfit* for his autobiography (1930) did not arise from this radicalism alone; it also indicated a consciousness of, and maybe a sensitivity to, his own perceived rejection by society. He began with a stance that precociously suggests the postmodern:

> I have undertaken to write this book in 'a perfectly straightforward manner'. I take this to mean to suit the taste of people who believe that the past governs the future but *fail to see that the future, much more drastically, governs the past.*[5]

Having declared his willingness to conform, he goes on to blithely ignore this stricture for the remainder of the work. The book is permeated with a bravado that might indicate a traumatic hurt that most adults either come to terms with or develop into a kind of tiresome braggadocio. White was too aware to indulge in the latter and yet reveals an immaturity that bedevilled his relationships, whether with his two wives or the many acquaintances that never seemed to develop into full-blown friendships. For all that, he was a man who stuck to his ideals; not grimly as the cliché would have it, but with a lightness of touch and indeed a humour that very often tempered the radical edges of the policies he pursued. In different circumstances with different opportunities he may have made a far greater mark. Certainly much lesser men than White have occupied much higher echelons in history's chronicles.

Chapter 1

Beginnings

An Act of Defiance

Doornkop ('Thorn Hill'), today a suburb of Soweto, was on 28 May 1900 the scene of what became known as the Battle of Johannesburg during the Second South African War, the Boer War. It was one of a series of ridges held by the Boers, and the British generals decided that it should be taken, not by cavalry but by the 'grunts', the original cannon fodder, officially known as the infantry. Fourteen rows of these unfortunates, spread across four miles, steadily made their way up the hill under a withering hail of bullets from the Boers. Comparisons have been made with Balaclava and the set-piece battles of that time.

Among the seven battalions were the Gordon Highlanders, and in the midst of these was a young subaltern, James Robert (Jack) White. Although fresh out of Sandhurst, White could clearly see that the Boer had a ready escape route behind the row of ridges they occupied, and while they had targets sufficiently far away to allow escape, they continued to fire. Eighteen of the Highlanders were killed and anything up to 100 wounded – there were at most about 600 of the enemy. Jack and his platoon were in the tenth row, and by the time they got to the top, most of the Boers had cleared off. Having been under fire, possibly for the first time in his career, he still managed with two of his men to be about fifty yards ahead of his line.

As he reached the dugouts that had been occupied by the Boer he spotted a rifle protruding from behind a rock and, quickly grabbing it, apprehended a very frightened youth. As the rest of his men caught up they were all for bayoneting this obviously shell-shocked fifteen-year-old; they believed he had been directly responsible for the death of a number of their comrades. The commanding officer arrived on horseback and immediately ordered him to be shot. White, as he said himself, was overcome with a 'wave of disgust' that 'swamped his discipline'. He turned, pointing his carbine at the officer, and said, 'If you shoot him, I'll shoot you.'

If proper procedure had been carried out at that time for this extraordinary act of defiance, Jack White would have been summarily executed. But a combination of good fortune, his forceful personality, and the fact that his father was a field marshal in the same war must have saved him; there is no account of even a reprimand. It does, however, give some insight into the kind of man Jack White was – a consistent supporter of the disadvantaged regardless of the unpopularity or danger to himself.

Origins

The grave of Jack White is to be found in the village of Broughshane, just outside Ballymena. He lies within a few miles of the foot of Slemish, a corruption of Sliabh Mis, the legendary Irish mountain, on whose slopes St Patrick tended sheep and swine. That his final resting place is there is one of those synchronicities of history that hints at grander schemes.

Although only just over 1,400ft and described unflatteringly by geologists as a volcanic plug, it dominates the landscape for miles around. Looking a little like the remnants of a volcano, its steep barren upper reaches contrast dramatically with the well-husbanded farmlands surrounding it. It is a suitable backdrop to finding God, as the founder of Christianity in this island did more than 1,500 years ago. Modern historians do not connect St Patrick with this place; the nearest acknowledgment is that the territory of Miliucc, the petty king who enslaved Patrick, extended to its slopes.

Mythology, however, does not defer to the discipline of history and has a young man escaping bondage from there and subsequently introducing an island to the 'one true faith'. Or maybe in more mundane terms, delivering Ireland, as it was later called, from the unconscious of prehistory to the modern world. Christianity either coincided with, or was the principal facilitator of, the introduction of writing to the island; the only evidence of the island's existence up to then, in the outlook of Graeco-Roman consciousness, lay in the glancing references of commentators like Strabo.

Lack of writing is not evidence of primitiveness (in fact a case could be made that this was a conscious abnegation), rather it is an indication of a culture and outlook that contrasted quite substantially with the familiar Euro-centric approach that has established itself over the past couple of millennia. It is fitting, however, that Jack White should be associated with this iconic, and seminal, figure of mythology on the Irish landscape. He was also a representative of alternative perspectives, as Patrick would have been albeit substantially different. He was a sceptic of the status quo who displayed through his actions and writings an empathy with the outsiders and the disadvantaged. This led along the way to charges of incorrigibility and even downright perversity. On the other hand, his conclusion, towards the end of his life, that he was an anarchist corresponds with a philosophy that would not have been out of place with these earlier, pre-Christian communities.

James Robert (Jack) White was born at Cleveland, Montague Place, Richmond, Surrey, England, on 22 May 1879, the only son of Field Marshal Sir George Stuart White (1835–1912) and his wife, Amelia Maria (Amy), née Baly (d. 1935).[1] He had four sisters, Rose, who was older than he, May Constance, Amy Gladys, and Georgina Mary.[2] Although the family's permanent residence was at Whitehall, Broughshane, Co. Antrim, Ireland, Sir George (or, as he was then, Major White), was campaigning in India at the time of Jack's birth. The later-to-become Lady Amy stayed with her parents for the confinement, and Jack White seems to have been quite influenced by his grandfather, an archdeacon, in those early years. George and Amy had actually met in India when he was first stationed there, and they were married in Simla in 1874.

Joseph Baly, Amy's father, held an MA from Oxford and had spent a considerable time in India in education before temporarily going back to England as Rector of Falmouth. In 1872 he was appointed Archdeacon of Calcutta. The position was essentially a sinecure, but Baly earned a reputation for social work; he was particularly concerned about the plight of Eurasians. He was a popular figure, being described as an extraordinary speaker in the pulpit, 'and in the dance hall he was an angel amongst mortals'.[3] He finally returned to England in 1883, having been appointed 'chaplain of the Royal Chapel in Windsor Park', retaining his post until his death in 1909 at the age of 85.[4]

Practically the only surviving records for that period concerning White are the reminiscences included in his autobiography. His elder sister, Rose, makes only one glancing reference to him when she mentions that she and Jack were read stories by Sir George from *Treasure Island, Little Lord Fauntleroy, Alice in Wonderland,* and *The Little Red Deer.*[5]

Rose compiled a memoir around 1914 as a kind of family history and this provides invaluable detail on Jack White's antecedents. The White family, according to their own lore, were originally of English Presbyterian stock, not planters in the strictest sense of the term, but refugees from the English Civil War:

> The Family of White is of English extraction, and from the County of York, in the West Riding of which they held considerable property in the reign of Charles the First.
>
> Hudson Hall was the name of their residence there, during the Civil War of that distracted period they espoused the Royal cause, and in the King's behalf raised and maintained a troop of Dragoons at their own expense, involved in their Masters ruin one individual sought refuge in Ireland, settled in the town of Antrim, and maintained himself and family by teaching a classical school, being a Clergyman of the Presbyterian Church he some time after he was chosen by the Broughshane Congregation of the same persuasion, and near that his descendants still live where he spent his last days. His remains were among the first interred in the Burying Ground at present surrounding the Meeting House at Broughshane. The above mentioned person who spelt his name Whyte was christened Fulke and left two sons, James and Timothy, both preachers.[6]

That was the year 1716 and this testimony, complete with idiosyncratic syntax, was written in 1829 by Miss Victoria White, great-aunt of Rose and Jack White. Rose goes on to relate that the same Fulke, despite being a Royalist, welcomed William of Orange 'on his landing at Carrickfergus'. She explains this apparent change in loyalties by noting that the Pope himself had congratulated William after the Battle of the Boyne, adding that 'I think it would be a fearful shock to most of the Orangemen of today to hear that.'[7] It could also indicate an ancestor demonstrating the unconventional behaviour that was to be Jack White's trademark.

Rose's elegantly written account of various antecedents does have its share of characters displaying an eccentricity and often obduracy against complying with conventional mores. In passing it has to be noted that Sir Mortimer Durand helped himself to extensive passages reproduced verbatim in his authorised biography of Sir George with only the barest acknowledgment of Rose.[8] At one stage she summarises her own perception of the family dispositions:

> One of the oldest inhabitants of Broughshane says that 'the old Whites' (referring principally to my great-grandfather and his children) were 'quare people' but the word queer has a double sense in Ireland and implies quite as much admiration as criticism. To judge my forbears by what I have heard about them and from the characteristics of their descendants I should say they had very marked individuality and idiosyncrasies without any wild eccentricity, great dash and fearlessness combined, in some cases, with considerable indecision, especially in the smallest details of life and almost hypersensitiveness in social relations.[9]

Written around 1913, after Sir George's death and prior to the publication of Durand's biography, these observations could have been applied directly to Jack White himself, and although hypersensitivity is not commonly associated with White, it might explain some of the rash actions he took. Even a detached account like Arthur Mitchell's from the *Oxford Dictionary of National Biography* comments on White's temperament; writing about his precipitate departure from the Irish Volunteers, Mitchell notes, 'characteristically, his involvement was short-lived and ended in his acrimonious departure'.[10] There are numerous accounts of White's disruptive behaviour in relationships, political or otherwise, and the reasons for this may lie in the family tendency to sensitivity rather than the more common attribution of perversity on his part. White acknowledges what he frankly calls his own 'immaturity' at various points of his autobiography. In one of his later letters in 1945 to his niece, he mentions that he went to a play with his second wife Noreen (*née* Shanahan) and admits to an inordinate timidity:

> Noreen and I, of course meet, as far as we do meet, on the artistic plane and largely for her sake, I forced myself to conquer the frightful inferiority complex, the sense of being a loathsome worm on which the kindest thing is the stamp [of] the heel.[11]

Certainly, his grandfather displayed remarkable extremes of diffidence and rashness. For example, on one occasion, having taken umbrage at the attitude of the judge, he precipitately ended his career as a barrister:

> [H]e was called to the bar and was always referred to, about Whitehall, as 'The Councillor' but he certainly did not do much to earn this title.

One story is that he once pleaded in Court and was so much upset by being told by the judge to speak up that he never repeated the attempt. But another story, as told us by the son of the solicitor who sent him his first brief and who thought he had the makings of a brilliant barrister. The brief was returned by my grandfather who said he could not possibly take the responsibility of it. Yet this man when very old and after several periods of feebleness each of which had been supposed to be the beginning of the end, could terrify both his sons by the reckless speed at which he drove a car over a wild mountain road at night in torrents of rain and a heavy thunderstorm. They dared not interfere until at last he suggested himself that it would be well for them to keep a look out as he could neither see nor hear.[12]

Sir George White

Jack's father, Sir George, was a remarkable man who achieved the highest level of success in his chosen profession. There was little to distinguish him from other Antrim landowning stock as he languished in various minor military posts from Cork to India. Then, when well into middle age, in an act of madness by any normal standards, he charged up a hill in Afghanistan to attack, single-handedly, a group of Pathan 'rebels' and was awarded a Victoria Cross. From there he ended up as a personal favourite of the Queen, and family lore has it that near the end of his life he refused an earldom.

Regardless of his tardiness in joining the ranks of the careerists, there appears no evidence of a willingness to step unthinkingly on others. In fact he seems to have earned a title, most rare among the ambitious, that of a perfect gentleman. Among the more unusual of elegies to him is a letter written long after his death by archive staff employed by his daughter Gladys, who by this stage had become Lady Napier. By the time they had sorted his papers they had come to form an attachment to him that they had not experienced with any other individuals whose papers they had handled before. Allowing even for a certain deference to Lady Gladys (a formidable woman) in this letter, it is still a remarkable tribute to a long dead man. They wrote:

> He must have been an exceptionally charming person to have left such an impression behind him. One always gets interested in the people whose papers one's working on, but one doesn't necessarily like them in the way we came to like Sir George.[13]

The goodwill he generated was not due to a charming manner alone; he, with his brother John, were noted for treating their tenants in a most considerate manner. They had to actively persuade these people to buy out their farms when the Land Acts provided for this; the tenants felt they were so well treated that they did not want to take over their own holdings. Earlier still, in 1881, the *Belfast Morning Telegraph* reported:

> Major White, who lately so gallantly distinguished himself in Roberts' famous march on Candahar, has made a generous abatement in rents to his tenants on his Cushleak estate here – giving 25, 20 and 15 per cent reduction respectively [...] Last year his brother Mr John White, of London, gave his tenants here 33 per cent reduction. The White family have certainly shown themselves sympathetic and generous to their tenantry in these depressed times.[14]

This article was filed under a column called 'Land Agitation', and directly underneath it was a report of evictions in County Armagh, indicating that the Whites' actions were far from conventional practice.

Sir George was not free of the social inhibition seemingly typical of the Whites. Rose recounts an incident where he excused himself 'for leaving a party early on the grounds that he could not bear to keep his wife waiting up for him and quite making his hearers believe he was married though only eighteen'.[15] For all his seeming urbanity, he had considerable problems with socialising, which became more and more a requirement as he rose through the military ranks. Rose again treats of the mannerisms of Sir George and his brother John:

> The Whites have an unsociable side to them which is rather hard to explain as they are sympathetic and interested in their fellows. Everyone who met my father and uncle socially seemed to find a peculiar charm in them and they took pains too to make themselves agreeable, but my uncle would hardly ever spend a night under anyone else's roof (including ours) and Father always had a dread of 'other people's homes' especially in anticipation. When the ordeal was over he would often realise, quite as if it were a pleasant surprise that he had been markedly well received and 'got on alright' but, never, even at times when he was being very much lionized did it seem to dawn upon him that his presence would be missed if he sent his womenfolk alone to any social function.

Father liked to meet interesting or lively people (more especially in his own house), but it bored him to have to conform to other people's habits of life or to go in for any social round and my uncle simply would not face it. Yet, when they were in society neither of them ever showed that he was bored. My uncle was especially impatient of what he called 'a platitudinous dog' but while talking to such a person would be almost extravagantly courteous.[16]

Again this analysis may throw light on some of Jack White's behaviour. Referring, for example to D.H. Lawrence's accounts of him, including, most famously, White punching the author in what appears to be a thuggish act, the fact that he was ill at ease and under stress might provide mitigating circumstances.[17]

Unlike his son, George White pursued a lifetime career in the army. He was appointed an ensign when aged eighteen in 1853 in the 27 Foot and, although quite ambitious, took five years to become a lieutenant, another five to reach captain, and was 38 before he became a major. Instead of being posted to 'a real war in the Crimea', he found himself in India which he detested, at first telling his sister that if he 'had known what sort of a place it was I should have left the army and taken to breaking stones in Ireland'.[18] Things changed, however, and he did see action in the Indian Mutiny of 1857–59 in which he won a medal, but it was not until the Afghan War (1879–80) that his much-desired career took off when he had attained the mature age of forty-four. The citation for the award of his Victoria Cross runs as follows:

> George Stuart White, Major (now Brevet Lieutenant-Colonel), 92nd Regiment (Gordon Highlanders). Date of Act of Bravery: 6th October, 1879. For conspicuous bravery during the engagement at Charasia on the 6th October, 1879, when, finding that the artillery and rifle fire failed to dislodge the enemy from a fortified hill which it was necessary to capture, Major White led an attack on it in person. Advancing with two companies of his regiment, and climbing from one steep ledge to another, he came upon a body of the enemy strongly posted and outnumbering his force by about eight to one. His men being much exhausted and immediate action being necessary, Major White took a rifle and, going on by himself, shot the leader of the enemy. This act so intimidated the rest that they

> fled round the side of the hill and the position was won. Again on the 1st September, 1880, at the Battle of Kandahar, Major White, in leading the final charge under heavy fire from the enemy, who held a strong position supported by two guns, rode straight up to within a few yards of them, and seeing the guns, dashed forward and secured one of them, immediately after which the enemy retired.[19]

It is clear that White displayed a total disregard for the conventional instincts of self-preservation on 6 October 1879. Of course this is a primary requirement for such an award, but, as the citation makes clear, he acted in this fashion on more than one occasion. This lead some to mistakenly believe he had won a double VC; family documents maintain he was recommended on both occasions and 'his VC bears the two dates'.[20] At the age of 44, and with a newly-born son, White displayed a character that could appear enigmatic, at least to a modern sensibility. There are numerous other examples, but these occasions are the most dramatic indications of dedication to a cause that would have to be called selfless.

What *The Times* called 'his readiness for any service' manifested itself in accepting an offer of duty, 'when at home in command of his own regiment in Edinburgh (a very pleasant duty)', in Egypt where 'the post assigned to him was less important than he deserved, and afforded little opportunity for military distinction'.[21] A family record of his subsequent career provides details:

> In October 1885 he was given a Brigade in Burma and six months later, in March 1886, he was given command of the field force in Burma with the local rank of Major General and remained in this command till 1888, when the subjugation of Upper Burma was complete […] From 1893 to 1898 he was the Commander in Chief in India after which he was appointed Quarter Master General in the War Office. At the outbreak of the South African War in 1899, he was appointed to command the Natal Field Force and defended Ladysmith in the famous siege.[22]

For more than twenty years, despite his ambitions, his career had been undistinguished – a rank of major when his compatriot Frederick Roberts (Bobs), just three years older, was already a major general – but from the moment he charged up the hill of Takht-i-shah, his path to eminence took a similar trajectory.

Although earning the soubriquet 'Hero of Ladysmith' could be described as the apogee of his fame – he was probably the most famous man in the United Kingdom in 1900[23] – he continued to earn further plaudits and became a field marshal in 1903. When he died in London in 1912 his body was brought for burial to Fulke Whyte's plot in Broughshane and his funeral was described as one of the biggest ever in the north of Ireland. Crowds met the ferry at Larne and accompanied it to the graveside; the town of Ballymena, en route, was completely shut down for a number of hours.[24]

Sir George, despite being known as the 'Hero of Ladysmith', had been the subject of questions about the wisdom of his actions in the Boer campaign. Even his obituary in *The Times* mentioned that 'he had never commanded an army in the field against forces armed with modern weapons' and acknowledged that 'criticisms ha[d] been directed at him' during the siege.[25] However, his popularity overrode any such misgivings and on his return to England, Durand said, 'it would serve no purpose to describe the various complimentary ceremonials' that Sir George received except 'a great dinner given in his honour by the Ulster Association in London' where he was congratulated 'upon the way in which he had acted upon the motto of Ulster, "No surrender"'.[26] Queen Victoria commissioned a portrait of him by Philip De László, and it still forms part of the royal family painting collection today.[27]

On 11 July 1900 Sir George White 'was sworn in as Governor and Commander-in-Chief of the City and Garrison' of Gibraltar.[28] This strategic promontory had been occupied continuously by the British since 1713. It was a staging post for anyone travelling by sea to the Mediterranean, and since the completion of the Suez Canal all shipping bound for the Far East passed through its waters as well. France and Germany during this time were competing for influence in Morocco and a considerable amount of diplomatic activity took place prior to the Algeciras agreement in 1906 shortly after Sir George retired in 1905. The British Empire made its presence felt with flotillas of naval ships steaming around the area in various maritime exercises. The governor's visitors' book is replete with a list of the 'great and good' as well as those of a more commercial disposition; the fact that it features both King Edward and the Kaiser (twice) indicates the importance of the posting.[29] Jack White joined his father there in 1902 as an aide-de-camp and it is probably the only occasion that the two were together for any extended period. It was there also that Jack saw at first hand the real face of imperialism, that is, those operators, those 'movers and shakers' whose creed was the garnering of the resources of the world towards primarily themselves.

Chapter 2

Training for Imperialism

Childhood and Education

White's first reminiscence consists of what he calls his 'consecutive memories' at the age of seven when he was told either that no one could stand on a three-legged stool or that he specifically was not allowed to do so. Having done so, and having fallen and cut his head, he still persisted in maintaining that authority was wrong. The floor was uneven; if it had not been so, he would have been unhurt – therefore he was correct in his refusal to accept the edict handed down to him.[1] In the early schools he attended he recalls the constant corporal punishment, and although the amount of beatings he took would not have been exceptional in those days, there does seem to have been a rebelliousness in him that made him stand out from the other children.

At the same time, his autobiography demonstrates a remarkable good-naturedness about his recollections of travails, a readiness to accept that people found themselves at the mercy of forces over which they had no control, whether these were external pressures and conditioning, or internal in the sense that it was their nature to behave so. This attitude is one that persisted right through his life, showing itself overall as a lack of bitterness about various injustices that he suffered, coupled with a deep appreciation of kindnesses that were shown him. Of course, this could have been with the hindsight of many years – he was 50 when he wrote *Misfit*; on the other hand, there are numerous occasions when he attempted to concentrate on what he imagined to be the good side in some recalcitrant opponent. More interestingly, he demonstrated sensitivity to the suffering of others from a young age. He recalls, for example:

> periodical killing of pigs in the farmyard that adjoined the school. Pig-killing day was a red letter day to the other boys and myself, but in different ways. They loved it and I dreaded it, I used to shut myself up in the class room and close the shutters to shut out the pigs' screams.[2]

He describes, with affection, his first schoolmaster, Dr Williams of Summerfield. Although having 'flogged enough Latin and Greek' into him, White still demonstrated an appreciation of what was done for him despite the various grades of punishments he received, ranging from slaps on the hand to more serious lashings. All administered in a courteous way, as he would have it.

He believed he had a dual relationship with another headmaster, Dr Fearon, the 'Bear', at Winchester; one was of two equals discussing the vagaries of school, the other was of master and pupil that involved a chronic history of transgression and punishment. White's account of the conversations he had with the 'Bear' is amusing; he suggested that he negotiated his expulsion from the school. At first, this was to avoid expulsion and, then, when he deemed himself tired of the whole system, to actively encourage it. White's rendering of the bewilderment of the teacher and his subsequent resignation to behaving in a manner contrary to his kindly disposition by expelling the boy is a masterly piece of writing in its overturning of conventional expectations.

White's accounts of his battles with the housemaster Smith, 'The Prowler', are evidence, if there is much substance in them, of a very high-spirited youth, including stories of attempts at setting off explosions and taking unauthorised trips to town to sample everything from drink to the local girls. However, the most illuminating story details his succumbing to ennui while fielding on the cricket pitch:

> It seemed to me I had been there since the world began, and the sun sinking towards the horizon was about to terminate a cycle of creation without incident or meaning. Something must enliven, or, if need be disrupt, this aeonic monotony. The cycle must not close carrying my ego with it to unbroken nothingness. I began to

make water for height, not, I think, with any intention of outrage of display, but anaesthetized from the mass-consciousness by my own boredom, and wishing to revive in myself the atrophying faculty of interest in something. I was soon observed, there was a roar of delighted amusement from twenty-two boys; [...] I was flogged of course. I was always being flogged.[3]

This anecdote elevates a conventional account of schooldays to something more significant. Along with the consistent rebelliousness, there was a conviction that he did not really fit in and was in any case disliked by the majority. He appeared to require a continual stimulation and this was often provided by getting into trouble for reasons that puzzled him as much as others. He continues about his punishment:

Thus it has always been, I possess the capacity of being bored to desperation, which moves me to break the mechanical routine under which others silently suffer. They rejoice for a moment at a glimpse of vicarious revolt, then round on the rebel.[4]

Singled out for general derision, he is sore and surprised to be once again unsupported by his schoolmates. It is as if his display was a desperate foray to achieve popularity and this, briefly attained when they roar with laughter, is again denied him when they realise what he has done.

He puzzles over this, not his seeking of the popular vote, which he probably could not admit to himself, but the fact that even to himself he is incorrigible and incomprehensible. He talks about reaching a 'desperation point where I knew I was no longer responsible for my actions' and quotes a previous teacher who said, 'White, you are in for more trouble than any boy in the school, but you are not the worst boy in the school. For whatever you do you are always found out.'[5] Then White goes on to consider if he might have wanted to be found out and finally surrenders by saying, 'I wanted to preserve something, though I don't know what', and there is no explanation, thirty-five years later, of what that might be.[6]

There were further adventures, including an abortive attempt to blow up one of the teachers and another story of having returned to the school dressed up as a prospective guardian. While probably daring escapades judged by any criteria, they are such that a large number of schoolboys could admit to having been involved in without any great sense of achievement; it does, however, indicate high spirits which in view of some episodes from his adult life are not surprising.

In recounting his struggles with various authorities and his almost automatic rejection of anything that was presented to him as received wisdom, White never mentions his parents except when he is finally requested to leave Winchester. Earlier in the text he writes about his doting grandmother, Archdeacon Baly's wife, and the good priest himself, as a man who had no idea about children, but beyond that he seems to have perceived his life as a solitary, almost orphan-like one. His son Derrick has commented when he first read the autobiography (late in life) that he was taken aback by the seeming self-centredness of the man, but this could also be seen as self sufficiency.[7]

Winchester has no records of note about White except that he featured in several of the school magazines as a member of the debating team where he seems to have performed adequately. The one speech of his whose substance was noted (without being recorded) was a spirited defence of Oliver Cromwell. Winchester could provide no evidence or record of his expulsion, but it is possible that public schools would perceive a need to expel a pupil as some sort of failure on their part. The school confirms that he got 'an exhibition' but points out that this was not as elevated as a scholarship.[8]

Sandhurst

White related that despite his absence from formal education for six months after his departure from Winchester, he still succeeded in gaining a King's cadetship for Sandhurst. Whatever other admissions he made about being incorrigible or even mad, or later, cowardly, it was always important for him not to be seen as a fool.

His becoming a soldier could be seen as puzzling, and he does not comment on it, although his radical tendencies soon caused him problems. More than likely the decision arose from a combination of his father's influence and the fact that there was little other choice open to him. There is a general consensus that the august military academy of Sandhurst was far from being an efficient training ground at that time. Like Sir George who, at the outset of the Boer War, 'had never commanded an army in the field against forces armed with modern weapons',[9] Britain itself had had very few serious military engagements for nearly fifty years. This became evident in Africa when the general flabbiness of the military thinking in the college was shown up. The historian A.P. Thornton quotes Admiral of the Fleet Jackie Fisher, who said in 1903 about the Boer War that it was 'accepted and continuing opinion in naval circles' that:

> One does not wonder at South Africa when one sees every day the utter ineptitude of military officers. Half the year they are on leave and the other half of the year everything is left to the sergeant-major and the NCO's.[10]

White's apparent perversity came to the fore when faced with what he might have believed to be a totally unnecessary task, but there was a justification to his discontent. The study of fortifications in particular aroused his ire, and he saw all the instruction as outdated by at least fifty years.[11] This recalcitrance was reflected in his marks, but the most notable evidence was his rustication for riding in a point-to-point when he had been specifically forbidden to do so because of some previous infringement. He relates meeting at this time with his father, about to become Quartermaster General at the War Office, who had come back from India having broken his leg in seven places in a horse race in Calcutta (this man was now sixty-two). When White went with his mother to meet him off the boat, Sir George had already heard about Jack's suspension:

> Lying in his cabin with his leg in plaster of Paris, he greeted me 'Well, Jack, I hear you've made a damned fool of yourself'. I knew I had, but I had learned the futility of too much self-abasement. 'Well, Father,' said I, 'I heard something of your coming to grief in a somewhat similar manner'. My father smiled and the incident was closed.[12]

This is one of the rare comments on record of his father's attitude to White's exploits, but it does not appear to be inconsistent with the other details of Sir George's attitude to his son's behaviour. The telegrams (discussed in Chapter 4) that Sir George sent to Dollie, White's fiancée, display a tolerance of, if not even some kind of resignation towards his son who seemed to be bent on a self-willed course regardless of any one else's feelings.[13]

Alan, Jack White's second son, believed Sir George was indulgent, particularly because he was both an absentee father and one who came to parenting rather later in life.[14] It is possible nevertheless that Sir George saw something in his son that was not going to respond to any direct discipline, that is, an intransigence in the face of authority. Of course another perspective could see Sir George, faced with an obdurate son and an adoring mother, as taking the path of least resistance.

White certainly served his father loyally in his own way; there is not a single critical word about him anywhere in White's writing, but the same cannot be said for his mother. In a letter to his niece, Pat English, he said that it was 'the force of female suction that killed Rosie [his eldest sister]' and implied that it was also responsible for his 'father's stroke'.[15] This seems to be a reference to his mother, which is borne out by his niece who remarks that 'from what I remember of her (and I was very fond of her) she would by any normal standards have been called a greedy selfish woman and a very powerful vampire'.[16]

It appears that Lady Amy White was a dominating woman who lived into her eighties. Certainly she was a very energetic woman; her diary in 1935, the year of her death, is filled with entries of social meetings and household tasks: 'today I did out the boudoir cupboard, a long and tiresome job which I had not finished by luncheon […] after which I rested for one hour, […] I then dressed for Mrs MacGregor's tea party'. She goes on to fill an entire foolscap diary page with details of people met and discussions had, before going back to finish the cupboard before dinner.[17]

At the end of his account of his Sandhurst days, White mentions two revealing incidents. The first describes the company he kept while awaiting his commission: he 'gravitated towards the higher ranks of the aristocracy'. Their appeal, he conceded frankly, was 'a certain recklessness' and his 'whole hearted snobbery'. This frankness runs right through all his writings and was the very essence of his disposition. Although at times endearing, it also provokes suspicion about its sheer manipulativeness. On a number of occasions he confesses to some unattractive behaviour on his part and it seems as if he is using it to forestall later criticism or in some way make it excusable. Certainly it adds weight to his credibility, and incredulity about some of the incidents related is often put in abeyance by the honesty he has demonstrated elsewhere.

In recalling his days mixing with 'aristocratic friends' he refers to his 'unexpected bit' as preventing his success as a snob. Having dressed immaculately to dine, he could not find a properly fitting top hat and so wore a bowler hat, which would appear to have been a deliberate social faux pas and probably looked ridiculous as well – 'an outrage'. He wrote presciently,

'I was never secure against this latent anarchist. He kept cropping up until he got me altogether in the end.'[18] This was written at least six or seven years before his experience of Stalinism in the Spanish Civil War convinced him that he was an anarchist, at least politically. However, he seems to have been aware of his 'unexpected bit' long before that and it formed an explanation of sorts to himself for the various adventures he found himself involved in.

He finishes his account of his experiences in Sandhurst with another revelation of recalcitrance. He had been 'gazetted to the 1st Gordon Highlanders then quartered in Edinburgh Castle' and claims:

> I did not like my brother officers and they did not like me. [...] I disliked the self effacement which was the tradition for newly joined subalterns. I disliked being drilled over again. [...] I disliked the salt I was obliged to eat with my porridge. I disliked everything and every one.[19]

He seems to have missed entirely the point about military training, which demanded a monastic-type obedience and submission to the will of whatever the soldier perceived to be his ultimate authority. He was completely unable to comply with any kind of subordination demanded of him unless he could establish an acceptable reason for it; orders for the sake of orders were a nonsense. His resistance was such that when his colleagues performed a mock court martial of him he was prepared to rebel to the point of killing someone: 'the light irresponsible feeling had come to me,' is how he describes the murderous emotion as if it was some kind of possession or even insanity over which he had no control.[20]

This was the autumn of 1899 and White, born into privilege and educated and trained as an executive of empire, now found that the time had come to support all that he had been conditioned to hold dear. *Dulce et decorum est pro patria mori* was a concept that he would almost automatically question, but there was a generosity to his character that would have found him complying with the demands being made on him. Although his ideology, complicated though it was, found its allies in peoples and movements that were fundamentally alien to him, his friends formed a bond with him that he never quite abnegated despite his differences. Even in the experiences which he was now about to undergo for the next couple of years, and in which he could never have believed in, there is a striking lack of bitterness or even critical comment about most of the characters he met.

The Second South African War

The Second South African War, more commonly known as the Boer War, began on 11 October 1899. Although it would be another twenty years before the British empire had reached its apogee in terms of territory, in South Africa there occurred the first indications of fragility in what was, up to then, a belief in the inalienable entitlement of the British people to govern more than one quarter of the entire globe. Thomas Pakenham described it as 'the most humiliating war for Britain between 1815 and 1914'.

Although E.P. Thompson's 'enormous condescension of hindsight' can readily perceive the inevitability of war, it is presumptuous to pick on one specific *casus belli*. For all that, the fact that an independent sovereign Transvaal, run by Boers, had discovered gold in 1886 has to be of especial significance. By 1898, the year before war started, it had become 'the largest single producer of gold in the world'. A Cecil Rhodes inspired adventure, the 'Jameson Raid', had attempted a few years before that to win back the mines from the Boers. According to Pakenham, Dr Jameson, the eponymous leader, was going 'to lick the burghers all round the Transvaal but instead had been humiliated by having to raise the white flag and weeping ... was led away in a cart to the gaol at Pretoria'.[21]

The conventional opinion (conventional as in any enterprise that begins in the early autumn) that the war would last until Christmas indicates the general lack of awareness of the task Britain had set for itself. The Jameson Raid itself seemed almost a harbinger of what awaited the British Army in their encounters. Arthur Conan Doyle, while working as a medical doctor with the army, wrote an account of the affair with an immediacy that is impressive even by today's standards. He stated that 'Napoleon and all his veterans have never treated us as roughly as these hard bitten farmers with their ancient theology and their inconveniently modern rifles.'[22]

The criticisms that White had about the practices at Sandhurst were further compounded by his accounts of what was, at its least, a marked inefficiency by the military in the field.

But there were other aspects of the war that would later have enormous relevance to White's thinking. It is unlikely his political consciousness had started to develop as early as this, but, the dominant elite that he was to encounter in Gibraltar a couple of years later would have been representative of what J.A. Hobson wrote about in his critique *–Imperialism: A Study*. Completed in 1902 and although writing more generally on imperialism

Hobson's remarks are very relevant to the Boer War – and, it has to be noted, almost eerily appropriate to today, post Iraq.

> The vast expenditure on armaments, the costly wars, the grave risks and embarrassments of foreign policy, the stoppage of political and social reforms within Great Britain, though fraught with great injury to the nation, have served well the present business interests of certain industries and professions.[23]

Although tainted with anti-Semitism, Hobson's Marxist analysis, where he saw the whole exercise of imperialism being of heavy economic cost to the nation but hugely profitable to a very tiny minority, is acknowledged even today for its validity.[24] In South Africa, White was about to see the fundamental driving issues of war, particularly at Doornkop, where the gold mines were located.

He served first in the Gordon Highlanders and then as a member of a scratch collection of various companies to make up a mounted infantry (6th M.I.) column. Among the engagements he was involved in were the battles at Magersfontein (December 1899) and Doornkop (May 1900). His regiment, the Gordons, formed part of the Highlanders force in both of these engagements.

In Magersfontein more than 3,000 men broke lines and ran. In the face of such an outright and sustained retreat the military powers seemed to have had no choice but to ignore what happened and carry on as normal. Pakenham relates that Lord Methuen, the overall commander, believed he was unlucky and could just about have achieved a victory but for the fact that some of his officers had insisted on carrying on a night march in close formation for too long. This brought them to a position where they were a very soft target for the Boers. After nine hours of marching in very difficult terrain at night and then finding themselves under sustained fire without any hope of responding and with a confusion of orders being given, it was regarded as understandable that a general panic eventually ensued.[25]

Of course White's perspective on the whole catastrophe was quite different: 'it was not a fight; it was half massacre, half farce'.[26] He and his troops had landed in South Africa barely a fortnight before, but they were very experienced, being mostly veterans from the Afghan campaign (Dargai, they were called). Their job was to back up the force of Highlanders that had been involved in the night march, and White's first encounter with them involved coming across groups of men lying around the great plain, 'which crackled with musketry like a fire of dry sticks', playing cards and complaining they were fed up. Eventually White and his comrades found themselves taking cover under fire and encountering scattered groups of dead Highlanders. After a period where there was absolutely no communication White found that the original assault force had turned back. He seems to have made some attempts to stop them but eventually found himself joining what he sardonically termed the 'homers'. He was scathing about the complete lack of communication from the command and pointed out that the *sangfroid* demonstrated by his men was as impressive as any of the newspaper reports made them out to be. Their 'nonchalant gallantry' was totally wasted, he said, because 'nobody told them to go anywhere'. Methuen, he said, 'disclaimed giving any such order [to retreat] as well he might. He had no means of giving any order at all. It was the days before loudspeakers'.[27]

Whether White was absolutely critical of Methuen as a commander or of the system that pitched men into battle without either clear organisation or instructions is debatable. More importantly, he instinctively had seen the whole phantasmagoria for what it was and questioned why such an activity should be regarded as praiseworthy: 'Oh very singular military mind! Most amazing of all I could not find my dumbfounded wonder at it all reflected in the minds of those with whom I subsequently discussed it.'[28]

White, for all his scepticism, did not refrain from a kind of jingoism in describing his own involvements: 'though I had never been under fire before [...] All the better; this was rather fun, and my section, nearly all old Dargai men, seemed to enjoy it too.' This can be interpreted as the language of one who has not experienced the realities, or more correctly the horrors, of warfare but in White's case it could be argued that this was not so. He was either a member of that peculiar, but nonetheless real group, who relish these types of conditions, possibly from some kind of adrenalin addiction, or else he believed that this was the type of attitude to aspire to in coping with the stresses of battle. He certainly openly acknowledged his own fearfulness: 'I recognized my own cowardice indeed cowardice begot the courage of self preservation' and perceptively went on to observe:

> I was naturally sympathetic, therefore, to the cowardice and self preservation of others. But those who are unwilling to recognize their own cowardice hide it from themselves by cruelty to others. Yet they will go to amazing lengths of self deception and mendacity.[29]

The engagement at Paardeberg, which, according to Pakenham, displayed a callous and obtuse Kitchener at his absolute worst, was a horrific blunder where, on Kitchener's orders, suicidal charges were made against almost unbreachable defences.[30] Although his regiment took a relatively insignificant role there, White was involved and treated it very summarily: 'At Paardeberg I got a little glimpse of what the Great War must have been like, for we had about a week in mud filled, corpse surrounded trenches, sapping up to Cronje [The Boer commander].'[31] News of his father's relief at Ladysmith came in the last days of Paardeberg and at his point White does not expand any further on the horrors of his own experiences there. This is the only time when White's comments on military matters include a criticism of Kitchener who surely warranted something far stronger than White's comments about Methuen. His loyalty to his father seems to have been conflated with a similar feeling for Kitchener who, although treating White well later on in India, did not return any loyalty on the outbreak of the Great War when White looked for an audience to explain his plan for the Irish Volunteers. It is also possible that, although later battles had their fill of horror, Paardeberg had a uniquely nightmarish aspect to it that would have jarred with the rather jaunty tone he adopted through the rest of the war.

In the next engagement he writes about in detail White, again, omits criticism of the commanding officer, but, in this case, he displays a certain admiration for General Sir Ian Hamilton, not as a military man but as a friend of White's family. Although Pakenham is scathing of Hamilton's order to storm the heights at Doornkop, there are no adverse comments from White except to point out that the cavalry had decided it was a job for the infantry. 'It was not, but no matter' he said curtly.[32] Winston Churchill, working as a war correspondent, found his naïve patriotism challenged when he saw the slaughter that had ensued, and all for the possession of the gold mines in the area. The Boers had occupied a high ridge at Doornkop: '*the* Doornkop, the actual kopje, beside the farmhouse, where Jameson had raised the white flag, five years before'.[33] This was Jameson of the infamous Jameson Raid which had gone ridiculously wrong and which Hamilton had now the opportunity of avenging. Whether the cavalry had any part to play in the tactics is not clear, but they were led by Sir John French. (He was later the commander of the British Home Forces who dealt with the Easter Rising in Ireland and certainly, in South Africa, displayed the callousness that distinguished him in Dublin.) In any case, the 'grunts', the old reliable cannon fodder, were the unfortunates selected to avenge Jameson, and they were ordered to storm the hill, leaving themselves exposed to a rain of bullets from the Boers. According to White, the Gordon Highlanders 'had lost a hundred men in ten minutes, but they had done the trick'.[34] They were rewarded by the presence of Hamilton himself that evening telling them how proud he was of them and that they had done, in that adverb reserved exclusively for the military commentator, splendidly, and, of course, the gold mines were secure. Leo Amery, that irredeemable exponent of the imperial *grands écrits*, is worth recalling, as Pakenham says, for his commentary with 'its ghastly anachronistic ring'. He wrote of 'the steady enduring discipline of the men under fire, [and] their absolute indifference to losses, contributed to carry on the glorious tradition of the British infantry'.[35]

White, as a child of his time, was certainly not completely free of these kinds of values and despite his dismissal of most of the constructs of the dominant hegemonies, whether it was the Catholic Church or the British Empire, betrayed an ambivalence to the radical forces he espoused whenever his old comrades hove into view. He was continually torn in his loyalties, and this probably contributed significantly to the irascibility of his demeanour. He describes Doornkop as 'the first of the only two real hot fights I claim to have experienced till I came to Ireland [...] [although] it had its farcical element'. He called it 'very unhealthy', and although he makes little of what must have felt like a suicidal procession up the hill, he again expresses his empathy with the misfits: 'I found on these occasions the drunkards and the religious fanatics had a way of standing out.'[36] (White's war writing has a vibrant realism, recalling Orwell in *Homage to Catalonia,* but would have benefited from some judicious editing.) His perspective on the action was that the Boers had a ready escape route behind the row of ridges they occupied and, while they had targets sufficiently far away to allow escape, they continued to fire. White was part of the tenth row of fourteen spread across about four miles, and by the time they got near the top, most of the Boers had been cleared off; nevertheless, he certainly came under fire and along with two others had got fifty yards ahead of his own line. The three of them were either in the act of charging or contemplating a charge when the rest of his regiments behind charged also.

This all leads to the incident referred to at the beginning of Chapter 1 and that arguably defined White as no other has. There have been no corroborating accounts uncovered, but it is an event in keeping with his character, and White's frankness lends credibility to what he has to say. For example, his later account of how he came to be awarded the Distinguished

Service Order (DSO) for bravery is not told with any self-deprecatory modesty but rather with an apparently genuine detachment from his own fright and foolishness, which lends further validity to this earlier event at Doornkop.

As he charged up the hill believing, as he said, that most of the Boer had made good their escape at this stage, he had contemplated the possibility of a VC, gained under false pretences. He then spotted a gun protruding from behind a rock. He grabbed it and apprehended a very frightened youth. When his men arrived they were all for bayoneting the young Boer on the spot, and White's superior officer actually ordered the youth be shot. White describes what happened next:

> A wave of disgust swamped my sense of discipline. 'If you shoot him,' said I, pointing my carbine at him, 'I'll shoot you' and he passed on. He is now a General, that officer and I am a Bolshevik, or reported as such.[37]

Whether it was White's own forceful personality, or more likely the fact that his father had become famous only a few weeks before, it typified the kind of defiance that he practised all his life. Of course it must be acknowledged that he displayed a great sense of justice. To balance this, he also included a counter report, purportedly written by one of the soldiers present, which appeared in a local paper, the *Bloemfontein Post,* about the incident, which was not at all flattering to him:

> I will now mention an incident that has made a good deal of bad feeling in the regiment. During the final charge, one of the Boers was seen to pick off five of our lads with his last five cartridges. Then he held up his hands and surrendered. Our boys were going to avenge their comrades when a young officer [White] came up and insisted that his life should be spared.[38]

His comment about writing like this preparing him for 'the truths of psychoanalysis' twenty years later is typical of the kind of obtuse remarks he made from time to time. Although White's account is extraordinary in that it has him escaping from being charged with mutiny, his version still has a more authentic ring to it than the newspaper's pat and ready tale of five bullets finding five of 'our lads'. Whatever version was closest to what actually happened, and assuming that both White and the *Bloemfontein Post* are referring to the same incident, it shows him in at least a favourable humanitarian light and demonstrates his willingness to defy the general consensus even under the most stressful of conditions.

Having subverted the authority of the British Army, and with his account of mutiny providing an antithesis to the regimental chronicle of glory that Doornkop became, White then continues to strike a more realistic note when relating how the sixteen bodies of the dead men were laid out the following morning (the seventeenth body, that of the officer, St John Meyrick, had been granted more decorum). These were the same bodies that Churchill witnessed which led to his temporary epiphany about the real reasons for the war. He does not corroborate White's story, however, about the competition for the boots of the dead men among their surviving comrades. White also relates that 'an elegant figure drew up beside' him:

> the Duke of Marlborough, known to me by sight, for my crammer was at Woodstock and we had sat immediately behind the ducal pew in church. He gazed at the ranks of death. 'C'est magnifique mais ce n'est pas la guerre' he said. No your grace, it was not even magnificent. Its magnificence was of the same order as your own.[39]

Being a horseman of renown, White was automatically seconded to the oxymoronically named mounted infantry (MI) which, according to him, Kitchener had formed. Pakenham, however, states that it was General Sir Redvers Buller who had first recognised the need for a more flexible infantry than the one they had, which quite often was unable to move much more than eight miles from a railway. Originally called the Imperial Yeomanry, it became the first real response to the mobility of the Boers.[40] White commented: 'War according to the text book may have been over; hard and continuous fighting was just beginning.'[41] He joined the 6th M.I. and it seems to have suited him eminently, galloping around the countryside engaging in guerrilla tactics similar to those employed by the Boers, and with little of the irritating discipline that brought out the worst in him.

On one occasion White was sent on a scouting mission and was captured by some Boers who deprived him of his trousers and horse. He barely escaped being shot but managed to run away and covered a distance of six miles to summon reinforcements to attack the enemy. It is difficult to establish exactly what White did because of the light-hearted way he treats the whole incident. He maintained, for example, that when he was spotted by some local people they were awestruck, having never seen a white man near naked before, and came to the conclusion he was some kind of deity. He was also laughed at by his own forces when he eventually caught up with them.

This unlikely account does not take from the fact that his fellow subaltern, an Irishman called Cameron, whom he described as fearless, was killed in the same adventure. Cameron was mentioned in despatches but it was White who was awarded the DSO.[42] There must have been some behaviour of military significance on White's part for him to win this; a DSO is a level two award in the hierarchy of military awards, ranking just below a VC and above the Military Cross.[43]

In his resumé of his feelings during the whole event, he is particularly harsh on himself, describing how he lost heart when separated from his comrades and how frightened he was. He said that to do himself justice he did his best to prevent himself getting the award and told his commanding officer that he had behaved like a coward. Accentuating his alienation he says, 'I was already becoming accustomed to the non-acceptance of my standards of merit or demerit.'[44]

This is an impressive piece of openness, something far beyond the false self-deprecatory stance of many so-called heroes. Protesting that he had behaved as a coward, he speculated that 'Kitchener seems to have been so tickled at the idea of me running away in my shirt that nothing would do him but to recommend me for the DSO.' [45] (There is another later light-hearted notion that, as his father had been awarded every other decoration, the DSO went to the family to make up the collection.) Again one is reminded of Orwell in his accounts of military action and their depiction of destructiveness and logistical insanity.

There is no political analysis of the war itself offered anywhere. He is brief but honest about the depredations engaged in by the British under the directions of Kitchener in an attempt to crush the Boer resistance: 'We led the life of filibusters and stole everything we saw' and talks about his unit as one of 'the "pastoral" columns [that] had been at work, taking the women into concentration camps, burning the farms, destroying every living thing, except the men, whom we couldn't catch'. [46]

Of course it is far too early to detect any kind of philosophy in a period prior to much consciousness on his part of the struggles of the world, whether in defence of class, country, or vested interests, although his taste for the metaphysical is first recorded when he recalls lying in the Crocodile River and having the 'most complete sense of physical well being' he had ever known.[47] As his life developed, he began to place more and more importance on these transcendent experiences. But even from the vantage point of thirty years later, White still makes little or no comment on what was essentially a serious reversal of Britain's place in the world and possibly the earliest harbinger of fragmentation in the Empire. His critiques are concerned with warfare, its practice, and its administration, rather than as a political weapon per se, although that perspective was to change later with his rather idiosyncratic adoption of pacifism.

This apolitical stance could also be taken as a demonstration of where White's original loyalties lay and where they remained to some extent right up to his death. There is little evidence of any sympathy on his part for nationalist causes in Ireland at any time, and it could be argued that his antipathy towards the Unionists lay in what he saw as a movement inimical to the interests of the United Kingdom despite its overt agenda. He said in a letter to the new Northern Ireland Prime Minister J.M. Andrews on 16 December 1940:

> I was Red – I was never Green, I never had any use for neutrality in this war, so little indeed that though I have done all in my power to forestall such a terrible possibility, I believe I would fight against Eire if it came to the pinch.[48]

Although written to impress upon a sceptical government his value as a soldier in the fight against Nazism and probably causing consternation among his nationalist admirers, it displays little that could be said to be inconsistent with his actions and speeches down through the years.

Chapter 3

Awakenings

Gibraltar

Sir George had been appointed Governor General of Gibraltar but, because of his poor health after the siege of Ladysmith, he was not able to take up the position until well into 1900. He appointed his son as an *aide-de-camp* (ADC) when Jack had returned to the Gordon Highlanders' barracks at Aberdeen after his own campaign had finished in 1902. White described himself as an 'invitation ADC; managing the invitation list, making out the plan of the table, writing the menus and dancing with the plain women'.[1] Gibraltar was a port of call for the northern European aristocracy who might be heading for the Mediterranean by sea for their vacations and for more important diplomatic missions in North Africa. In fact, Sir George's autograph book for that period is filled with illustrious signatures and provides a comprehensive list of mainly British but also some European members of the dominant elite of the time.[2] His daughter Rose, along with her three sisters and her mother, Lady Amy, provided in-house diplomatic services for visitors, and Rose describes a visit by King Edward VII when he commented on what a fine looking woman Lady Amy still was. The king had a penchant for inviting ladies to dinner specifically without their husbands, 'to equalize the party a little' according to the innocent Rose.[3]

France and Germany at that time had been wrangling over the benefits they wished to bring to Morocco, and although the conference of Algeciras did not take place until 1906, the year after the Whites left, there was much activity and sabre-rattling in the meantime. Even the British Royal Navy, whose country had even less business in the proceedings, was occupied in steaming up and down in battle formation through the straits and carrying out various naval manoeuvres. Here Jack White, so reticent in his criticism of his military commanders in Africa, emerges in full iconoclastic regalia. He maintained that 'the royalties were the business agents to get their countries a place in the Moroccan sun, and Gibraltar was the jumping off ground'. He goes on to critique generally and analyse specifically some of these people, with a particular emphasis on the 'courts' that accompanied them:

> My experience included Edward VII of England and William II of Germany and one or two minor lights. It would be presumptuous to say I had seen through them and what they stood for; but they no longer interested me. I was inoculated against that particular form of hypnosis. They were no different from other people. They were the summation of, shall we say, the most ordinary and least interesting side of other people. Their function, I had seen as invitation A.D.C., was to bring out in strong relief an aspect of other people which at other times lurked in decent concealment. Far be it from me to claim that I was exempt from this undesirable aspect myself. I was as big a snob as the rest; but with one eye open.[4]

This development in perception he claimed had come about through a transformative experience, Damascene in its suddenness and scope. He described it as something that 'changed the very mechanism of my consciousness and the whole course of my life'.[5] It will have to be examined in greater depth later because it remains as a continuing theme through the rest of his writings, in particular those at the end of his life. However questionable his powers of perception may be in analysing the types of individuals who made up the two principal entourages in Gibraltar, it is compensated for by the colourfulness of his descriptions:

> I was struck with the greater *naivete* and greater sincerity of the [Germans]. That the Kaiser was a bit of a mountebank I could see even then. I am convinced that his gentlemen could not. When the Kaiser would summon one of his suite to be presented to my mother with an 'Ach, you have not met *my* Admiral von Tirpitz' even that bewhiskered old pirate evidently became 'the proudest man that ever scuttled a ship'. These immaculate military or naval chromographs,

hung with decorations principally for lunching with people, literally glowed with pride at any sign of this Imperial notice. And they spoke of the Kaiser with a reverence, watched him with a henchman's tenderness, that was obviously genuine.

Edward's atmosphere was quite different. His inner circle, or the men I saw nearest to him, were either intimate or privileged jesters like Lambton or Charlie Beresford, or very well bred superior flunkies like ahem! some others. Certainly there was nothing naïve about either themselves or their attitude to their master. The flunkies could and did demand from others the reverential attitude they assumed themselves, but one felt it was an assumption. The jesters in their intimate gossip constantly undermined it.[6]

The analysis of the latter is probably the more accurate; there seems to have been affection in his portrayal of the Germans that possibly biased his outlook.

Certainly the purpose of the visit of Edward, father of the empire, positioned there only for the convenience of the likes of Admiral Charles Beresford, resonates with a very probable reality. Beresford combined his employment as a sailor with the political duties of a member of parliament and the commercial interests of a representative of the Associated Chambers of Commerce.[7] In fact, the visitors' book from that time, apart from the signatures of both Edward and the Kaiser and minor royalty like Charles of Denmark, the various princesses, daughters and granddaughters of Victoria, ladies of the bedchamber (Charlotte Knollys), and minor foreign figures (Admiral Valois), also includes those of a considerable number of what could be at best termed entrepeneurs.[8] The copperplate signature of Hedworth Lambert (1856–1929), described by White as an intimate jester, is there.[9] He, apart from a dilettantish career in the Navy, inherited a considerable estate on condition that he assume the name of Meux on the death of Lady Meux who, childless, had taken an inordinate fancy to him which was unlikely to be maternal – they were roughly the same age. He died, also without issue, so her manoeuvre was unsuccessful, and the title died out.[10] Another, less elegantly autographed name, was Horace Farquhar, First Earl,[11] described by *Burke's Peerage* as 'a cavalier financier [...] lucky to have] escaped prosecution for fraud while alive' and certainly an undiscovered bankrupt who was extremely unpopular 'despite his wealth and his honours and his generous hospitality or perhaps because'.[12] White had few illusions about these people. Interestingly he makes no comment on one of the purposes of the king's visit at that time (8 April 1903), which was to promote Sir George to the 'highest rank a soldier can attain', field-marshal. The king remarked to Lady Amy, 'I do hope that Sir George will now desist from risking his life in point to point races', yet nearly a year later, at the age of almost seventy, he finished tenth in a race which Jack won.[13]

In Jack White's summary of the change that had begun and was taking place in him, he writes that he 'had seen two people too close – God and the King', and this was also to play a part in another seminal moment in Gibraltar, his enchantment with Dollie Mosley. A short story by White, published in 1912, has survived, entitled 'A Ride in Andalusia'. It describes a journey on horseback from the coast to Ronda, nowadays a well-known tourist town high in the Spanish hills.[14] There is little to recommend the story, but it is of interest because Sir George's biographer, Sir Mortimer Durand, records a visit by him and Lady Amy to Andalusia for one weekend where they stayed overnight in Ronda with Mr and Mrs Mosley, the parents of the same Dollie. Leonard, the father, was later to become estranged from the Whites over their son's betrothal to her.[15] It was inevitable that Dollie would appeal to the king's 'predilection for pretty women', and, as White wrote, 'half of me was proud of the notice' taken by Edward.[16] Rose White also makes note of it in the aforementioned letter to her Uncle John: 'Mrs Pablo Lorios and Miss Dollie Mosley (the king more or less hinted that he would like to have the latter two ladies both of whom are very pretty and one or two ladies without their husbands)' to his private dinner party.[17] White's fidelity to king and country was undermined: 'This pimping for princes might have its limitations',[18] and was probably further damaged by an incident related by Rose on the same night:

'What did you put in that?' asked the King when Jack handed him a whiskey. 'Oh' said Jack, 'My father's whiskey is very white, Sir, there's more there than it looks'. 'It's not the look, it's the taste' said the King. 'And you a Gordon Highlander!'[19]

The inevitable laughter must have rankled with White and the anger probably still lurked deep within him when, a couple of years later, he was swearing two young recruits in Aberdeen to 'an allegiance to their liege Lord Edward, his heirs and successors'. This was all 'irrespective of Lord Edward's moral condition', of which he did not approve, so it became the actual moment that precipitated White abandoning his military career.[20]

White at this stage of his life was living what can only be described as a sybaritic existence. He was the governor's son with duties of the pleasantest kind and a licence to indulge in his passion for horses. As an old Wykehamist, a graduate of Sandhurst, a decorated war hero, on familiar terms with most of the military powers of the moment, including Kitchener himself, and clearly intelligent, he was set for a very successful career. He had dined with royalty and had become familiar with the affluent power-brokers that accompanied Edward. He was an ideal product and future custodian of the British Empire, the greatest socio-economic structure the world had ever seen. Although it would be another two years before he left the army and formally began to part ways with almost everything he had been bred for, White, according to his autobiography, had already abandoned the values of this society to pursue what he could not articulate.

Inner Life and the 'Liqueur Sensation'

From a young age White displayed an inability to accept any instruction or diktat without questioning and examining the alternatives. Although his life took a course that seemed to have cancelled out his earlier misgivings and unease, and he had found himself as successful as any other young officer in his position, there lurked under the surface a rebelliousness or an unwillingness to accept the ready path laid out before him. This seeming perversity led him on a road to self-destruction. That is, of course, if the conventional criteria of success being wealth and fame are applied. White's daemons appeared to urge him to pursue matters beyond the mundane; he had little interest in the social aspirations of his peers. R.B. McDowell, biographer of Alice Stopford Green, the nationalist historian, wrote that White 'was in many ways a most unworldly man' and this is probably as perceptive an observation as has been made about him.[21] While in Gibraltar White had a transcendent experience which he maintained justified the path he took and somehow blessed his eccentricities despite his friends' and family's misgivings.

Displaying what must have been at times an unnerving certainty, White never shrank from the challenge of confronting himself, even in his most egregious behaviour. John Cowper Powys, commenting on a piece of White's writing, now lost, said it was 'the most honest attempt he had ever read of a man or woman attempting to explain themselves'.[22] This seems to have been the hallmark of White from his time in Gibraltar. His autobiography is replete with musings over the conundrum that he saw himself to be. Unlike many autobiographies, White's makes no attempt at justifying his actions, which he spelled out, sometimes in their sheer indefensible ugliness. It is doubtful, for example, that many other writers would recount the incident where he had an Indian whipped whose only crime was the irritation he caused White.[23] A review of his autobiography in 1930 described it as 'the most egotistical work which will be published this year', arguing that

> It would be difficult to admire Captain White. Probably he does not admire himself. But, despite certain shocking errors of taste, despite borderland vanity, and despite a blindness to the interests of others which simulates cruelty, there still emerges from this acute and witty monograph the shape of a man whom many have loved and followed, a figure not without grotesque heroism, and a soul that followed its star all dismayed.[24]

While some comments are disputable, the acuity of these observations leads one to suspect that the writer John Still had an insight into White based on more than the book itself. The next period of this 'soul that followed its star all dismayed' began in a wandering both geographical and psychological, that, for all his subsequent adventures, was primarily spiritual.

White's enthrallment with Maria de las Mercedes Ana Luisa Carmen Dolores (Dollie) Mosley coincided with the first occurrence of the 'liqueur sensation' that he placed so much emphasis on for the rest of his life, or at least until the time of his autobiography in 1930. There are few references to it in his late letters, but it is not unreasonable to accept that as a seminal experience it served to give a coherence to his inner beliefs, which remained more or less consistent to the end. Although caution must be adopted by recalling that the only records of substance of his inner life were not written until he had reached the age of 50 or thereabouts, questioning their reliability too much would be to cavil unnecessarily.

White described this phenomenon for the first time as a 'most pleasurable sensation in the middle of my chest, as if I had just drunk a strong liqueur'.[25] It seems to have lasted at least an hour or more and reached some kind of intensity as he was reading a telegram about the Russo-Japanese War, which, oddly, was the topic that initially sparked the experience. Whatever it was, it served White as a satisfactory explanation for later behaviour that contributed to his reputation for incorrigibility; he believed it was the driving force that lead him 'out of the army, to Canada, in to various prisons and awkward predicaments beyond number'.[26] When he left India, barely avoiding a charge of desertion by getting the personal permission of Kitchener to return temporarily to Europe in order to pursue Dollie, White gave this sensation as the justification for what appeared to be a 'mental aberration'. He developed it into a kind of personal spiritual guidance which, although not as dramatic as the 'absolute faith [...] that is reported of Joan of Arc', still was 'wonderful evidence of intelligent guidance' beyond the ordinary. He did not lay claim to 'actual clairaudience or clairvoyance. The impulse to action was always this sensation in my chest accompanied by a mental sensation of co-operation with a scientific law beyond my formulation or comprehension'.[27]

It is not within the ambit of this work to theorise on the nature of this experience of his, or the fact that he placed such credence in it, but undoubtedly it is a more common occurrence than is generally acknowledged. From the time of William James's *The Varieties of Religious Experience* (1902) there has been a regular academic reporting of similar phenomena. White himself maintained that American transcendentalists like Ralph Waldo Emerson and Walt Whitman experienced this, as had others like the English poet, socialist, and mystic Edward Carpenter. He recorded his attempts to find references to it among the philosophers. Henri Bergson's perspective on the higher intellect provided him with some insight into his 'sensation'. He dismissed Richard Bucke's *Cosmic Consciousness* as too elitist, 'confined to a handful of notorieties!'[28] However, more recently, Alan Watts, Protestant clergyman turned Zen Buddhist, comments on Bucke in a manner that suggests similarities to White's experience:

> The most impressive fact in man's spiritual, intellectual, and poetic experience has always been, for me, the universal prevalence of those astonishing moments of insight which Richard Bucke called 'cosmic consciousness'. There is really no satisfactory name for this type of experience. To call it mystical is to confuse it with visions of another world, or of gods and angels. To call it spiritual or metaphysical is to suggest it is not also extremely concrete and physical, while the term 'cosmic consciousness' itself had the unpoetic flavour of occultist jargon. But from all historical times and cultures we have reports of this same unmistakable sensation emerging, as a rule, quite suddenly and unexpectedly and from no clearly understood cause.[29]

White's penchant for religious conviction and experience lasted all his life, and towards the end, aware that he was dying, there is a continual stream of references to resources beyond the temporal. Characteristically, there are none of the more conventional pleas for relief for his terminal illness or expressions of confidence in being taken care of. He did not appear to believe that the spiritual had anything to do with his personal concerns, which must have been pressing, considering the pain he was enduring. He describes particularly unpleasant experiences to his niece, but without recourse to religion:

> returning from [...] Ballymena, having weathered the strain, as I thought, pretty well, I was suddenly seized with a violent fit of nose bleeding in Ballymena station. Luckily I had just rang up a cab which I bled over all the way to Broughshane, and the bleeding has gone on at intervals since, making me frightened and weak.[30]

This was in August 1945, six months before he died of prostate cancer; his own diagnosis of what was happening gives an indication of where his interests lay at that time:

> I interpret this as part result, part safety valve for the abnormal strain of the messianic consciousness on the brain, and this rise to the brain of the later stages of it is closely connected with the virgin birth, as I grope for its true meaning.[31]

There is little evidence of his attending religious services, although he would have described himself as Presbyterian and professed a faith in God, but he seems to have perceived his own spiritual beliefs on a kind of political basis, heavily supported with biblical references and mythology. The concept of messiah had an enduring fascination and, it must be stated, in particular as it applied to himself. This raises doubts about his mental stability towards the end of his life, although the more likely explanation is regular overindulgence in solitary drinking. (His daughter-in-law Jennifer, Derrick's first wife, informed me that the landlady of the local public house had related that, not only did White do a considerable amount of late night drinking in Broughshane in the 1940s, but that the village was accustomed to the clip clop of his horse in the early hours of the morning going on journeys to no-one-knew-where.)[32]

Dollie

Allied to White's spiritual leanings was a conviction that whatever course of action he had decided upon was going to be taken without any consideration for the discomfort – or worse – that he would cause others. According to himself, he wooed Dollie Mosley against the explicit wishes of both families,[33] although in the surviving correspondence on the matter there is not the slightest recrimination from either of his parents. This is probably an indication of the indulgence they continually granted their wayward son. White had been posted to India after his father had retired as Governor General of Gibraltar in 1905. When Dollie called off their engagement, he decided, filled with conviction inspired by his 'liqueur sensation', to leave India and return to Europe to repair his fractured relationship, a harbinger of the match to come and decades of marital turmoil. (This had been the second such occasion; previously he wrote in detail about getting leave from Kitchener to hurry back and persuade Dollie to change her mind soon after he had arrived at his posting.) This time there was a flurry of letters between Dollie and Sir George and Lady Amy, all written with the spectre of White returning by steamer from the East, undeterred by either the blandishments of his mother or Dollie's letters. Dollie had been living with the Whites in London when she had changed her mind and agreed to marry White after his first return from India. However, she had once more decided to cancel the engagement sometime in late 1906 or early 1907 and had returned home to Gibraltar. She wrote to Lady Amy on 15 January 1907:

> I don't want my day of arrival to pass away without writing you a few lines. Well here I am! It has been a very sad home coming. […] I could never forget you all and all the kindness bestowed on me when I have been the principal cause of all your anxiety and worry.[34]

By the beginning of March White was on his way back and Dollie had notified the Whites of her concern because at some stage he had given the impression that he was going to call to Gibraltar. This was, for some reason, totally unacceptable to Dollie's father, Alexander Mosley. Sir George telegraphed Dollie:

Royal Hospital Chelsea

Miss Mosley, Library Ramp, Gibraltar.

Your letter and telegram received. Jack on Mongolia. We have telegraphed Port Said all we could to prevent him going to Gibraltar but he is intent on learning your unbiased decision from yourself and I recommend your telegraphing decisively to Marseilles your unbiased personal decision about seeing him disclaiming all other influences. We will do our best from here. Show this [to] your father, George White.[35]

It seems that Dollie then informed her father and came to a decision, because Sir George received two telegrams despatched within minutes of each other. The first, from Dollie's father, was blunt:

Mar. 6th [1907] At 10.15 a.m. Received 1.00 p.m.

Regret [your] sons proposed action which must inevitably end in grave scandal positively refuse allow him enter my house have done my duty in warning you and am not responsible consequences.

Alexander Mosley.[36]

The second demonstrated that Jack did not have a monopoly in the future partnership on precipitous decisions:

Mar 6th. Gibraltar at 10.25 [1907]

To: Sir George [...] Royal Hospital Chelsea

Have shown your wire to father decided to marry at once against every ones wish nowhere to go will you take me in will wire Jack meet me London – Dollie.[37]

Sir George replied to her demonstrating the innate kindness of the man together with a commendable lack of animosity towards Alexander Mosley (or Jack, for that matter). He telegraphed her that same afternoon, dispensing with the conventional foreshortened telegram style presumably to ensure that she understood the import of what he wanted to say:

> I cannot bear to think you may be taking this vital step to prevent trouble with Jack at Gibraltar without whole heartedly wishing it yourself. Your last telegram suggests this to me. I advise your writing a letter to him here saying exactly what your feelings are as regards marrying him. Wire to him Marseilles that you have written fully here that if he comes Gibraltar you will not see him and he will irrevocably alienate you. If this and what I will wire to him does not keep him from Gibraltar nothing will. Don't leave your home until you hear from him and also from me from London.
>
> George White – dispatched 6/3/07 5.30p.m.[38]

Dollie responded in kind in a letter:

> I cannot thank you enough for the fatherly interest you have taken in me and for your kind telegrams. […] I am prepared to marry him at once, but I am not disposed to undergo all the worries of another engagement – this would have to be with yours and Lady White's consent and in your house as my father refuses to have anything to do with it and blames me very much for all the worry I have brought on him and my people. So hoping that we have been successful in stopping Jack at Marseilles and that he has come away with leave and not placed you in worse troubles over me.[39]

The fact that she was concerned that White might have returned from India while absent-without-leave seemed to be of concern to both Dollie and Sir George; it is an indication of their opinion of his intemperateness. It has not been established what aroused Alexander Mosley's grievous antipathy to White, but it is unlikely that religious differences were the underlying cause, although Dollie was a Roman Catholic, probably from her mother's side, which was Spanish. She had written earlier to Lady Amy that 'father is still very, very angry with me and will listen to no reason, he declares if Jack turns up he will hand him over to the police'.[40] It is obvious in that letter that her mother, on the other hand, was well disposed to the Whites. Dollie wrote that 'Mother is so grateful to you for all you have done for me.'[41] This, of course, would be surprising if it were otherwise; Sir George, as war hero and as Governor General of Gibraltar, would have established the White family as the cream of high society there. It is probably a good example of Jack White's ability to exasperate people in even the most favourable of circumstances. White himself often appears puzzled at this tendency of his. He describes a meeting on his earlier mission to Dollie and a subsequent contretemps he had over some religious point of dogma with a Reverend Mother in Kensington Square who was Dollie's spiritual director. He said to himself, that he was a 'Fool, having gone to such trouble to get the girl, to be obstructive over these premature details'. But he appeared to be pathologically incapable of compromise on certain beliefs:

> I was willing to give up all I had gained [Dollie] rather than compromise the right of my hypothetical hopefuls to extend this new consciousness free of dogmatic shackles. Rome too stood pre-eminently for the subordination of the inner light to external authority, individual vision to collective prudence. Rome was the enemy despite this charming and remonstrant lady.[42]

Although he was describing his new-found enthusiasm for some kind of divine guidance, he reveals his inability to grasp any notion of diplomacy or compromise. When he concedes that he 'fell in love' in Monte Carlo but did not admit it to himself until the object of his attentions informed him he had a soul the 'size of a peanut',[43] Alexander Mosley's reservations appear to be well founded. White's honesty in reporting the fact that he could consider a relationship with another woman and, at the same time, cause havoc in his amorous pursuit of Dollie, is remarkable for its frankness. One can only speculate that this dalliance caused the seeming delay in his arrival that the telegrams refer to: Lady Amy complains to him at one stage, 'have not written or forwarded letters as expecting you daily'.[44] Several undated copies of telegrams record Lady Amy's attempts to contact her son, until she finally writes to Dollie announcing that she had 'received letter from Jack last night first communication since Sunday saying he expected your answer to his letter sent via Mongolia [the ship carrying him from India] [...] wired him previously your letter awaiting him here'.[45] White responded, somewhat enigmatically: 'insist seeing Dollie this condition come home inform Marseille'.[46] This appears to say that he is demanding to see Dollie whatever the consequences. In return, his mother tells him that 'Dollie has written me imploring you not to go to Gib now and appeals to you not to place her in a false position.' She continues that this 'would destroy every vestige [of] hope Come home direct'.[47] White appeared to finally relent, and Lady Amy reported to Dollie:

Mar. 11th. 8p.m. to Miss Mosley, Library Ramp. Gibraltar.

Yours received. Jack wired from Marseilles Saturday begins. ['] *Never dreamt of going unasked* [to] *Gibraltar please write removing false impression if created by you. I remain here* ['] ends. I then wired again urging him come home. We have heard nothing his movements since. Did you wire to him Marseilles saying you had written to him fully here [?] Amy White [emphasis added to indicate White's words].[48]

Lady Amy finished the correspondence by advising both parties that arrangements would have to be formalised before they were admitted to the White household. In a telegram to White she wrote on 16 March 1907:

Captain White care King Company Marseilles.

Your letter wire received. Had expected you here daily. Letter from Dollie for you been here several days. She writes most hopefully for you. But father won't invite her here till all preliminaries definitely settled with you both. Come wire movements, Mother.[49]

A similar message was despatched to Dollie. Surprisingly, because of all the concerns, White 'went home overland from Monte Carlo and stayed', as he said, 'with my people at Chelsea Hospital. From there I corresponded with Gibraltar and things began to come right'.[50] However, further disruptions had to be faced before matters were completely resolved; the intransigence of the Catholic Church in insisting on the offspring of a mixed marriage being reared as Catholics met an equal obduracy in White. Despite his father's urgings, White refused to give way. Even his grandfather, the Anglican archdeacon and chaplain to the royal family at Windsor, pleaded with him to concede, because 'his God was as mellow as himself and able to tolerate the most foolish practices in people who hadn't the discipline of a study of Sanskrit roots'.[51] However, White, pleading his 'fundamental Protestantism', stated that 'It is indecision, moral uncertainty, which breaks the spirit', and going further than Johnson asserted that 'any fool should be able to face hanging, once he knows there is no chance of a reprieve'.[52] Eventually, Dollie 'accepted' his conditions, which meant that a 'church' wedding was not possible and they were duly married at the 'Chelsea Registry Office [where] the only representative of the Mosley interest was an uncle [...] invited by wire. The uncle replied in kind, "Coming, but absolutely hostile" '.[53]

White emerges from this account as domineering and stubborn, but it must be noted that Dollie herself was more than capable of intemperate outbursts, if White's account of their sea voyage from India after his final stint there is to be accepted:

> Somewhere about Malta I was developing Dollie's intelligence by means of a game of chess with a set of the captain's chessmen he valued deeply. Suddenly the chessmen were swept off the board and flung into the Mediterranean [by Dollie …] The captain, if he is still alive, may see the humour and pathos of the situation better now than he did at the time.[54]

Departure from Army

There is little evidence of White's activities from his marriage on 24 April 1907 up to his return to Ireland after his father's death in 1912, except for what he chooses to tell himself. A considerable amount of this time was spent in what could be called a 'grand tour' but not of a type that resembled the aristocratic perambulations around the culture sites of Europe up to the middle of the nineteenth century. It was a journey closer to that taken by Western school leavers of the 1960s who left for the East in an attempt to fulfil some need to search for alternatives. He described his mental condition at the time:

> I read a good deal, especially Tolstoy. My own condition was a good example of his simile of the bird seeing the light through the closed window of a room. It dashes towards the light, encounters the glass and falls back dazed. To me freedom for spiritual adventure was the light, the army and my complete economic dependence upon it, my lack of training for anything else, was the glass.[55]

Having returned from India, White had been stationed in Aberdeen as a training officer for part-time soldiers in a Territorial Battalion. It was here that he resigned his commission in 1908. This was precipitated by the incident already related of his swearing in a couple of callow recruits, and he concluded that 'it was simply childish nonsense to seek love and draw a captain's pay and allowances for teaching people to kill each other'.[56] Naturally his father opposed the idea; Jack White, with his war record, had a future and the army was an important career at that time.

In fact, in a line of thinking that his son Jack would never have supported, Sir George believed that the United Kingdom was particularly under threat because of the paucity of its armed forces. A speech he gave to an unidentified audience around 1906 reflects the insecurity of those running the empire at that time (and the subsequent arms race). He argued that in 1805 Napoleon had demonstrated England's inability to exercise 'any effect upon the balance of power or on the destinies of Europe'.[57] This he believed was because of the inadequate size of the British army itself which at that time had a 'total number of men under arms [of] about 800,000 or about 1 in 4 of the men capable of bearing arms'.[58] In 1905, he said:

> the effectives were less by some 50,000 than 100 years before in the United Kingdom. But [...] the area of the Empire had increased tenfold and the population 16 fold. [And] our present armed force is still more insufficient if we compare it with the colossal expansion of the continental powers. The armed strength of France is now 7 times greater than it was in 1805, of Russia about 8 times greater, of Austria about 7 times greater and the armed forces of Germany are some 10 times greater than those of Prussia in 1805.[59]

It must have been incomprehensible to Sir George that his son wanted to leave the army. Jack displayed some filial diplomacy in writing to ask his permission first. Sir George's response was remarkably mild; he told Jack that he was quite odd enough, adding that 'I should be a little less odd, if I were you, and go on with your work.' White himself, even recounting it twenty-odd years later is petulant; it was 'always the same story "be a little less odd", "be more like other people" '.[60]

When White did finally make his mind up to leave, he typed, as he said, his reasons and gave them to Sir George, having already been told by Gladys, his sister, that 'it would kill father'. Sir George returned the document 'with his usual high courtesy after he had read it and said "I don't deny you a certain skill in argument, my boy, but ..."', and White does not elaborate on what was said after that.[61] His uncle John also hinted that there was a considerable amount of discussion of the matter by Sir George but again there is no record of what was said. Sir George's perspective on authority as expressed in his speech, 'the first duty of loyal citizenship is to make some sacrifice for the State to which we owe Service and Allegiance',[62] indicates a gulf between father and son that was possibly unbridgeable. For all that, the absence of any record of critical comments by either party indicates an admirable mutual fidelity. White records that he sent the same document to Tolstoy and received 'a charming letter [stating] that I was one of those nearest to his spirit'.[63] White's family had a different perspective, evidenced by his admission that they paid for his head to be examined by a surgeon, Sir Victor Horsley. White, without saying so exactly, gives the amusing impression that it was some kind of exercise in phrenology, but Horsley was a very eminent physiologist, knighted for his medical services, who 'founded in Britain the modern study of the thyroid gland'.[64]

Chapter 4

Wanderings and Home

Peregrinations

According to White, the next four to five years of his life consisted of a peripatetic pursuit of what he believed were Tolstoyan principles, although nowhere does he attempt to articulate what these were except to acknowledge that vegetarianism and celibacy were ideals that he singularly failed to put into practise. He eventually came to the conclusion that Tolstoy's notion that it was humankind's lot to live by the sweat of its brow was something at which he was particularly inept. Working for a farmer, White overheard him one day to remark that

> he 'couldn't turn Mr White out because he was such a perfect gentleman'. This was about as nasty a knock as I could receive. I was training as a farm labourer to become a peasant in the approved Tolstoyan fashion.[1]

On another occasion he and Dollie set up a chicken farm, and when he carried out a costing exercise discovered that each egg cost eight pence to produce. 'Luckily we didn't produce many', he said.[2]

During these wanderings he encountered a number of people whom, with a sardonic but affectionate eye, he fashioned into a set of picturesque characters. While teaching English in Bohemia he met Prince Raoul de Rohan, an exotic refugee, 'a bit of flotsam', as White would have it, from the French Revolution.[3] The prince was a devout Catholic who had married a

Mary Agnes Rock in Dalkey in 1888.[4] The couple told White he could stay as long as he liked after he had been sacked from his teaching job, but this friendship was abruptly ended after an argument about religion in which Tolstoy was attacked by the prince with 'that peculiar self-satisfied assurance that the spoon-fed mind uses to the first-hand seeker'.[5]

In answering an advertisement for the 'goodwill' of a school for sale, White met A.M. Cogswell, whom he delicately refers to as C–. His description of Cogswell, though scathing, is not unsympathetic and is worth quoting for its literary content alone. He had, White wrote:

> no presence or training for anything but the lower walks of intellectual slavery, with a genius for morbid self-torture, he was handicapped by birth, by nature, and by circumstance, and admirably adapted to taste the dregs of all three. His soul was a camera obscura, lit by one little window of genius, where his imagination let in the suffering of others and intensified it by his own.[6]

Cogswell wrote a novel after the Great War entitled *Ermitage and the Curate* (1922). H.G. Wells, according to White, said, 'it was one of three war books which would be remembered one hundred years after the war'.[7] T.E. Lawrence referred to it as a book that impressed him.[8] George Russell (Æ) reviewed it favourably and provides a summary:

> The curate who preached war sermons and then felt compelled to volunteer, and the teacher he shamed into enlisting by his sermons, are the chief characters. We can feel the torture of exasperated nerves all through the book, sensitive men bullied, disciplined and yelled at, the vast military machine grinding remorselessly because it must, and yet at the end, for all the agony, we are not certain that the crushed souls are not better for all the torture of mind and body.[9]

Cogswell, according to White, 'wanted to be a conscientious objector, not from cowardice but inherent conviction'. He prevaricated about joining the army in 1914, and White, by now his friend, 'advised him to let himself be shot ten times over rather than go out to the shambles'.[10] He did eventually, unlike White, join up and was 'drafted to a Labour Battalion', that is a non-combat section often used to employ pacifists. 'There', according to White, 'he descended into objective hell and observed it with his subjective hell.'[11]

Drawing from these experiences he produced the book, 'written lying on his bed in a room without a table'.[12]

Abandoning the idea of owning a school, probably the most inappropriate job that White ever considered, he spent some time tramping the countryside and working as a farm labourer before Dollie and he headed off to Canada. After a week she 'cabled to her father for funds and returned home'.[13] White remained there for another twelve months doing various jobs working as a horseman and in the logging camps. Dollie joined him again and persuaded him to return to Britain. He did not attempt to hide his utter failure: 'I was not a backwoodsman. I was not a peasant, I was not a farm labourer. In respect to that abortive incarnation, I cursed Tolstoy and died.' Not relishing 'the prodigal son business', he said, on the boat on the way back, 'Dollie sat at the captain's table, so I sat there too; but I felt like a slice off Lot's wife.'[14]

Probably White's most significant experience in those years was his sojourn in the Whiteway Colony:

> a community of 'free-thinkers' which was established on the Cotswold Hills near Sheepscombe in 1898. The colony was conceived as an experiment in practical communism and the original members were strongly influenced by the teachings of Tolstoy with which they had become acquainted through the Croydon Brotherhood Church. However, the colony attracted a diversity of people as no single religious, philosophical or political creed was prescribed and over the years the lifestyle of many colonists evolved away from early principles.[15]

It has been variously described as an anarchistic community with a particular belief that sexual partnership was a flexible arrangement dogged by authoritative regulation in conventional society – free love, in other words. 'Rumours of nudity and sexual orgies brought journalists and sightseers as well as hopeful applicants to live.'[16] Even White's description, which leaves the impression of a louche place, was possibly unfair to the sincerity of its members:

> It started on a basis of pure Communism, with the usual admixture of pure crankdom. The 'purest' specimens debated such points as whether it was lawful to support the State by putting a postage stamp on a letter, or whether the moral legitimacy of gathering firewood in

the adjacent landlord's game-preserves was invalidated by the risk of angering the game-keeper. Meanwhile, the more mundanely-minded did the cooking and washing. [For this, read women]. Ultimately the latter kicked. [...] The place had a reputation for looseness that was largely unfounded.[17]

White formed a friendship with Francis Sedlak who lived with Nellie Shaw 'in a very adequate shack he had built with his own hands'.[18] Described in his obituary (he died in 1929) as a 'rebel Czech' and 'Hegelian philosopher', Sedlak had formed a 'free union' with Shaw.[19] White said Sedlak claimed to be 'married but not legally, my wife objecting to chattel slavery'.[20] Shaw was described as an 'anarchist-feminist seamstress from Penge', who, along with a number of other young women, was attracted to Tolstoy's advocacy of 'non-violent anarchism, the rejection of the state and of private property in favour of a simple and ascetic life lived on the soil. The aim was freedom for the individual'.[21] Nellie Shaw saw

> the founding of the Tolstoyan community at Purleigh in Essex in 1896 and visited it frequently. Aylmer Maude, translator of Tolstoy and a friend of Russian exiles, was living near Purleigh at Great Baddow and, under his influence, the colony provided a home for members of the Doukhobor sect and other Russians. Nellie Shaw and other young women found Tolstoy's ideas compelling enough to abandon their lives in London and pursue the ideal of commune life. In 1899 Shaw, however, rejected Purleigh and, along with a few others, took part in the founding of Whiteway.[22]

According to White, Aylmer Maude 'had apparently interpreted the master's negative attitude to sex too severely. The more vital spirits had kicked, and there had been an exodus of the more amorously inclined to Whiteway'.[23] This was probably a very personal interpretation; Tolstoy's proscriptions on sexuality appeared to have caused White the greatest difficulty. Shaw herself maintained that in search of 'something warmer, more vital, more appealing to the idealistic side of our natures than mere economics', and feeling that Purleigh 'was affected by class prejudice, and disagreeing with its anti-sex (and anti-woman) ideas', she left with some others and formed Whiteway.[24] Although White wrote in detail about Sedlak and his adventures, finding a common outlook with him in his perspective on authority and the army in particular, the colony itself seems to have been a genuine attempt to come to terms with the ideals of an anarchist society and must have left an impression on White. Sedlak wrote a book with the remarkably unsellable title, *A Holiday with a Hegelian,* 'which no one on earth but himself could understand. I as little as any; but I could understand that Francis understood. He had entered a world of pure thought', said White.[25] More importantly, Sedlak had been to visit Tolstoy who had advised him to go to Purleigh, which is probably where he met Nellie Shaw for the first time. White was amused and felt that the impracticalities of the master's diktats were illustrated when Sedlak was asked how he intended to return to England from Iasnia Poliana, Tolstoy's estate. On replying that he would walk, Tolstoy asked him had he any money. Sedlak said, '"No, have you?" "No" said Tolstoy [and] eventually three roubles were borrowed from the master's cook, and Francis set out to walk to Purley [sic]'.[26]

Living by the sweat of his brow had proved to be beyond White, and, in a phrase as elegant as it is eloquent, he said that as regards 'free love' anyone 'not by birth an aristocrat or gypsy lack[ed] the right balance of confidence or nonchalance'.[27] (It was not to be his only deliberation on free love; there is a report of a lady turning down his offer in the twenties to stay in a republican free love commune. Her response was that she had no objection to the latter, but felt that the former meant living in Ireland, something she could not accept.) He concluded:

> I had tried out Tolstoy. Doing so had convinced me that if Tolstoy had tried himself out as a younger man, instead of breaking away to his tragic death at the last, he'd have seen the snag he left people like Sedlak and me to find out for him. He sent his mind out on adventures and left his body with his wife and that convenient cook.[28]

'From this Tolstoyan anarchist colony of Whiteway' White turned from a pursuit of inner peace for his turbulent mind to a searching outside for social justice, which, as he said, took him into the 'thick of the fight in Ireland'.[29]

White emerges from this time as someone who is desperately seeking some personal form of fulfilment but also with an awareness of himself that insists he must have a role to play in the grand scheme of things. Although a quarter of a century would elapse before he openly acknowledged his beliefs to be that of an anarchist, his demeanour was already of a nature that resisted centralised authority and was robustly sceptical of all grand narratives. Despite being married to a Roman Catholic, White opposed that body vigorously and in particular because of its centrally authoritarian structure. On the other hand, he had little patience for social constructs or ideologies that boiled down to a lot of '–isms', whether it was Catholicism, nationalism, or the sectarianism that polluted both sides of the political divide in Ireland.

Home

In the spring of 1912 Sir George White 'caught a chill at a flower show in the [Royal Chelsea] Hospital grounds, and became seriously ill'. He died on 24 June of that year and it is a mark of his prestige that while he lay seriously ill he had a visit from the king and queen, 'who had both come in person to express to his wife their sympathy in her trouble'.[30]

At the beginning of 1912 Jack White was still at the Whiteway Colony. A letter he wrote to some of the Irish papers in Belfast, dated 15 April 1912, gives his address as c/o Francis Sedlak, Whiteway, Nr Stroud, Gloucestershire.[31] Probably since his return from Canada, but certainly during his time in Whiteway, Ireland had begun to play a part in his thinking. He did at that time express a hope 'to return to Ireland shortly'.[32] Having spent holidays in Whitehall when young, with all the attendant attractions and, as importantly, securities of childhood memories, it would have represented for him somewhere he could find his bearings or at least gain some peace. The fact that at this stage his father's 'health had failed, and in the general breakdown he had been attacked by some form of that mysterious malady, aphasia' (a disorder of speech and writing),[33] would have indicated to White that the time was imminent when he would have to take over as head of family and the duties of care for the White estate at Correen, outside Ballymena. Although the Whites were not exactly well off by ascendancy standards – Sir George having taken the Chelsea Hospital governorship 'because he was not a rich man, and he felt that a comfortable house and an extra £500 a year were not to be thrown away'[34] – Whitehall and its revenues would still have represented alleviation from the penury he and Dollie were enduring.

In those days, White, if his perspective of twenty years later is to be accepted, believed that he was inspired in some way. He wrote, 'I had been dowered with liqueur sensation which freed me from the necessity to stop my processes in order to examine them.'[35] He felt that this inspiration manifested itself in a power that assisted him in carrying out whatever his 'sensation' indicated to him. Convinced by his success in persuading Dollie from afar to marry him, he believed that 'such a power' at his disposal 'could not stop at these long distance amorous assignations'.[36] Identifying it with sexuality of a sort, he wondered that his

> deepening and widening amorousness might hit on the exact time and place, say, to cut a country out from under the batons of twenty thousand policemen, or a church out from under a Pope, or a class out from under a carefully-nourished lie. I would be led to meet the men who would co-operate with me as surely as I had been led to meet Dollie.[37]

He postulates that 'if action was no good without intelligence, intelligence was even less good without action',[38] and recollects his feeling of being 'very much alive, and [I] suspected that my life impulse was derived from a highly intelligent Person, who was also alive'. Unnervingly he then states that 'I decided more and more to trust my half formed wishes.'[39]

It is at this time that he addresses the Irish problem for the first time and in typical idiosyncratic fashion identifies it as 'the sex problem writ large'. He sees the two 'warring creeds and races' as partners in an unstable marriage where 'Ascendancy, male dominance, must disappear and with it the submissive, irresponsible, or the nagging, hysterical woman. Comradeship must take the place of male dominance or female emotional hysteria'.[40] Reminiscent of Arnold's gendering of the Celt and Anglo-Saxon, White's analysis was not original, but it demonstrated both an objectivity and a precocity for its time: 'Obviously they [the warring creeds] could not meet, while one partner was attached to a foreign king and the other to a foreign pope.'[41]

Political Debut

As both an outsider born and educated in England and someone whose roots were in Antrim, White was positioned to contribute substantially to resolving the 'Irish Question'. As in the case of James Larkin and James Connolly, White represented the return of the diaspora but from a different tradition. The only evidence of his first foray into the Irish political scene comes from his own report of his speech delivered at the Memorial Hall in Farringdon Street, London, a well-known venue for political debate. *The Times* reported the meeting on 6 December 1912 but despite the lengthy list of speakers on the platform there is no mention of White. *The Manchester Guardian,* 3 December 1912, gave advance notice of the meeting, mentions White's name and, interestingly, Yeats's, but there was no follow-up report. Certainly, George Bernard Shaw, Arthur Conan Doyle and Stephen Gwynn were present, and Shaw's speech is reported in brief. It was an addition to the initial resolution of the meeting of the Irish Protestant Home Rule Committee which

> expressed its abhorrence of the methods employed by Ulster Unionists, and wishes to assure the British electorate that the grant of self government so far from endangering Protestantism in Ireland, will further the spread of mutual toleration and trust among all creeds in the country.

Shaw, in typical fashion, reworked the old saw that England was nominally supposed to govern Ireland, but 'that was a fiction'. He went on to say that

> the fact he was an Irishman filled him with a wild and inextinguishable pride. He was assured that as a Protestant he would be protected by Englishmen. He would sooner be burnt at the stake (Cheers). He did not want religion banished from politics, particularly from Irish politics; but he wanted to banish much that was called 'religion'.[42]

Conan Doyle, by then Sir Arthur, (whose origins were Irish), said that the Catholic Church in Ireland had never been a persecuting one, conveniently ignoring its singular lack of opportunity.[43] White's own speech, which was not reported, was a fine one but displayed some of the kind of independent thinking that earned him a reputation for unreliability among his fellow platform speakers. Connolly, for example, on at least one occasion refused to speak until after White had finished, because he felt he might be required to undo some damage White might cause.[44] There is no doubt that White was a very accomplished public orator, from his days at Winchester on the school debating team to the late thirties when as a member of the Anarcho-Syndicalist Union, Albert Meltzer described him as one of the 'excellent speakers' the movement had.[45] Like any good speaker, he was sensitive to his audience, but there is no evidence of him ever conforming for the sake of diplomacy, or even co-operating with whatever group he was involved with, for that matter. On this particular occasion, he takes what is a convoluted point – for a speech, that is – and elaborates it for what he described as a mainly Catholic audience. Whether they grasped the point he made or not, he believed that he was received with great enthusiasm. This is almost certainly true because his closing lines demonstrate all the gifts of a demagogue: 'I hear the spirit of Catholic Ireland crying to the spirit of Liberalism: Give us some of the freedom you have won, and we will give you some of the reverence and beauty you have lost.' [46]

This address at the Memorial Hall address was his maiden public political speech and is of some interest because it demonstrates how his analysis of the political system was to change over the next five years. It was an ecumenical speech with a tolerance and understanding of Catholicism that probably was dictated by the composition of the audience. White said he saw Protestantism and Catholicism as 'complementary and, if they but knew it, mutually necessary parties'.[47] He maintained that all religions were not equal 'in the sense that it is a matter of indifference to which one, one belongs', but rather that different religions cater for 'the needs of the universal human spirit at different stages of that gradual evolution of the spirit'.[48] The difference to him was that Protestantism had

> arrived at a recognition of having within itself its own supreme law, had glimpsed within itself, however dimly, the Logos or higher creative reason, whereas [Catholicism] had not, and consequently objectified its supreme law in a Church and priesthood external to, and having authority over itself.[49]

Protestant individualism proved a natural habitat for the liberal approach, and it was astonishing then that when the normally 'authority'-embracing Catholics demonstrated a desire for autonomy, the opposition came from 'some Protestants who exclaim the forces of hell are being let loose'.[50] Maybe White was a little disingenuous in conflating political and religious mindsets, and it is difficult to imagine any audience grasping the sophisticated tenets of such an argument at a political gathering, but it indicates an original mind. White, even twenty years later, was still pleased with his speech: 'The predominantly Catholic audience cheered it to the echo. At that time I was so fresh and ingenuous I would have got a blessing from the Pope for a eulogy on Luther.'[51]

White's earliest comment on Irish affairs was in the letter he wrote from the Whiteway colony in April 1912. This made no such attempt at appeasement when denouncing a Protestant refusal to allow Winston Churchill to speak in the Ulster Hall, Belfast, earlier in the year as 'the naked spirit of Popery'.[52] White saw this as his entry into Irish politics, indeed all politics, because he almost never adopted any kind of nationalist perspective, seeing all struggles more or less, as he asserted in the Memorial Hall speech, as essentially against authoritarianism of one kind or another. The letter, although in one sense a crowd-pleasing exercise, is consistent with later utterances, lauding the ethos of Protestantism, but condemning bigotry and damning the perpetrators as doing Ulster 'incalculable damage in the eyes of all to whom the true spirit and mission of Protestantism is most dear'.[53]

Preparation for Ballymoney

At this point White's antagonism was directed almost entirely against unionism and in particular Carson and all the sectarianism that he seemed to foment. Although he held no brief for Catholicism, White's entire efforts in finding a resolution to the impending strife seemed to lie in Home Rule. This support, it has to be reiterated, was not that of conventional nationalism; at that stage White would have had little, if any, sympathy for an independent thirty-two county Ireland. His socialism was at an embryonic stage; his notion of equality would have been freedom from religious discrimination for all the people in Ireland. The later influence of Connolly, coupled with his natural sympathy for the underdog – which would develop into an extremely radical political position – was never allied with an enthusiasm for Sinn Féin or any of the earlier Irish nationalist positions. He later indicated his lack of sympathy with nationalism, not just in the afore-mentioned letter in 1940 where he declared that he 'was Red, I never was Green', but there were occasions when he openly stated that under certain conditions he would take up arms, either for Carson (in his first speech in Dublin), or against the Free State (again in the 1940 letter).[54] For all that, it would have been difficult to distinguish his actions, or at least the motives for his actions, from those of some of the nationalist activists he was involved with. On the other hand, and typical of the man, he writes about an enthralment to the country that would rival the emotions of someone like James Clarence Mangan:

> With my Bible and shillelagh I went to the Route [the environs of Ballymoney] to chase [...] the spirit of '98. This spirit, though a potent intoxicant, is not the product of the local distilleries at

> Bushmills and Coleraine. To define it fully would take a history of Ireland and more than that. It would take one of those flashes of Kathleen Ni Houlihan's eyes, which have been known to bind even full-blooded Englishmen under a spell for life. To some, these flashes come by way of the mind. To some they come lying out on a Donegal or Connemara mountain by way of – what? the aesthetic sense, a sexual susceptibility to something powerfully female in the Irish earth? Why bother to define it? Especially if, in these disillusioned days, one is almost tempted to suspect that Homer with his tales of Circe and the sirens knew at least as much about it as Yeats with his bean rows and his beehives. *Enough to say that to the genuinely spell-struck, it disturbs the knowledge of how many beans make five. It disturbs the balance.*[55]

White's willingness to court the irrational, the transcendent, is always lurking under the most pragmatic positions he might take. It probably is this that fuels his ready embracing of anarchism, 'a vital unreason', in the phrase that George Dangerfield, the English historian, used to describe a related radical strategy, syndicalism.[56]

Making no mention of his father's death, White recalls that when he returned to Ireland that he 'knew little of the history of Ireland, nothing of her current parties and personalities'.[57] He must have been reading up on the country around that time, however, because in his first speech on home soil he demonstrated not just a sense of history, in particular about 1798 and the subsequent Act of Union, quoting Lecky among others, but, more significantly, also mentioned Connolly's writing. This direct reference in the speech appeared to be more for effect rather than of any particular relevance; he quoted Connolly: 'The English were not yet eight years in Ireland [...] [and] already the Irish were excommunicated for refusing to become slaves.'[58] White's speech was given at a meeting in Ballymoney in County Antrim on 24 October 1913. Apart from marking Roger Casement's Irish political debut and maiden speech, the meeting was an event of some significance because it was an attempt, initiated by White, to demonstrate that there was a substantial opposition to Carson among the Protestants of the north of the country. It is an event forgotten now but of interest and of some pertinence because of the alternative voices it recollects – voices, that is, that acknowledged the very different history of the smaller of the two main islands off the European continent but simultaneously embraced some of the traditions of the larger. A less important note is that White's recollections confuse parts of his speech with that given by Alice Stopford Green. The pamphlet *A Protestant Protest* is accepted as the definitive account of the speeches delivered at the meeting.

In attempting to set up this meeting, White met a number of influential people including, in early October 1913, the Liberal Home Ruler, the Reverend J.B. Armour, who, despite his position, appeared to be far more concerned than White with the Lockout in Dublin. White was probably unaware of the crisis at that time. Armour, in a letter to his son, gives his analysis of the strike as a 'kind of foreword of the future [when] the question before an Irish Parliament will not be Catholicism versus Protestantism — but labour against capital with a by-play, clericalism versus anti-clericalism'. He follows this with a description of a meeting with White who was mainly concerned about Carson's sectarianism. This must have seemed to Armour almost the antithesis of the socialist analysis of his letter, yet it was also of some concern to him:

> Captain White, son of the late Field-Marshal Sir George White, was here on Monday evening to see if a meeting could be got up against the Carson policy. I have not heard what was done as Dr Taggart [the North Antrim Liberal electoral organiser] did not seem anxious for me to be present, though on what grounds I cannot say, as the captain is anxious to enlist a number of Protestants who may not be ardent home rulers but who are opposed to Carson's histrionics. I saw Captain White. He is strong for Home Rule and has been in communication with Lord Dunraven, though whether he is a Dunravenite pure and simple or not, I could not say. There was talk of holding the meeting immediately after Carson had discharged the last of his wooden guns in Ulster. His concluding play is to terminate during this month.[59]

While not exactly the wholehearted support that White maintained it was, it could be said that the subsequent meeting held at Ballymoney was White's brain-child, and it is a mark of the feeling of dismay among liberal Protestants opposed to Carson that such a meeting could be held so readily. White was joined by Sir Roger Casement on the platform, and from the very beginning White's talent to exacerbate and disconcert was evident. He maintains that his original idea was to protest against the creed of 'lovelessness' that Carson promulgated but that on the insistence of Casement it was changed to an anti-Carson lawlessness.[60] White's appeal, he said, was to God, Casement's to Caesar.[61] His latent millenarianism, which becomes evident in his later letters, comes to the fore here in an esoteric flight of fancy about 'Ireland as the pivot of a great world change':

> Her little parochial rebellions achieve nothing but a morbid intensification of the martyr-mania of her people. Her real upheavals come in unison with world wide movements and connect her effort towards internal unity with the unity of mankind.[62]

'We'll get on alright if you're honest', he told Casement whose response was that this was 'most insulting'; nevertheless, White, surprisingly, believed it cleared the air for 'affection and humorous tolerance' to develop.[63]

White wrote that he was in Pentonville Prison serving three months for sedition and in an adjoining cell to Casement the night before he was hanged, and a note of criticism still lingered about the planning for the Ballymoney meeting, even after all the years. Casement, he said, was a man of 'kingly presence' marred by his training as a diplomat. 'Do all diplomats think they can wrangle anything?'[64] he asks when pointing out that Casement's objection to the lawlessness of Carson was inconsistent with an incident in Cork when he called for three cheers for the same gentleman. White believed that Casement was mistaken, not just about the nationalist cause, which White never embraced; he also believed that Casement, when failed by the British Empire, turned to the Kaiser. Then, in his own idiosyncratic way White stated, 'I knew by intuition, before I knew by reason, that the destiny of Ireland had nothing to do with Caesars or empires except to outlast the lot and rise on their ruins.'[65]

A clue to White's more ready antipathy lies in his frank remark that there was a 'rival messiahship' between them.[66] Armour, who was more than aware of friction between them, wrote in a letter to his son that it was he who had invited Casement down after receiving a letter from him about a similar meeting to that which White was planning. After various discussions about the constitution of the panel of speakers and in particular the 'lawlessness' clause, Casement later told Armour that White had (some time earlier in Belfast):

> opened on Sir Roger, accused him of every kind of crime, winding up with the charge that he was not an *honest* man. [...] Sir Roger told

me that and bound me over to secrecy, [Casement's] explanation of the matter is that there is a slate off. Certainly White is peculiar.[67]

It seems clear that White felt Casement was interfering with his original plan; there is also no doubt from the tone of the letter that Armour was most impressed by Casement. What White seems to have been unaware of was that Casement had met not only Armour, but also a committee of 'fifteen of the stalwarts' in the Minor Hall at Ballymoney where the feasibility of such a meeting was decided 'by a unanimous yes', and speakers and other details were discussed.[68] Casement later maintained the confidentiality of this meeting by describing himself during his speech as 'being invited down'. It has to be noted that Casement, although a charismatic character, had his share of critics as well, in particular as regards his temperament. Alice Stopford Green (now remembered as a historian and inspiration to Connolly), his co-speaker on the platform and a close confidante over the years, observed that

> he had spent an evening in her house delivering 'a particularly vehement Irish tirade'. Immediately 'the hall door had at last closed on him' she exclaimed, 'sometimes when I listen to that man I feel I never want to hear the subject of Ireland mentioned again'.[69]

Elsewhere there are other examples of a fieriness which rivalled anything White might have been accused of and undermine Armour's earlier version of a one-sided attack by White; Casement appeared to be just as capable of performing a prima donna routine:

> To the staff of the *Irish Review,* when it printed one of his [Casement's] poems incorrectly, he appeared as 'an Etna vomiting a most devastating lava of boiling hot abuse'. The young Cork nationalist, J.J. Horgan, introduced to him that winter, admired and liked him, but felt he gave an impression of instability and restlessness; and Erskine Childers's young wife, when they met, thought him crazed.[70]

There is no record of Casement anywhere being generous about White, and he 'charitably assured [Green] that White was not a lunatic, but that there was not "much in him save goodwill and a strong desire to knock Carson out"'.[71] An examination of the speeches at Ballymoney should belie this judgment, and it should also be noted that White appears to have, in typical fashion, buried whatever animosity lay between them and, apart from airing what could be argued as a justified grievance at the hijacking of his meeting, never mentioned Casement again except in the most complimentary fashion. Green herself, incidentally, was more than capable of delivering an acid commentary, and she 'told an old friend':

> I would like to let fly at all Irish Protestants. There they sit isolated on their little mounds of self-attributed virtues and boasting of their superior means of grace [...] [while] for lack of grace or graciousness their influence is nothing at all (unless they have a rifle to play with).[72]

Armour, regarding Casement as the more agreeable and understanding of the two principals, concentrated on assuaging White's temperament: 'As [White] is to be in the forefront of the orators and as there is no mention of a chairman, perhaps the wrath of Achilles may be soothed. I am anxious to hear what he says.'[73] As it happened, the meeting was eventually chaired by a Mr J. McElderry, JP. This was after a number of candidates were rejected for various reasons of unsuitability under a process that appeared to require the Machiavellian skill of Armour who, in his letters to his sons, displayed all the manipulative talents of a successful politician. McMinn saw it merely as 'evidence of the jealousy and animosity which existed' within the Antrim Liberals.[74] Armour was particularly concerned about security and insisted on County Police Inspector Morrison coming to Ballymoney to discuss policing tactics. He was worried about the Orange Hall across from the meeting being occupied with drumbeaters and, impractically, wanted the police to prevent people from entering it.

Painting a picture of rioting mobs on both sides, Armour was equally uncomplimentary of the police, maintaining that his analysis of the potential mayhem 'let a little light into their skulls tarred with political prejudice'.[75] On 22 October, two days before the meeting, the all-ticket affair had been almost sold out completely. No Catholics were allowed at the meeting and although McMinn suspects ambivalence on Armour's part towards Catholicism it certainly made sense to exclude them on the grounds that this was a statement specifically by Protestants attacking Carson's attempted monopoly of Protestant politics.[76]

Chapter 5

Unionism and Nationalism

Ballymoney meeting

White's account of Ballymoney bears out Armour's concerns. A strong police force surrounded the building and an Orange drum was banging loudly in the hall across from the meeting as White arrived 'in a two-seater Ford in which I had recently invested',[1] accompanied by Dollie ('a handsome woman, a Spaniard it is said', recorded the appreciative Armour).[2] However, the required police, about seventy strong, stationed strategically, caused 'the hooligans [to take] fright and everything in the town in all its parts was as quiet as on a Sabbath day. *Disturbance none'*, and Armour went on to report that

> The meeting was a success [although] the reports even in the *Irish News* are very poor. The speaking was high tone and earnest and everybody said it was the finest gathering ever held in the Town Hall. Captain White spoke well. As he and Sir Roger had had a tiff I insisted that he should lead off which he did.[3]

It was actually Casement's maiden speech, by his own admission, and it was reported in great detail by *The Irish Times*. White and Alice Stopford Green were the other two principal speakers and, according to the *Manchester Guardian,* White, speaking in a 'ringing voice', received numerous ovations.

The 'local' speakers were Alec Wilson (admired by Armour), John Dinsmore, 'one of Ulster's "captains of industry"', and William Macafee, an 'unsuccessful Liberal candidate for North Antrim in 1910'.[4] Although the hall was filled to capacity by all accounts, 'a building three times the size could have been easily filled', according to the *Guardian*. Though 'it was held in the most Unionist county in the country', it seemed, as Armour mentioned, to be regarded as a very insignificant event by most of the press. *The Irish Times* noted about the gathering that 'their voice was not the voice of North Antrim. The meeting did not appear to excite much interest locally'.[5]

That newspaper's political position in those days is very clearly evident. It is difficult not to be a little disturbed at the entrenchment and obdurate refusal to allow for any other perspective, in particular from a quarter that purported to represent the authoritative, balanced view. Even allowing for the objectivity acquired from hindsight there must have been some resonance felt at the time from the points expressed at the meeting. What appeared to be stalwarts of the northern Irish Protestant community stood up in the face of what must have been considerable intimidation and expressed an outlook that sadly even today has been buried under the dominant narratives of nationalism and unionism. That they should have been at best patronised contributed as significantly to the ensuing turmoil as any of the rabid fundamentalism that flourishes in times like that. The various speeches are of interest even today; the ideas and the viewpoints are, in some cases, surprisingly familiar and for that alone are worth recounting.

Both Casement and Green spoke about the inevitability of Home Rule: 'whatever happened to the actual Bill, the old government of Ireland was dead. Dublin Castle was an empty tenement today – the tenement of a vanished rule', according to Casement.[6] Green added to this by talking of 'a Christian minister [who] had called [the Carsonites] from the pulpit to a "holy" war'; she quoted speeches where Catholics had been 'denounced in these last days as "an alien race", as "our hereditary and implacable enemies", [and] as "our ancient and most treacherous foes"'.[7] Green, whose historical works had had a very significant impact on Connolly, took examples from the past where Catholic and Protestant had co-operated:

> Remember the critical days when Belfast was beginning to build up its commercial position – in 1784 – how the leading Protestants of the town subscribed towards the first Roman Catholic chapel allowed to be built after the penal days – how the Belfast Volunteers, in full

uniform, lined the chapel yard as a guard of honour, and presented arms to the priest as he passed into the church.[8]

She related how in 1851 the Tenants League of north and south consisted of both Protestants and Catholics, of how Isaac Butt led both religions in the demand for Home Rule, and how it was predominantly the Catholics who had fought the long battle that culminated in the relief of lease holders in 1886 which had benefitted all sides. 'What a scandal', she said, 'would it be for us Protestants to push aside such men from joint public service to our common country.'[9] Now, she maintained, Carson, using threat of force, was going to repudiate all cooperation and alarmingly told of his 'sinister warning that the Irish Roman Catholics were to be held by his government as hostages, much in the manner of mediaeval times'.[10] Casting doubts on the level of his support, 'Sir Edward Carson knows well that his Provisional Government could not hold a single county – no, not a single half county even in North East Ulster – for a week except by military force.' Green concluded with another glance at the past and the opportunity that they, as Protestants, now had to

> be the friend, the helper, the uplifter of those it so grievously wronged in the past [...]. This land of sorrow – we have in old days added to its griefs and attempted the degradation of its people. It has given to us [its] riches [...]. Let us now give our people peace instead of a sword, law instead of disorder.[11]

The thrust of the 'lawlessness' charge was regarded by some as giving validity to the notion that Carson could be charged with treason, which had been mooted by Armour when organising the event. He wrote about 'an able letter giving Lord Halsbury's idea of what constitutes high treason – which idea clearly points to Carson as guilty'. Ironically, as White pointed out many years later about Casement, the next speaker, 'the rulers of Britain hanged him while they honoured Carson'.[12] Casement in particular pleaded for a unity of both north and south, both Catholic and Protestant. He had commented a fortnight earlier that 'the will of a fragment of a section of Ireland must now transcend in value not only the wish of the Irish majority, but the declared will of the Parliament of Great Britain and Ireland'.[13] At Ballymoney he aspired to an aloof perspective with a declared intention to discuss 'aspects of the question, far higher than politics' and averred that he was looking only for 'peace with honour'. Denouncing the notion that the 'two Irelands cannot be united' as un-Christian, he went on to maintain that the canard, 'Protestant Ulsterman are being told that they have been bought and sold over their heads', was the reason he had 'accepted the invitation to be present' at the meeting. Referring to the Volunteers, he said that 'Protestant Ulstermen are being armed and drilled' to fight against an enemy that is 'in very truth [...] their own brother, and the best friend they have in the world'. Ireland, he said, was falling apart: 'surely some evil power has been at work in our midst'. He suggested that the madness lay in 'sectarian animosity [which] is, as Lecky called it, the "Master Curse of Ireland" '.[14] According to Casement:

> While the Empire has been expanding and consolidating, Ireland has been contracting and falling apart. A hundred years ago there was only one Ireland. The Wexford Catholic and the Antrim Presbyterian were then equal rebels in the cause of that one Ireland. [...] Where do they stand today? Disunited and severed [...] while the Ireland they died to make one, has lost millions of her people to build up greatness abroad, she has been growing poorer in men, poorer in heart, more abject in spirit, until today it is actually hailed as a triumph of Unionism that here at the very heart of Empire [...] there are not one Irish people, but two.[15]

He noted the merging of the Briton and the Boer in South Africa and 'the closest bonds of unity and goodwill' between England and the United States while 'Ireland is to be rent asunder by her Imperialists in an orgy of hate.'[16] He acknowledged that 'it is they [the Ulster Protestants] who are building up the healthiest and most prosperous part of Ireland' but suggested that they should 'with goodwill in the heart and instruction in the hand [...] guide and help and sustain those less instructed and possibly less capable other Irishmen'. Casement occasionally appears condescending toward the Catholic peasantry, believing they had still to recover fully from their 'long contact with the penal swamp'.[17] He told them that 'the old government of Ireland is dead' and the new one, under the inevitability of Home Rule, 'lies largely in the hands of the men of Ulster'.

In an extraordinary step he suggests that 'Rather than Dublin Castle, Ireland I verily believe would accept government from the Old Town Hall of Belfast.'[18] *The Times* correspondent records laughter at this stage, presumably supportive of the pronouncement. If the Ulster Protestants put aside the 'petty thought of a Provisional Government of Ulster, based on enmity and ill-will', was it 'too bold an idea to put before the men of Ulster' that they should 'take over [...] the provisional government of all Ireland, to hold not Ulster only but all Ireland for the Empire'?[19] Bold it may have been for the northern Protestants, and although it must be borne in mind that the speaker had to take cognisance of the audience, it is unlikely that the majority, as he referred to them, in the South would have perceived it as any more acceptable, although Padraig Pearse expressed exactly the same sentiments just a short few weeks later.[20]

All in all, the *Times* reported, Casement displayed his 'citizenship of the world with an enthusiastic attachment to romantic nationalism'.[21] The remaining three speakers lived up to the image of the pragmatic northern Protestant; although repeating some of the historical precedents of tolerance and unity related by the others, they made some cogent comments and were unanimous in their condemnation of Carson and what they saw as his rabble-rousing tactics which would lead all into perdition.

Alec Wilson, JP, earned Armour's approval with a practical analysis of what the Carson threat amounted to. He questioned how such a 'Provisional Government' was going to gather taxes, for example. He was concerned about the impression given abroad that 'Ulster is a province full of dangerous lunatics'. He spoke about the 'delusion' that was fostered about the Carsonites being under siege and perceptively remarked that 'if you cut the Pope out of Irish Unionism there is nothing left but a handful of rubbish'. The idea that the Act of Union had protected the Protestants was a nonsense; it had been passed when Catholics were at their weakest, and in a unique argument for Home Rule, Wilson said that 'ever since the days of Lord Randolph Churchill our English rulers have used the Bishops of Rome as their advisers and helpers in governing Ireland'. In a spirit of common sense he predicted that Tim Healy's 'biting epigram' would be correct: 'Religion has been keeping us apart in Ireland; pigs and cattle will bring us together.'[22]

Dinsmore, with remarkable socialist acuity for a 'captain of industry', in an examination of the wage levels for the various industries, maintained that the remuneration in the linen trade was almost as much as forty per cent lower than some of the other industries. This showed 'what a good business bigotry was' and that 'the Pope, the greatest asset the linen lords have, is worth at least half a million per annum' to them.[23] The divisions of sectarianism had allowed the working classes to be exploited. William MacAfee, barrister, failed election candidate and suspect, according to Armour, because of his 'attending a Redmond meeting on the Sunday and speaking',[24] stoutly declared his opposition to Carsonism, describing it as 'the embodiment of civil ascendancy, political domination, and religious bigotry'.[25]

White's own speech is provided in detail by him from a report in the *Ulster Guardian*. He described Home Rule as not a religious question but ' a question of human rights'.[26] He said it was 'not the lawlessness of Carsonism but the lovelessness ' and 'its wholesale falsification of the facts of history'.[27] Although he uses the *Ulster Guardian* to recount his speech and quotes himself as saying that 'The Land Acts were the outcome of ceaseless agitation by the farmers of all Ireland. [...] In that fight north and south fought side by side. The victory won, the Protestant farmers were bidden to forget their allies';[28] however, this was actually part of Green's speech. Apart from quite an amount of duplication of points in the speeches, it is probable that the pamphlet printed privately by Green is the most reliable version. In any case, White makes a point about the Act of Union that is worthy of some note:

> the rebellion of 1798, though it failed and was stamped out with inhuman severity, visited on Presbyterian and Catholic alike, had come too dangerously near a successful combination of the Presbyterian and Catholic people to be risked again. The means taken to stop this combination was the Union [...][which] was consummated by the expenditure of 1.5 millions in bribes, voted against by 13 out of 17 of the Ulster members at the time – 'opposed,' to quote Lecky, 'by all the unbribed intellect of Ireland' – protested against by 32 Orange Lodges on one day, but according to Mr Plowden, a Catholic historian, viewed with favour by a very great preponderance of the Catholic body, particularly their nobility, gentry, and clergy.[29]

He was saying to Carson that if the Protestants opposed the Union one hundred years ago, there was little legitimacy to their hysteria now. Ignoring the fact that the anti-Catholicism of the French Revolution must have played some part in Catholic support for the Union, he saw it as 'the policy of England for centuries to rule Ireland by fomenting religious divisions within her borders'.[30]

Then, in imitation of the Carson movement, the assembly signed a covenant, read out by White, which began, 'Being convinced in our conscience that Home Rule would not be disastrous to the national well being of Ulster', and went on to pledge all to stand by each other, Protestant and Catholic, in the 'troublous days that are before us'. This is hardly the most defiant or ringingly inspirational of historic documents, but it at least stated its opposition to unionist objectives and bravely stood against the coercion that, according to Armour, was rife:

> That Carsonism is not really popular outside the ranks of the Orange Lodges is true and that his provisional government is the most outlandish proposal ever made by a sane man is also true but the terror is so great that sane men prefer to sit silent and say nothing. The right of free speech does not exist in Ulster.[31]

Aftermath

White's comment that 'Ballymoney made something of a stir' cannot be denied, but from all the press accounts it did so in a relatively small way.[32] *The Times*, apart from emphasising some different points made by the speakers, gave a similar account to *The Irish Times*, concluding:

> One felt that the pick of the Protestant Home Rulers present on the platform [...] were somewhat out of touch with everyday life and feeling in Ulster, and might be called cranks and faddists by the Philistines and muscular Christians in Sir Edward Carson's following.[33]

However, it was 'The Thunderer's' leader that probably dealt the most damaging blow to any positive effect from Ballymoney. It belittled the town, saying 'it was probably the only place in the whole province where such a gathering could be held with any prospect of success' and described it as 'a small and isolated "pocket" of [...] Ulster Liberals of the old type [...] like the Cheshire Cat [which] has vanished until only its grin lingers furtively in a corner of North Antrim [...]. The one small effort of Protestant Home Rulers [...] reveals the scantiness of their numbers'.[34] Speaking of Carsonism, in essentially a dismissal of White, Casement, Green, and company and their concerns, it said 'the most remarkable feature of the movement in Ulster is its extraordinary restraint. No man's hand is being raised against his neighbour', and in a very early version of what was to become a wearily familiar cant, maintained that 'The people of England will never consent to the forcible coercion of the loyal population of Ulster.' In an unconscious acknowledgment of the first part of White's argument, the article, in contrast, saw Home Rule as once having plenty of support in the struggle for land reform but now, outdated and backward looking, it represented 'the menace of an internal upheaval [...] [and] will throw Ireland back for many decades'.[35]

It is probable that *The Times* would not have devoted so much space to such an event except for the fact that the whole article was meant as a warning to Asquith who was giving a speech at Ladybank in Scotland that day. The prime minister had to withstand a series of threats from the unionists, stating that they would insist on the north-east of Ulster being treated as an exception, or even externally altogether to the Home Rule Bill. Probably for the first time in Irish history the word 'partition' was being realistically mentioned. But, in the words of the *Sunday Independent,* whose proprietor William Martin Murphy's sympathies could be described as nationalist but of a distinctly economic hue:

> conciliatory, yet firm, was the Premier's declaration and the probability is that it will be all the more appreciated by the responsible section of the men of Ulster. [...] He stuck to his guns and avowed his intention of keeping faith with the Irish people.

The paper also made the point on the same page about Ballymoney itself:

> The 'Times' reporter tells his readers that the meeting, as compared with the assemblies of covenanters, lacked impressiveness, but dull, indeed, must be the imagination of him who is not impressed by the fact that the expressions of opinion voiced by such sincere and prominent Protestants as Sir Roger Casement, Mrs J.R. Green and Captain White find endorsement among hundreds of their co-religionists.[36]

Possibly a better indication of the underlying agenda of *The Times* leader is a report that Redmond, who, because he would not have two nationalists contesting one seat, ordered the withdrawal of his party candidate in a Cork by-election. This allowed *The Times* to comment critically and unreasonably about his claim of popularity there (and exposed its partisanship): 'we notice that he does not care to send a candidate to contest North Cork'.[37]

Their special correspondent, apart from reporting on the actual meeting, also filed a commentary on the proceedings. The article, although perceptively remarking on White's 'very individual views [...] [which] appear to be Tolstoyan rather than Redmondite', confines itself to categorising the participants and making the occasional barbed aside.

While all were Home Rulers, Casement, Green, and the words of the covenant itself were nationalist in persuasion; the remainder were Russellites. These were recalcitrant Presbyterians who did not respond with the rest of their co-religionists to Gladstone's Home Rule bill by becoming unionists. Instead they formed the Ulster Farmers' and Labourers' Association, 'supported by Mr T.W. Russell between 1902 and 1909' (hence presumably the use of the term, 'the solitary Ulster Liberal', to describe Russell, who was an MP).[38] In the classic mode of the aspersion caster, the special correspondent wrote that 'they are *said* to dominate the present Liberal Association, which Unionists are *inclined to describe* as a mere clique of place hunters [emphasis added]'.[39] He does reasonably point out, however, that although a number of the participants spoke about the 'unity of Ireland and of the folly of sectarianism [...,] they made no attempt to answer Ulster criticism of present-day Nationalist politics'.[40]

Casement responded in a letter published on 31 October in *The Times*. He said that the crowd, although filling the hall, would have been much larger only for threats of violence; there were only two 'Ulster Liberals' on the platform and if he was an out of touch crank, it was his 'romantic humanitarianism' that drove him 'up the Congo and Amazon rivers' to expose the exploitation occurring there. He was an Ulsterman, unlike Carson and some of the others, and a 'Nationalist' not associated with any party who represents 'far more truly [...] a growing number of the sturdy people of this kindly part of Ireland than those who misrepresent them as being aliens in their own land'.[41]

As a further enlarging of the perspective on the whole debate, White quotes a letter by a Lord Charnwood as the 'respectable view' of the Protestant Home Rulers and uses it to demonstrate 'the deep sincerity of the Ulster people'. Charnwood, although theoretically a Ballymoney supporter, accepted the notion that 'Home Rule means Rome Rule [...] and the influences which the Pope unquestionably symbolizes to Ulster have unquestionably their ugly side.'[42]

Though home in Broughshane for no more than six months, White was already beginning to create an impression. Armour mentions in one of his letters that John Baxter, one of those considered for the chairmanship, was suspicious of White and thought that he had some ulterior motive in the matter, to which I said – supposing he wants to contest this constituency the next time should we not rejoice that somebody would give Kerr-Smiley [a Unionist MP, North Antrim] a run for his money.[43]

White makes no mention of this, but it does indicate how quickly he had made his mark in political circles if someone like Armour would consider White had such potential.

Ballymoney had been a failure, in spite of the reputation of participants of the calibre of J.B. Armour and Sir Roger Casement. *The Times* had damned the whole effort in its support for the allies of the unionists, the Conservative Party. The historian A.P. Thornton's mordant comment on the Tories was appropriate, and in this case maybe a little too kind: 'Ulster was an issue on which men could distribute their emotions freely without having to exercise their brains.'[44] It is pointless to speculate how different things might have been if Carson's impact had been diminished; the ideas and concepts expressed at the meeting were at the least cogent and even inspirational at times. It is difficult to accept that its protagonists had erred so badly in their assessment of the support they had. Rather it seems to have been that other forces imposed their will, which resulted in an outcome that reverberates tragically even today.

National University Meeting – Nationalism

Following on the heels of Ballymoney, and presumably on the strength of his performance there, White was invited to Dublin to speak. He later noted that, 'On the platform also speaking were John Dillon [MP], Tom Kettle, and a number of leading lights of the National struggle.'[45] This was the fifty-eighth session of the Literary and Historical Society of University College Dublin, held on the night of 6 November 1913; the topic was 'The Healing Power of Freedom' and among those attending was Dr Douglas Hyde. At the time White was taken to be sympathetic to the nationalist cause. This is one of the remarkable features of the man, something his wife noted in a letter many years later after he died,[46] that he appeared to be all things to all men, and yet this usually means someone who is incapable of taking any kind of firm stance on any matter. White's case was usually the opposite: he seemed to be totally incapable of lining up with any party to the point of perversity and this was instanced almost immediately at the meeting:

> John Dillon's speech was interrupted several times by suffragettes, whose rather rough ejection was greeted with approving glee by the occupants of the platform behind me. This angered me so much that I turned around and shouted 'Shame' at them.[47]

White had no qualms about upsetting his new supposed friends for the sake of protesting against injustice. Up to this point there had been no indication of his interest in the women's movement but, after the war, he did align himself with the Pankhursts. There is no evidence that White ever followed any line other than one completely independent of the particular movements he might appear to be associated with. It must also be recorded that *The Irish Times* did not report any rough treatment of the women who protested. Although judging by the contrast between White's version of some of the other asides at the meeting and what the reporter wrote, it seems that the paper saw itself in an ameliorative role, dampening any rancour after the event with a calming report:

> A lady in the audience shouted – 'Why not uphold the liberty of Irish women?' A good deal of excitement prevailed as the lady stood on a chair, with numerous stewards around her. She was finally escorted out of the hall amid loud cheering. Mr Dillon was then about to resume when he was again interrupted by another lady suffragist, who was also quietly ejected. [Not much later] another lady interrupted and as she was being escorted from the hall she handed some suffragist literature to Mr Dillon [who] said he believed that the ladies who interrupted were not students of the University. Certainly, their idea of the methods by which they could serve a cause was not calculated to support their claim. (Applause.)[48]

It is possible that White's instinctive sympathy for the underdog was often accompanied with resentment against whomever he perceived was on the opposing side. Dillon appeared to have no argument with the women except for an old-fashioned reserve, whereas White, according to himself, opened his speech by, ironically, one has to presume, congratulating 'the meeting on the gentle and chivalrous treatment shown to the suffragettes'.[49]

From White's perspective, the opening address by the auditor, a Michael J. Ryan, utilising the typical anodyne rhetorical flourishes of an embryonic politician, such as, 'the soon to be a Home Rule Act, is replete with safeguards for the Irish minority',[50] appeared to have had no comprehension of the very real fears of the Protestant community. Dillon, a politician of experience, pragmatically claimed, 'I am ready to give, and have consented to give guarantees, but I do not believe that the Protestants of Ireland themselves care three straws for guarantees.'[51] Then he went on to analyse the resistance to Home Rule:

> They were not such weaklings to be afraid of their faith under an Irish Parliament, and they knew it, under it, their position would be one of power. (Applause.) The truth was they would not accept equality. The old spirit of ascendancy still existed in certain classes in Ireland, and those who would benefit most, or, at least, as much as what was called the majority, were those who were clinging to an ascendancy which could not be maintained in any country at this period of human progress.[52]

Finally, as if to make sure he was not misunderstood, Dillon trumpeted, 'The men in Ulster who were opposing Home Rule were living in the seventeenth century and not in the present.'[53] There would have been considerable support for this contention but even if this could be said to have acutely identified the problem, it was not in any way conciliatory; rather, it was merely setting down a marker from which the Carsonites were to be attacked. There was little or no gesture of reconciliation except for a few platitudes earlier in his speech where he suggested that 'such was the healing power of the gift of freedom that within five years [of Grattan's Parliament] the Catholics and Protestants were close friends'. Again, like Ryan earlier, there was no acknowledgment of the potential tyranny of the Catholic Church and the Protestants' concern.

White, apart from his defence of the suffragettes, was uncharacteristically diplomatic at first, suggesting that if the Catholic Church attempted 'supremacy over the State', 'the Catholic people of Ireland would not be one whit behind Protestants in resisting it'.[54] Although he himself was convinced of this, he said, the people of Ulster needed reassuring and this, in a direct response to Dillon, would have to come from 'the Catholic politicians themselves, and in the clearest and most unmistakeable terms'.[55]

Of the three options open, he believed the first two could operate together, that is, the convincing of the Ulster Protestants of the good intentions of the south and, secondly, 'to prepare to fight their own battle for a united Ireland if Ulster stood out against it'.[56] The third option, that is, allowing the British troops to subjugate Carson and his followers was, surprisingly, something that he himself would resist: 'he would offer his services, as leader or private trooper of irregular horse or any body of horse or foot, to Sir Edward Carson'.[57] It is difficult to establish whether this is an atavistic reaction to what is essentially 'his own' being attacked or again his almost automatic support for the besieged, even though only the Carsonites could have perceived themselves that way.

It may also have indicated that he felt surrounded by people whose political positions were even further away from his than Carson's. What is noteworthy is that it is probably the only occasion he can be found supportive of what he called bigoted unionism which he found repugnant at other times.

Whatever his unease, Kettle's speech did nothing to alleviate it; in fact, White would have had to have taken it as a personal attack on himself: 'the problem with Ulster was not a problem of irregular horses, but a problem of regular asses (Laughter)'.[58] The remainder of what he had to say is covered in *The Irish Times* and goes further than Dillon in displaying absolutely no conciliatory attitude towards the northern Protestants:

> He would ask nothing better than that the staunch, determined, and grim men of north-east Ulster should have an opportunity of learning that there were grim and determined, but less self advertising, men in other parts of Ireland. [...] They [the nationalists] wanted freedom, and they were going to fight for it, and no squalling group of reactionaries could prevent the inevitable rising of the tide, and Sir Edward Carson could not lay fetters on the feet of the coming dawn.[59]

Even if White did not believe he was being attacked personally, he would surely have had difficulty approving such a speech, despite the idea being expressed that the Carsonites should not be allowed to stand in anyone's way. As White said, Kettle's speech made it evident that he did not command unqualified approval, and he then went on to make a comment that lies at the core of the tragedies of the time:

> Yet in a few months from that National University meeting, Tom Kettle was fighting England's battles in Flanders, while I was drilling Irish volunteers in an Ulster county. That is odd, is it not? Yet the explanation is simple. For the real fight, as I was soon to discover, was not between England and Ireland at all, nor yet between Ulster and the rest of Ireland. Kettle and his like never got down to the real fight.[60]

This is the first record of White expressing a social concern, and it is probable that this was the first time he actually became aware of the Dublin strike that came to be called the Lockout. Typically up until now his analysis of the tensions that bedevilled political relationships in Ireland was almost academic in its perspective and seemingly of little interest to the public at large. Once again, as at Ballymoney, the core of his speech about the essential contrasting natures of the two religions with regard to authority, which is detailed in his autobiography, appears to be ignored and does not feature at all in the report by *The Irish Times*. In fact, again, he seems to have been the only speaker who made an attempt to directly address the topic of the meeting, the healing power of freedom. It seemed to him that while Catholicism laid

> stress on cohesion and the limiting of the liberty of the individual, which was necessary to secure the order of the whole, be it a nation or other smaller community, Protestantism laid stress on the liberty of the individual, which he held to be equally necessary, that each might be free by progressive experiment, the essence of which was to make mistakes, to extend and enrich the common life.[61]

Here is, as in his Ballymoney speech, a suggestion of anarchist thinking. The advocacy of liberty, in contrast to the rigidity of control and regulation, allowed for progress even if it only arose from mistakes that were made precisely because of that liberty. Now this view was to be allied with a concern for the social injustices, so evident in the Dublin slums, and the alleviation of which, he believed, the nationalists were almost completely indifferent to. They, in their enthralment with the grand narrative of Ireland in chains, were easy prey to other more life-threatening constructs, like the notion that to take up arms for the United Kingdom against Germany was to defend small nations. Repeating his assertion that the real fight was not 'a political fight at all', he said it 'may not even be a National fight but a class fight'.[62]

Chapter 6

Dublin – the Cast

William Martin Murphy

White mentioned the Dublin slums for the first time in his speech at the meeting at University College Dublin, although he could hardly have been unaware of them up until then.[1] It was from there that the Dublin employers drew a great part of their manpower and from there that Larkin received substantial support for the strike action by the Irish Transport and General Workers Union (ITGWU) on Tuesday, 26 August 1913. This began when tram drivers deserted their vehicles in the middle of Sackville Street during one of the busiest times in the city, the Horse Show. It was precipitated when the owner of the Dublin United Tramway Company, William Martin Murphy, attempted to prevent his workers from joining the ITGWU and had surreptitiously begun a campaign of dismissal against those workers he perceived as troublesome.

Murphy, certainly the best-known example of a rare species, that is, the Irish Catholic individualist, was an 'international contractor of railways and light rail (Africa and South America), an international financier, a press baron who revolutionised the Irish newspaper industry, and a fearless patriot who helped bring down the Irish Party, defeat conscription and, so it seemed at his death, prevent partition'.[2] His opponents would have said:

> Murphy's opposition to Parnell, Larkin, Yeats, and Redmond left him with an extremely select group of admirers by the time of his death in 1919. His role in the downfall of Parnell had not been forgotten

in Dublin (the main centre of the uncrowned king's posthumous support). He was one of the few anti-Parnellites to lose his seat in the 1892 election. His heavy-handed victory against Larkin in the Dublin Lockout of 1913 assured his position as the anti-Christ of Irish labour history. Larkin described him as the 'most foul and vicious blackguard that ever polluted any country [...] a capitalistic vampire'. To compound his bad name in perpetuity, Murphy angered Yeats by opposing a proposed gallery development in Dublin in 1913 to house Lane's pictures.[3]

Murphy, despite his patrician appearance and success on the commercial world stage, represented all that Yeats targeted with his contumely about the fumbler 'in the greasy till'. However, a reassessment is due of this remarkable character, who, although very much on the wrong side of a number of historical events, displayed at other times a steadfastness and intelligence of position and certainly was an individual of more substance than many occupying the pantheon of the Irish state.

He had been a nationalist MP and more importantly owned several newspapers, *The Irish Independent, Evening Herald* and *The Irish Catholic,* with which it would be naïve to imagine he did not employ to promote his own views on current events. Although 'he had no time for employers who created labour unrest by abusing their workers, he enjoyed a reputation as a progressive and moderate employer, a reputation at one time acknowledged by the Dublin Trades Council',[4] his despotic rule over employees could be described as benign only by those who unquestioningly complied with his wishes:

> Murphy was [...] harsh and ruthless when it came to trade unionism, and it is not too cynical a view that suggests that he never faced a strike because he never used unionised labour where unorganised labour could be had instead [...] [he] had a strike free record to 1913 because his absolute authority was not challenged until Larkin challenged it.[5]

About 150 to 200 of the 700 tram drivers had become members of Larkin's union, and it was they who took strike action. In view of the kind of man they were in effect rebelling against, and regardless of the encouragement of Larkin, it was an act of great courage to behave as they did. Although they were relatively well paid compared with unskilled workers, their wages were still 25 per cent less than those of tram drivers in Belfast or Glasgow.[6]

Dublin Metropolitan Police

Retribution occurred immediately with the arrest of Larkin and others; all were charged with sedition for their inflammatory speeches. Connolly was arrested on Saturday 30 August amidst violent baton charges by the Dublin Metropolitan Police (DMP) when two men were killed, one of them a trade union member. The following day, when the bailed Larkin made a dramatic appearance at a balcony in a hotel owned – ironically – by Murphy, the incensed DMP arrested him and the resulting mayhem earned the soubriquet of 'Bloody Sunday'.

The headlines in *The Irish Times* on Monday 1 September 1913 summarised succinctly the disorder of the weekend: 'Grave Labour riots in Dublin. Dramatic scene at Larkin's capture. Fierce attacks on the Police. Baton charges in the streets. One man killed and over 400 persons treated in hospital. Thirty Policemen injured.' The language of the paper leaves little doubt of the perspective being adopted towards the whole affair: 'After a long fight by the police against tremendous odds the rioters were driven off and scattered in all directions.'

The statistics of two men dead (a second died later in the week) and four hundred hospitalised as opposed to thirty policemen injured raised a question about who the 'tremendous odds' were against; such a disparity of casualties between two groups of combatants would suggest an imbalance of force. Certainly there were a substantial number of witnesses who wrote to praise the behaviour of the police but, without questioning either honesty or vested interest, the point has to be made that none of these reports could have a perspective on the overall picture. It is possible the letters critical of the police prove to be a better indication of what happened.

One letter, in that day's paper, written by Casimir Dunin Markievicz, husband of Constance, *née* Gore-Booth, painted a scene of appalling brutality:

> round the corner of Princes Street I saw a young man pursued by a huge policeman, knocked down and then while bleeding on the ground, batoned and kicked, not only by this policeman, but by his colleagues, lusting for slaughter. I saw many batoned people lying on the ground senseless and bleeding. Women, old and young, were not

spared, but were knocked down and trampled on. When the police had satisfied their bloodthirsty pursuit, the terror-stricken people and we, the passers-by, timorously sought shelter in the doorways, but the baton was still used freely.[7]

In view of his wife's relationship to revolutionary causes, Markievicz's presence in Sackville Street was understandably questioned in a leader on the same day, but the paper did concede that 'some of the police, harassed and wearied by the constant fighting, lost their heads, and did things which they would not have done in cold blood'.[8] However 'they [the police] have vindicated a reputation which is too secure to be hurt by casual criticism'.

This was the establishment line, and similar opinions probably represented the thinking of the general middle-class public of those days. It can be argued that analysis of some of the texts, even at a distance of a century, and conceding the dangers of applying social standards from a different era, can still reveal an entrenched attitude that seems unconscious of its own bias. Apart from the imbalance of wounded between both sets of protagonists – 400 to 30 (and bearing in mind that the majority of those 400 would have been most reluctant to be hospitalised) – there were other newspaper reports which indicate the activities of the police were possibly suggestive more of Markievicz's Cossacks than of upholders of public order.

As an illustration of underlying attitudes among the police, who seemed to believe that the gathering of crowds, especially those of the working class, were inherently illegal, the following article appeared in *The Irish Times* on Saturday 30 August 1913 before the serious riots took place. This appears, at least to modern eyes, a police attitude of intolerance coupled with a total disregard for the citizen's right to protest in a peaceable manner:

POLICE CHARGE THE MOB

After the meeting, and as the people were crowding up Eden Quay, a youth made an insulting remark to a police sergeant, who was standing alone at the corner of Marlborough street. The sergeant pluckily charged into the crowd after the youth and boxed his ears. The crowd, seeing the policeman charging into them, quickly scattered. Superintendent Kiernan, who had a dozen men under his charge at the corner of Lower Abbey Street, seeing the commotion, was quickly on the scene, and directed his men, without drawing their batons, to charge on the crowd. This they did, and drove the people at full speed down the length of Butt Bridge, where they scattered. For some time afterwards the crowd was kept on the move, but no further disturbance took place, and by half-past eleven o'clock the streets had resumed their normal appearance.

Taking the entire article at face value, the headline mentions a mob, yet there is no indication whatsoever of any disturbing behaviour by the crowd, who are leaving a meeting, apart from a youth who 'made an insulting remark'. In any case they 'quickly scattered' when the youth had his ears boxed (surely under different circumstances this could be regarded as an assault by the policeman). A superintendent directed a charge of a dozen men on the crowd 'and drove the people at full speed' until they scattered. They were then kept moving, but 'no further disturbance took place', a disingenuous remark, when no earlier disturbance had been identified.[9]

The article describes a police force pursuing a policy of oppression and a denial of citizens their rights to go peaceably from place to place, and all of this, judging from the tone of the article, is approved by the majority of the regular readers of that paper. It is difficult to withhold scepticism at the fact that the number of letters to the paper recounting brutality are balanced by other letters approving the police in doing a difficult job. The paper itself was unrepentant, even in its acknowledgment of the reported police brutality:

> It was freely stated in the City Hall that policemen had broken into private houses and wrecked them. Cases which were heard in the Police Courts yesterday showed that the police only entered private houses to capture ruffians by whom they had been murderously assaulted. We shall welcome an impartial inquiry, knowing that it will dispose finally of these and other cruel fictions. We shall welcome the inquiry for a further reason. In a very few cases individual policemen may have betrayed their trust as guardians of the public peace [...] if they are confirmed, this man is a disgrace to the force and should be expelled from it with the least possible delay.[10]

Then, as if to accentuate the position it was taking, the article reported that the Manchester trade unions 'espoused the cause of the Dublin hooligans' and it earnestly hoped 'that our Dublin working men, for their own sake, will give no encouragement to these new busy bodies. [...] Mr Keir Hardie's intervention is a gross impertinence.' It had no objection to trade unionism but saw the ITGWU as 'an intolerable tyranny over masters and men alike'.[11]

It is generally accepted that the behaviour of the DMP in that period was more than unusually brutal, and it would appear that this was not maverick behaviour by some superintendents or even by Sir John Ross, the Chief of Police, but approved and accepted tactics as far as the established powers of the city were concerned. Although it was consciousness of this that drove White to become involved directly in revolutionary politics for the first time, it is the condition of the Dublin slums that provided the humanitarian element, which was always his prime concern.

Slums of the Inner City

Within a couple of days of the aftermath of 'Bloody Sunday' a further tragedy occurred. On Tuesday evening, 2 September 1913, two tenement buildings at 66 and 67 Church Street collapsed without warning and eight people were killed and twenty hospitalised, including three who were critically injured. Four children were among the dead. Adjacent houses had to be propped up while the fire brigade tried to rescue those trapped inside. According to *The Times*:

> The affair created a profound impression when it became known in the city, and a searching inquiry will be held. The slums of Dublin are the worst in the kingdom. They are in the charge of the Corporation, who are supposed to provide for their regular inspection and to insist upon necessary repairs. It is quite possible that the present accident may lead to a full public inquiry into the state of the slums and the conditions of the poor who live there. It is a terrible fact that 20,000 families, nearly a third part of the population of Dublin, live in one-room tenements.[12]

In fact, a report by Sir Charles Cameron delivered on 16 October 1913 revealed that there were 21,000 single-room tenements in which 30,000 people lived in rooms with four to six occupants, 6,000 lived in rooms of seven-person occupancy, and another 2,000 lived in eight to twelve-person occupancy.[13]

Padraig Yeates writes that Dublin at that time had a sewage system so broken down that 'faecal sediment impregnated the subsoil of the city', creating a continual odour of filth and decay. The inner city had been deserted by the elite long before. Encouraged by various rates reliefs and more salubrious surroundings in the suburbs, they left their once-great mansions to deteriorate into tenements inhabited by over 70,000 souls living in the close proximity described by Cameron. Yeates quotes a journalist, Arnold Wright, reputedly paid by the employers during the Lockout, who described Dublin as a place 'where the degradation of humankind is carried to a point of abjectness beyond that reached in any city of the Western world, save perhaps Naples'.[14]

George Russell (Æ) described them as 'interesting experiments carried on in Dublin for generations to find out how closely human beings can be packed together, on how little a human being can live, and what is the minimum wage his employer need pay him'.[15]

White makes extensive use of *The Times* to describe the conditions and contrasts them with other cities of the United Kingdom:

> The average death rate in the city of Dublin during the past decade has been 24.6 per 1,000; in London the annual rate is 13.6. Last year 43.4 per cent of the deaths took place in the various workhouses, hospitals, lunatic asylums and prisons of Dublin; the proportion of deaths in public institutions in large English towns only averages 18 per cent.[16]

The paper describes such conditions as 'subversive to health and morality' and tellingly points out that 'they suffice to account for the haggard and despairing men who gather daily outside Liberty Hall or on the banks of the Liffey'.[17] It then details, in a series of points, where the problems lay. Firstly, there is the perennial problem of the surfeit of administrative resources:

> The irony of the situation is that Dublin, still by far the richest city in Ireland, maintains an elaborate staff to look after the public health and the sanitation of its precincts. There are 146 persons, most of whom are exclusively engaged under the direction of the Corporation in professedly caring for the health of Dublin. The city possesses twenty two medical officers of health and thirty six sanitary sub-officers armed with impressive certificates in sanitary science. The Corporation has ample funds, and is backed by laws which give it all the powers it requires. The net result of all this simulation of endeavour is the state of Dublin as we see it today.[18]

It then reveals its political agenda, in its support of unionism, favoured by the Conservative party:

> Home Rule will not right the wrongs of the Dublin poor. These are woes of Ireland on which the Nationalist party has always been studiously silent. Ardent Members of Parliament are always streaming from Westminster through Dublin, but they have never found time or inclination to expose grievances far worse than were ever found in Land League campaigns, grievances for which they know full well the remedy lies ready to hand.[19]

And finally it thunders: 'The churches, the employers of labour, the public men, the wealthy private folk, none can escape their share of the blame.' [20]

David A. Chart was a distinguished senior civil servant who worked in the Public Record Office in the Four Courts from 1912 to 1915.[21] He compiled a statistical study of the unskilled labourers in Dublin presented to, among others, the Lord Lieutenant on 6 March 1914. Although the Lockout had petered out at this stage, the study is relevant in its report of the economics of the lumpenproleteriat in the Dublin slums at that time:

> 24,000, more than a quarter of the adult male population, were engaged in unskilled labour in Dublin. [...] the average wage paid was about 18/- a week [...] the lecturer submitted a typical budget of a labouring household [...] Rent 2/6, fuel and light 2/-; bread, 4/-; tea, 9d; sugar, 9d; milk (usually condensed) 6d; butter (dripping, margarine), 1/6; potatoes or other vegetables, 2/-; meat, fish, bacon etc., 2/-; leaving a balance of 3/-.[22]

Clothes, shoes, furniture, medicine, and any entertainment, basically toys and drink, would all have to be covered by the 'balance' of three shillings (about 20 cents, maybe €15 in today's money). According to Chart, 'Hard Times' were unfortunately of frequent occurrence, usually caused by sickness (an inevitable result of living conditions) or unemployment (characteristic of the life of the unskilled labourer), and 'the housekeeper on eighteen shillings a week was engaged in a never ceasing hand to hand struggle with indigence'.[23]

Chart, though sympathetic to the labourers' plight, claimed 'that the blame for the state of the slums lay with the slum dwellers themselves, that the tenant of insanitary habits made the house noisome, and so on, and that such people, if admitted to a palace would turn it into a pig sty'.[24] The fact that he was no liberal bleeding heart makes his case about granting a wage increase all the more cogent. Suggesting a rise of four shillings a week for a carter, he calculates that this would add a halfpenny to the cost of a ton of coal. Pragmatically he determined that

> under such circumstances the Dublin coal merchants would, with singular unanimity, put up the price by one shilling per ton [...] and even if their coal were to cost [the public] the full shilling more, many of them would rather pay it [... than] be troubled with the thought of the carter's miserable home and half nourished children (Applause). If the only solution was to pay more, in Heaven's name let them do so and be done with it.[25]

Among the responses to Chart were the usual innocuous aspirations, most of all, and not surprisingly, by the Lord Lieutenant, who flaccidly concluded that, 'There was sympathy, and it should be evoked and directed so as not to give the impression that those who were better to do were unsympathetic.' Several displayed condescension: 'the claims of Bacchus and gambling were the first toll' on the household budget, while others argued that education was the answer. Charles Eason, however, spoke much more bluntly: 'They had got to recognise that the present industrial system had broken down [...] They had to face the question that men and women to a large extent were underpaid, and that their wages must be raised.'[26]

The most interesting response was that of the notable academic, Fr Finlay, SJ, who said of Chart's suggestion:

> to add a few pence per ton to the price of coal [...] might look a very simple thing [...] but it became a very serious matter for the conductor of a large business [... who could be operating on a] margin of profit on his invested capital that was exceedingly narrow. [...] Unless it could be shown that their business enterprises were conducted on such lines as to leave the employer a decent normal return upon his capital, he maintained it was absolutely out of the question for him to raise the rate of wages and still carry on in business. [...] It was a question above all else of business capacity.[27]

Allowing for the priest's position in attempting to portray himself as conscious of decisions that are necessary for the day-to-day life of business, it is still an unusual speech in that the flock seems to be of much less concern to the shepherd than the wellbeing of the owner of the field they graze in. His notion that 'whatever solution [...] had been proposed seemed to furnish difficulties' allows him to at least make a cursory nod to his calling, and he almost timidly suggests that 'when they got back to the old relations based on Christianity, rather than adopt the devices of modern statesmanship, they would arrive at the solution of this distressing problem. Applause'.[28]

Fr Finlay is identified by Connolly in *The Re-Conquest of Ireland* as a member, along with George Russell and Sir Horace Plunkett, of the Irish Agricultural Organisation Society who 'in their attempts to regenerate Irish agricultural life had no more bitter enemies than the political representatives of the Irish people, irrespective of their political colour'.[29] At this meeting he may have been a little ameliorative to people who would have supported these political representatives. Fr Finlay could not, however, be seen as a Connolly supporter. In 1899 he had given a paper in Maynooth on 'Co-operation' where he displayed a distinct lack of sympathy for the socialist perspective by stating that it was 'seen to have much in common with slavery'. Donal Nevin quotes from the *Workers' Republic,* 8 July 1899:

> As to Fr Finlay's claim that socialism had 'hopelessly broken down wherever it had been tried', Connolly responded that this was not so because being the fruit of an historical evolution yet to be completed, *Socialism has never been tried.*[30]

Children of the Lockout

As White began to engage with the various issues in Dublin, his desire to remain tolerant of all creeds was put under serious strain. Having seen the ugliness of bigotry, particularly in the north, and having spoken out against Carsonism, he was now becoming aware of the other face of sectarianism:

> The strikers were hard pressed, terribly hard pressed. A movement was set on foot by Socialist sympathisers in England to relieve the pressure on them by taking some of the strikers' children to be cared for during the duration of the strike in English homes. A Mrs Montefiore [...] and a Mrs Rand were sent over to Dublin as

representatives of the English movement to select children from the hardest pressed families and arrange their transport to England [...] a loathsome agitation convulsed Dublin. The priests with unspeakable indecency became the open tools of the bosses, who were slowly starving out the parents and used their 'sacred' office to ensure that the children should starve with them.[31]

Quoting from *The Times* again, White repeats that 'the physical characteristics of the slum children [is that] most of them wilt at a very early age, and the infant mortality is very great'.[32] Now, because of the rumours that 'the children were being taken away to England to be proselytized and weaned away from the true faith were spread and commonly believed',[33] the poor were to be denied the possibility of decent nutrition because of the power of the Catholic priests.

White's stance did not take cognisance of the feelings of a significant number of the strikers themselves. Although *The Times* mentions 'the extraordinary jealousy with which the Roman Catholic Church in Ireland regards any intrusion on its own social or spiritual field', it concedes that there is 'a widespread belief in Dublin that all English trade unionists are Socialists and that Socialism and Atheism are identical terms'.[34] Interestingly, opposition was not confined to Catholics, for 'much offence [had been given] to Protestants [...]. It is regarded as the last humiliation in a sustained process of holding up Irish poverty and misery to the gaze of people in Great Britain'.

Even in the strikers' camp misgivings were expressed: 'Mr Partridge, one of Mr Larkin's lieutenants, deprecates it today, and suggests that the children of distressed strikers might be taken into Roman Catholic homes in Ireland.'[35] All of this indicates that Mrs Montefiore, and Larkin for that matter, were challenging a hegemony at least as powerful as anything that William Martin Murphy could muster.

When it became known that 'six children were actually taken over by the mid day boat' to England, the 'Roman Catholic Church and Liberty Hall came into conflict'.[36] The following morning news reached the St Andrews' Parish Presbytery at Westland Row that prior to 'embarking for England [...] some fifty boys and girls were brought to Tara Street Baths [...] to be washed and newly clothed for their journey by the afternoon boat'. Five priests arrived on the scene and with a 'good deal of excitement prevailing, many women appearing to now object to the sending away of their children', only nineteen eventually went to Westland Row Station.[37]

Mrs Rand, daughter of a former US ambassador to Portugal, and companion to Mrs Montefiore, was briefly arrested. The papers featured a number of interviews with both parents and children, all expressing regrets for the fact that they considered leaving at all and implying that there may have been duplicity involved, or at least an unwarranted enthusiasm in persuading them in the first place, by either the Larkinites or Mrs Montefiore and her assistants.[38] *The Irish Times* reported that 'The Parliamentary Committee of the British Trade Union Congress deny that they are in any way concerned with the schemes for transporting the children of Dublin workers to homes in England', and in a statement, apparently made by the British Trade Unions, but lacking names or references of any kind, the scheme was described as a 'project [...] as ill advised in its conception as it was tactless in its execution'.

The statement also (conveniently) noted that its supporters 'are mainly Socialists'.[39] Providing a balance to mask its inherent distaste for the general activities of trade unions, the paper also suggested a latent hysteria on the other side when it reported that no fewer than twenty priests and a large number of members of the 'Ancient Order of Hibernians' manned the quays the previous day (that is, the day after the Tara Street Baths debacle). This was to ensure there were no further attempts to deport children. The following morning Mrs Montefiore appeared in court 'charged with having feloniously taken George Burke away from Liberty Hall on Wednesday with the intention of depriving his father, Terence Burke, of the custody of him'.[40] She had previously testified that it was she, and not Mrs Rand, who would bear the responsibility for any charges made about deporting children. White believed that 'they [Mrs Montefiore and her supporters] did take charge of one boy [...] whose drunken father was hunted up, made to state that he had given no consent to his son's removal, and this was made the basis of the charge. [...] I saw red'.[41]

His forbearance had evaporated, the 'sand of his gentility had run out', and in probably the most intemperate statement in the entire autobiography, he writes that 'the dirty reptile latent in priestcraft could not rest content with that [weaning children away from the true faith]. The children were being deported for the white slave traffic'!'[42]

Roy Foster attributes this penny-dreadful 'white slavery' to Maud Gonne, who, along with Countess Plunkett, 'supported the strike but opposed the removal of the children'.[43] However, the two letters he mentions that she wrote to *The Irish Times* about the children do not make this point at all. They actually, in a balanced way, express what appear to be reasonable concerns and reveal a Maud Gonne both pragmatic and concerned for the common good. Firstly she writes about the condition of the children:

> Year after year, Sir Charles Cameron [...] has pointed out that the high death rate in Dublin is due chiefly to the high rate of mortality among the children of the very poor, and that their deaths, in his opinion, are in great part due to lack of food. The lock-out has greatly increased the numbers of starving children. *The danger of actual starvation is less, probably, among the children of men belonging to trade unions who are getting strike pay and some food than among the children of casual labourers, who belong to no unions, but are out of work because of the general standstill in business.*[44]

This raised the spectre of the lumpenproletariat, those whom even Marx reserved judgment over, those who were actually worse off than Larkin's people but would not be sent abroad and who, of course, could potentially divert sympathy from their cause.

Furthermore, the image of the Church and its servile followers heedlessly sacrificing children's health was considerably diffused by Gonne lauding the nuns for the sterling work they were doing in looking after the children. (Without detracting from the nuns, it must be remembered that feeding the hungry offered untold opportunities for proselytism, and in 'the war for souls' in Dublin between Protestants and Catholics, there was 'little room for Christian charity'.)[45] Gonne also addressed the actual problem of feeding such numbers by practically suggesting that it should be done through the schools, a solution that heretofore had merited little attention in the debate. She firmly came out against the sending of the children abroad by stating 'it is our duty to see that they are fed at home'.[46] Then she went on to expose tellingly the ill-preparedness of the plan:

> Mr Larkin stated that I have imputed bad motives to the English ladies who proposed sending 350 Irish children to [...] England [...] in answer to Mrs Montefiore's appeal in the *Daily Herald*. [...] I am writing to Mr Larkin to tell him he is mistaken. [...] I never imputed bad motives to these ladies [...,] but after having heard Mrs Montefiore explain her scheme, I came to the conclusion she could not answer for all the homes she meant to send the children to. This was the reason why I advised Miss Larkin not to go on with the

scheme. I have the greatest sympathy with the Irish Transport Union, and believe that it has done a great public work.[47]

Certainly it would present an alarming picture today if some of the children being cared for were sent to homes that had not been vetted. The fact that the scheme involved only 350 children, when at least 20,000 families were starving, indicates that it was going to have little effect on the overall problem.

It appears Gonne may have been a victim of the demagogic zeal of Larkin, which White himself was shortly to experience. In any case, it is questionable whether the whole affair benefitted the strikers' cause and, undoubtedly, Larkin's challenge to the authority of the Catholic Church had received a severe buffeting. According to *The Times*:

> He has been badly beaten over the question of the deportation of the workers' children. As the *Irish Times* says to-day, he has exasperated public opinion and shaken the allegiance of his own followers. His prestige is hurt, and for a democratic leader prestige is everything.[48]

It could be argued equally, as in the still-raging contest with William Martin Murphy, that Larkin may have lost the short-term battle but emerged victorious in the war of images – the spectacle of little children being denied basic sustenance by a group of religious zealots probably defined the Lockout for years.

In any case, White, recollecting the affair nearly twenty years later, still held to the position that the Catholic priests, 'with unspeakable indecency, became the open tools of the bosses, who were slowly starving out the parents and used their "sacred" office to ensure that the children should starve with them'.[49] He maintained that this was the single motivating factor that galvanised him into supporting the strike even 'before I realised that here in Irish Labour was the medium destined at once to unite Ireland and link her cause with that of humanity at large'.[50] This phrase marks the first recorded conscious reference by White to a political perspective that was developing from merely combating Carsonism and supporting the 1913–14 strike to a Marxian belief that, according to Engels, 'the first and most pressing duty, as Irishmen, was to establish their own national independence'.[51] It was to cause untold turmoil in his allegiances for years to come.

Chapter 7

The Search for a Role

'A Liberty Hall Surprise'

White writes about the almost simultaneous occurrences of the tramway strike and the names of the general staff of the Ulster Volunteer Force being published, and he perceives:

> synchronisation [as being] symbolic of a deep connection which is not visible on the surface. Time, the invisible dimension, brought out the hidden link between the ultimate forces warring respectively to sever and maintain Ireland's connection with the British Empire.[1]

Reluctant to align with the nationalists for reasons of birth, upbringing and inherent individualism, and in the process of forming a political philosophy, White was frustrated with the seeming impossibility of resisting the 'lovelessness' of Carsonism, but he found an outlet for his need for action by turning his attention to the activities of the Dublin Metropolitan Police. As mentioned already, their dubiously legal behaviour in violently putting an end to what they perceived to be rebellious acts of malcontents rather than the legitimate protests of citizens of the state came very much into public consciousness around the events of 'Bloody Sunday'. The conventional support for lawkeeping which the bourgeoisie generally gave to the police came under severe strain with what White described as 'an amazing outburst of police savagery', and an inquiry was called for in a resolution passed by the Dublin Corporation.[2] The Lord Lieutenant replied that 'until order is fully restored and pending the issue of the legal proceedings now in progress in the Police Courts it would be impossible to institute the official inquiry which the Council suggests' but, of course, 'at the earliest possible moment [...] His Excellency would desire [...] a searching investigation'.[3] This conventional bureaucratic-speak would be interpreted by White as saying the authorities supported the actions of the police and would prevaricate and dissemble in an effort to inhibit any real examination of the behaviour of the Dublin Metropolitan Police (DMP).

The notion occurred to White that this was an area where he could put his considerable military experience to good use without compromising his pacifism. The strikers were like 'basking seals' being clubbed on their marches;[4] training them to become a disciplined force to resist the attacks of the police not only offered the practical benefit of allowing them to protest with more confidence, but also constituted a blow against some of those 'ultimate forces'. The night after the fifty-eighth session of the Literary and Historical Society of University College Dublin, White was on the platform at Liberty Hall with James Connolly and this was to lead, within a few days, to White offering his services in forming a citizen army. That night, however, the main topic addressed by Connolly was the need to respond to the strike breakers and a subsequent ratcheting up of the strike which led to his announcement that 'From Monday forward there would be massed picketing [...] and any man or woman who did not join in [...] would forfeit the strike allowance.' Connolly went on to disparage the 'six poltroons', who must have been members of the Irish Party, who stood by while the workers, the real Home Rulers, were 'brutally bludgeoned by the armed bullies of Dublin Castle'.[5] Then, consistent as always in his Marxist perspective of a class struggle, Connolly described how

> He had spent all his life trying to show the Orangemen of the North how they were being exploited by the capitalists and politicians, and he was as much opposed to Hibernianism in the South, for the workers did not want sectarian domination. They wanted a working class and democratic movement in which they would be able to hold out the hand of fellowship and comradeship to every man.[6]

White, who merited the headline, 'A Liberty Hall Surprise', was introduced as 'the latest adherent [to] the sympathy and support of the best intelligence in these countries'. Not overawed, he said 'it was not quite true to say that he was on the side of the men', although instinctively sympathetic, he needed to study the position. George Russell's writing and the 'faked up humbug that had taken place about the deportation of children' was what brought him to the platform. 'He had', he said, 'been fighting in the North of Ireland against the action of ministers of religion who sought to divide the people, and that was a thing he would always oppose.' [7] That was a Friday night and promptly on Monday morning (10 November) the *Irish Independent* produced a letter signed by the pseudonymous 'Ignotus' taking White to task for both the presumptions he had made in his speech and the people he had associated with. It was quite a respectful letter (White had yet to lose the immunity enjoyed by the upper echelons of society in matters like this), but it attempted to make a connection between George Russell's support for the strike and the fact that 'a certain employer wrote many letters […] expressing his disapproval of […] a scheme for a trans-Liffey Art Gallery'.[8] (William Martin Murphy, proprietor of the *Irish Independent,* could hardly be disturbed by such an argument.) Russell behaved like 'a pettish child' when this proposed art development was turned down. 'Ignotus' also damned Russell as 'somewhat of a mystic' and related that he was reported to have gone

> down into a subterranean chamber somewhere near Newgrange, and there endeavouring to invoke a visitation of the ancient pagan gods of Ireland, not desisting from his efforts until he was disturbed in his invocation by the arrival of two Presbyterian clergymen.[9]

White had a reply in Wednesday's paper, which should credit some impartiality on the part of the newspaper, although his aristocratic associations, surely fraying, may have dismissed any doubts about not printing it. Like 'Ignotus', he began by referring to William Martin Murphy, but without naming him:

> I am glad you commence your letter to me with the words: 'it is stated in the public Press', for between what is stated in the public Press and the actual facts, there is, in Ireland, a deep gulf fixed, across which, sir, your winged words and mine can with difficulty pass. For my part, I believe the filling of this gulf with the dead reputations of newspaper proprietors is the first duty of Irish patriots.[10]

Then, defending Russell against accusations of pettiness and spite, he exploits the ludicrous charge of mysticism to demolish his opponent:

> I learn that Mr Russell is a great master of magic.
>
> 'I can call the spirits from the vasty deep – Ay, so can I, but will they answer you?'
>
> Evidently they will answer Mr Russell, for a more direct reply to the invocation of the ancient pagan gods than the appearance of two Presbyterian clergymen could hardly be looked for.[11]

'Ignotus' replied again on Friday but his well-argued instances of Larkin and other trade union men reneging on contracts, which was his original main theme (this time annotated and added to by the editor), was surely lost in the derision that White had invoked.[12]

None of the foregoing can have endeared White to Murphy, and it is possibly a mark of White's naiveté that he later approached the leader of the employers in an effort to settle the strike. It could surprise nobody that Murphy reported giving him short shrift,[13] but it is an illustration of White's continuing unabashed belief that personal differences could be put aside when larger issues are at stake. This trait appears again and again in his treatment of the various individuals he encountered. Regardless of comments made in speeches or even letters written at a particular time, White displays a later willingness to, at least, allow for another point of view. He was now planting himself in the middle of the first important Irish political struggle of the twentieth century and firmly on the socialist side, although he probably would not have acknowledged that at the time. In a letter to his mother he attempts to explain his support for Larkin and Connolly, who

> for all the excrescences of their platform speeches, are men of ideals and ability. To earn their sympathy and trust now and to establish a bond between their class and the *progressively-minded people in ours* will, I believe, bear golden fruit when the time comes to construct.[14]

Not for him yet, or maybe ever, the abolition of class. White describes his equivocation, which must have dogged him throughout all this time and especially so prior to the Easter rebellion; although he found common cause with the nationalists, the strikers, and the socialists, his friends and family were, after all, the very stuff of the British Empire:

> In moments I saw the clear revolutionary principle; at others I was repelled by the bitterness of a philosophy fighting against the whole established order, imputing sinister motives to every 'bourgeois' action, including my own. I clung to the comfortable suavities of my own class. I was not innocent of patronizing the cause I had adopted. I was definitely guilty of emphasizing this note of patronage in intercourse with my family and respectable friends.[15]

There was an inexorable logic to White's next step. The Irish Citizen Army provided all that was fundamental to his requirements at that time; a way of articulating his concern for the disadvantaged in the sense that his role was to protect the poor. His own military experience was put to full use in training the strikers to protect themselves against assaults by the authorities. His target of battling bigotry was achieved against the employers of the city of Dublin. On another level, his idiosyncratic pacifism was satisfied because the role he taught the strikers was a defensive one. Although he was delighted to find experienced soldiers in the ranks of the Citizen Army, he, unlike the other principal protagonists, had seen violence in all its ugliness during the extremities of battle in South Africa. Finally, although he could still be scathing about Carsonism and the other brands of Protestant bigotry, it appears that he had concluded that the Catholic variety was even more dangerous. William Martin Murphy and his co-employers; Sinn Féin and Arthur Griffith; the nationalists of Tom Kettle's ilk, and the Irish Parliamentary Party all combined to form what he saw as a Catholic nationalism unsympathetic, at the very least, to the occupiers of the Dublin tenements. Up to now, White's thinking was marked by a practical approach to the immediate question at hand, informed by a philosophical stance that was heavily dictated by Tolstoy. Now the first signs of a political ideology began to colour his analysis which, although never without a spiritual dimension, was to become distinctly socialist. Typically, it was always coloured by his own highly personal interpretation and led him to describe himself in various original ways; his standing for election as a Christian Communist in 1923 surely raised some eyebrows in Moscow, for example.[16] However, it must be stressed that at all times he had considerable reservations about nationalism. His statement about Casement made in 1936 on the anniversary of his execution illustrates very succinctly the position White held consistently all his life: 'I, myself, have one criticism and only one to make of Casement. He loved his native land better than he loved humanity.'[17] I would argue that what White was doing was drawing a very clear distinction between the support for what could be called the grand narrative of nationalism and the support for some action that he believed would be of direct benefit to humanity. In academic critical theory this poststructuralist questioning of constructs is an important aspect of anarchism, that is, a robust scepticism for any of the banners that humankind throngs to, whether religious or political. This, I would suggest, is White's most important contribution to the whole story of Ireland in the early twentieth century: his belief that both sides, left or right, coloniser or indigenous, regardless of their justification, were bedevilled with unassailable ideologies that inhibited the prospect of resolution. He said:

> In the North I had raised a protest against the perversion of Protestantism to deny political freedom to a subject nation. In the South I broke away from politics down to the real fight in indignant horror at the perversion of Catholicism to deny even the freedom to control their own children to an economically subject class.[18]

There was a combination of guilelessness and sophistication in White's make-up; his ready enthusiasms and almost unworldly belief in his aims were counterpointed by an acute perceptiveness of the machinations that quite often lay behind the exercise of power. His second wife, Noreen Shanahan, wrote after his death:

> He had [...] the child's faith in God and the unshakeable conviction that whatever enterprise he was embarking on, was in fact not merely the work of JRW [his family referred to him thus], but of JRW as divinely-inspired vehicle of the Almighty.

But she also acknowledges him as 'a most brilliant diamond' in the same letter.[19] Despite his seeming gullibility in accepting the idea that the Catholic clergy were somehow primarily concerned with their own authority beyond every other consideration, including even the well-being of their congregations, he still consistently ignored the trumpet call to whatever standard seemed urgent and instead pursued a position that had the immediate purpose of alleviating some injustice. Unionism, nationalism, and Catholicism crystallised in his thinking as concepts that were not necessarily summonses to the collective at large for a better future. Rather, he saw them as notions that could be fostered by those advantaged few who benefitted from them to the cost of the exploited many.

Meeting Connolly and Larkin

Some time between White's surprise appearance on the platform at Beresford Place, Dublin, on the night of 7 November 1913, and his speech at a meeting of the Dublin University Gaelic Society on 18 November, he mooted the idea of a Citizen Army. White maintains he first proposed this idea at a meeting of the Civic League. This was a collection of intellectuals, artists, and academics 'in sympathy with the Strike', and was formerly known as the Peace Committee. White writes that 'the great George Russell (Æ) was a member of it, so was Padraic Colum the poet, Robin Gwynn of Trinity College, and Houston of the College of Science. Sheehy Skeffington was on it, of course'.[20] The members decided to disband soon after White had attended his very first meeting in Dublin on 6 November 1913, 'as peace was the last thing either of the contending parties wanted'. Tom Kettle was the chairman, but, according to White, he arrived very late and very drunk. White, who had been invited to attend and could hardly have been sympathetic to him based on their previous meeting, proposed Kettle should 'vacate the chair as unfit for proceedings', and was elected as chairman himself. The members 'reconstructed' themselves 'as the Civic League', and it was that 'innocent' body that passed White's proposal to 'drill the Dublin strikers' before he had offered his services to Connolly and Larkin.[21]

Andrew Boyd's version of the beginnings is as follows: 'O'Casey helped to organise the open-air rally in Beresford Place when first Jim Larkin and then Jack White appeared at an upstairs window in Liberty Hall to announce the inauguration of the Irish Citizen Army.'[22] This puts the date as after Larkin's release on 13 November. According to White, 'Connolly and Larkin welcomed the proposal to drill the men [...]. It was at one of these [Croydon Park] Sunday meetings I first propounded the proposal of the Citizen Army, to the huge enthusiasm and delight of the men themselves.'[23]

White saw the Citizen Army as a practical way of contributing his very substantial military skills to the strike effort, while at the same time not breaching his pacifism, a concept that he rarely refers to directly either in *Misfit* or in his other writings until much later.[24] Boyd relates that Larkin

> had already said the ITGWU should have weapons. On 27 August, two months before Jack White came to speak in Dublin, he told

the members assembled outside Liberty Hall, headquarters of the union, that if it was 'legal and right for Carson to arm in the North why should it not be right and legal for the men of Dublin to arm to protect themselves'. He warned the union members that when on strike they would have to face 'hired assassins' and would need therefore to be armed themselves. His advice was 'whenever one of your men is shot, shoot two of theirs'.[25]

Although allies, but for quite different reasons, Larkin and White, because of their impetuous temperaments, could never have been close, but White always had a tremendous regard for him: 'Jim at his worst [...] perpetually dogs the heels of his best. In those days [1913], at the height of his influence he was, what God meant him to be, great.'[26] An incident that was made much of in the press (and is detailed later on) occurred when at a series of meetings in early 1914 in Sackville Street, Larkin referred to White's father fighting under the 'Butcher's Apron'. White left the platform and gave an opportunity to *The Irish Times* to denigrate Larkin:

> the fact that Mr Larkin went out of his way, on the spur of the moment, to offend an ally whose services we suppose to be valuable to him, gives us a vivid glimpse into his hopelessly impulsive character. It is not surprising that the English trade union leaders should have decided to abandon the fruitless task of maintaining diplomatic relations with Mr Larkin.[27]

White reports that he got no apology for ten years, but then, out of the blue, Larkin made handsome recompense in an incident that illustrates the unconventional aspects of both men's characters. At a meeting in Battersea Town Hall where White was badly heckled having confessed to communists his 'belief in an intelligent Supreme Being', Larkin leapt to his defence and 'told the most heart rending story, entirely fictitious' about White being blackballed about his beliefs. Then, White wrote, 'finally he apologised for the Union Jack incident of ten years before, not to me, but to the audience. That is Jim'.[28]

James Connolly's own writings indicate that it was he who initiated the idea of the Citizen Army and saw White, appalled at the 'basking seal' treatment by the DMP, as a fortuitous arrival in the strikers' camp. Perceiving the entire affair as a class struggle, the logical step for Connolly had to be the formation of an army of the working class. Even the revolutionary redolent term 'citizen' is unlikely to have come at that stage from White, but most of all, for the syndicalist that Connolly was, this was a significant advance in the war on capitalism. This became obvious later when Connolly used the uniformed Citizen Army on the picket line.

Connolly's Influence on White

It has been suggested that White picked up whatever Marxism he had from Connolly,[29] but it has not been possible to establish with any certainty what he actually read of Connolly's work; clearly his tastes were very wide, as evidenced by the various glancing references he makes. Certainly White was profoundly impressed by Connolly to the extent that he was imprisoned for sedition after a naïve attempt to rescue Connolly in 1916, events which will be dealt with later. White's later writing and speeches became very radical. For example, his analysis of Sinn Féin in 1918 (also to be detailed later) indicates the possibility that it was Connolly who provided the principal inspiration for this approach. Connolly was by far the single most important thinker that White associated with on an ongoing basis at this time. Although in close association for a period of not much more than six months, it was during this time that White's innate questioning of conventional society and the authority that governed it developed into a radical critique of capitalism and imperialism as the main impediments to the just society to which he aspired. His reference to Connolly twenty-two years later in 1936 in Catalonia illustrates just how much White was affected by him. After a visit to 'revolutionary Barcelona', White wrote an article for a journal of the Confederacíon Nacional del Trabajo (CNT), along with the Iberian Anarchist Federation (FAI) the main anarchist force during the Spanish Civil War:

> You will have heard no doubt about the Dublin Rising of 1916. That rising is now thought of as purely a national one, of which the aims went no further than the national independence of Ireland. It is conveniently forgotten that not only was the manifesto published by the 'bourgeois' leaders conceived in a spirit of extreme liberal democracy, but, associated with the bourgeois leaders, was James Connolly, the international socialist, who some regarded as the greatest revolutionary fighter and organiser of his day. In command of the Irish Citizen Army, which I had drilled, he made common

cause with the Republican separatists against the common Imperial enemy. It is said that he threatened to come out with the Citizen Army alone, if the bourgeois republicans shirked the issue.[30]

And in that vein, he finished his article: 'Comrades of Catalonia [...] I greet you with the voice of revolutionary Ireland, *smothered awhile* but destined to regain its strength.'[31]

Connolly's Apostasy?

White believed that he and Connolly both saw the challenge ahead as a class struggle rather than a national one, although Connolly supported the idea that the British presence in Ireland was the primary obstruction to the success of the revolution. This may in some sense address Connolly's purported embracing of nationalism. According to Robert Young, 'When Connolly's involvement in the 1916 uprising became known, many European socialists were reportedly baffled, unable to understand how he could have got involved with Irish nationalism', and although Young explains that Connolly had already 'elaborated with some care his own position to Sinn Fein [...] and called for a political alliance between Sinn Fein and Irish socialists', he maintains that 'the prescription of Marx himself' justified Connolly's action, that 'you must attack [England] in Ireland. That's her weakest point. Ireland lost, the British Empire is gone and the class war in England till now somnolent and chronic, will assume acute forms'.[32]

Eric Hobsbawm, the Marxist historian, has no problem with this, although he points out that 'nationalist politicians and their opponents naturally like to suggest that one kind of appeal excluded the other'. However, he actually uses Connolly as proof that this is not so: 'it was perfectly possible to become simultaneously a class-conscious Marxian revolutionary and an Irish patriot, like James Connolly'.[33] This is a questionable statement, and White would not have agreed, seeing himself (and probably Connolly to some extent) as 'Red – [...] never Green'.[34] In any case Marx's advice was ignored or found unacceptable to quite a number of Irish socialists; even if England was to be a target, an alliance with any of the various bourgeois movements would not be acceptable.

Emmet O'Connor mentions that Connolly, less emotive and more pragmatic than most of his colleagues, concluded that 'under Eoin McNeill's command they [the Irish Volunteers] would never seize the moment'.

Determined to pursue his own course of resistance in 1916, 'It was only to forestall unilateral action by Connolly that, in January 1916, he was informed of IRB plans and the union of Easter Week was sealed.'[35]

The Lockout itself had revealed serious divisions in the broader nationalist struggle, with many of the strikers believing that the Irish Volunteers, for example, were at best indifferent to their problems. Several disputes broke out over training grounds: 'The Army failed to get permission to use those halls in the city where the Irish Volunteers drilled. They were informed they were in constant use.'[36] Class distinction was emphasised and there were very few members of the Citizen Army from either the artisan or petit bourgeois classes; Boyd notes that the 'leaders of the Irish Volunteers [...] of middle-class nationalist mentality [...,] were hostile to the working class ICA'.[37] The Citizen Army was 'Separatist and Republican and, besides this, it had militant Labour aims'.[38] The first handbill issued by the Citizen Army gives a good indication of their attitude. Among the reasons given why Irish workers should not join the Irish Volunteers were:

1. Because many members of the executive are hostile to the workers.
2. Because it is controlled by the forces that have always opposed Labour.
3. Because many of its officials have locked out their workers for asserting their right to join the trades union of their choice.[39]

This could hardly have been issued without Connolly's approval, and this level of opposition almost certainly indicates that some change occurred later in his attitude towards the Volunteers. Sean O'Casey, who would have personally observed the 'singular change', as he saw it, foregrounds what many of the socialists must have seen as, to say the least, a puzzling change of heart:

> [Connolly's] determined attachment to the principles enunciated by Sinn Fein and the Irish Volunteers, which were, in many instances, directly contrary to his life-long teaching of Socialism, was the fixing on the frontage of Liberty Hall a scroll on which was written the inscription: 'We serve neither King nor Kaiser – but Ireland.' [...] the appeal of Caitlín ní hÚallacháin [...] was in his ears a louder cry than the appeal of the Internationale.[40]

White deals with this in his own fashion. He first quotes O'Casey from the same source, in an even more direct attack on Connolly:

> all proclaimed that Jim Connolly had stepped from the narrow byway of Irish Socialism on to the broad and crowded highway of Irish Nationalism [… its] high creed became his daily rosary, while the higher creed of International humanity that had so long bubbled from his eloquent lips was silent forever and Irish Labour lost a leader.[41]

White points out that O'Casey himself 'had left all armies for the art of the dramatist', so he is, ironically, absolved from any charges of compromise. White is not, because he actually joined the Volunteers, 'long before Connolly identified the Citizen Army with the National Cause'. (This is a kind of faux self-deprecatory statement, for even O'Casey himself did not blame White for his move.) But White goes on:

> Jim Connolly's strongest defence [was when] he realized that the National Movement was the reservoir of the nation's subconscious power, that amalgamating with it he could tap ore in Ireland, even if mixed with a mass of sentimental dross. He was a realist. He saw the British troops in Ireland. They are out of the twenty-six counties now. That is Connolly's defence against O'Casey or even against me.[42]

After quoting scripture about judging not, White delivers, under the guise of self-criticism, an *ad hominem* attack on O'Casey: 'I judged O'Cathasaigh once because he took a literary prize from Asquith, Prime Minister of the Government that shot Connolly, his old chief.'[43] Although White's view of the 'twenty-six counties' would hardly have been very favourable, the above passage indicates his appreciation of the pragmatic benefits of nationalism. This and his address to the Catalans indicated that he believed Connolly also saw the nationalist cause as primarily a means to an end.

White's Relationship with Connolly

White, at the point of meeting Connolly, could best be described as a Tolstoyan. His leanings to anarchism would have been evident in his demeanour rather than in any political position. It must be pointed out, of course, that Tolstoy is generally accepted as an anarchist, even though, according to Woodcock, he 'did not call himself an anarchist, because he applied the name to those who wished to change society by violent means'.[44] Tolstoy, when arguing against any form of government, wrote with irony that 'the very idea of living without a government is a blasphemy which one hardly dare put into words; this is the – for some reason terrible – doctrine of anarchism, with which a mental picture of all kinds of horrors is associated'.[45] The only indications of White's political stance at that time were his speeches in London and, in particular, Ballymoney. There is no acknowledgment of any socialist ideas in them; indeed, he could probably quite comfortably have been accommodated within liberalism.

In his own way White would have been as disadvantaged as Connolly; although well educated, his own background and conditioning would have militated against ever acquiring a truly socialist view, and a good-natured naiveté created a misleading impression of innocence. His awareness, or honesty, or both, recognised this weakness in himself, and with this, mixed with a not-inconsiderable opinion of himself, he recounts how:

> If I had stayed with the Citizen Army instead of going off in a huff to the National Volunteers when the Transport Union appointed a committee to clip my wings and control me, I believe I could have merged National in Labour ideals instead of leaving the merger to come the other way around.[46]

This is not as grandiose as it seems at first. White at this stage, from late 1913 until mid-1914, featured in most headlines that were concerned with either nationalist or labour topics and could well have presented a figure that was acceptable to both sides. Despite his evidently stormy temperament, his position on most matters seemed to be acceptable, to the press at least. Even a report on a speech of his in *The Irish Times* on 2 December 1913, at the height of the tensions of the Lockout, portrays a man of some restraint:

> When violent orations were expected, the men were told to meet the employers half-way. [...] The doctrine of rebellion was not preached, and when the audience heard from Captain White that he was not a rebel, it afforded them much food for thought during their leisure hours yesterday.[47]

Meanwhile, his relationship with Connolly was at times strained. He describes a row between the two of them when a training schedule of the Citizen Army had been interrupted:

> What Connolly said to me one day, when I remonstrated about my army being taken off to a political meeting without my being notified, was true enough, 'You're nothing but a great boy,' said he. 'Go to hell,' I replied. The incident was the first beginning of the dissipation of the class-suspicion and the establishment of warmer relations between us.[48]

The contrast between the six-foot-three White with his received pronounciation – scion of a field-marshal and daughter of a clergyman to the Royal Family – and the five-foot-four, Scottish-accented, shabbily dressed Connolly,[49] presented the oddest of pairs and hardly suggested a meeting of minds, but White was to position himself as one of Connolly's stoutest supporters.

As already mentioned, writing in 1930, he had defended Connolly's supposed apostasy from socialism, maintaining that Connolly had 'realized that the National Movement was the reservoir of the nation's subconscious power'. But he also pointed out that 'Connolly was, of course, more definitely revolutionary than I, and more prepared for violent methods.'[50] In an extended metaphor he contrasted Larkin with Connolly:

> They were two different types of lover. Larkin was the troubadour serenading with love inspiring poems. If the lady proved difficult they turned to vicious lampoons. Connolly could sing a little, very little, rather raucously, like a crow in the mating season. But he held the caveman in reserve and relied on the caveman, not the troubadour.[51]

The 'caveman' in Connolly is probably what gave him his power, but it was not surprising that, even if only in sheer desperation, he resorted to this persona when the Lockout, with its starving participants and the ultimate lack of any resolution after its collapse, must have produced the bleakest prognosis of the disadvantaged in Ireland. Some of White's own passionate despair is captured in a letter of March 1914:

> I heard today of a man who had just died, according to his wife, 'of a broken heart' from the attempt to feed himself and his family on

a loaf of bread per day. The people prefer death to going into the workhouse. Would to God they would seek their death in violent protest against the devilish apathy of those responsible for their relief. Every avenue is blocked to them [...]. The attitude of the Dublin public is little short of devilish. The Lord Mayor of Dublin told a friend of mine today that he thought feeling was too bitter to make an appeal by him for funds from the public likely to be successful. I have had evidence myself of the attitude of a large section of the comfortable classes. It can be summarized as 'Let then starve; it will teach them a lesson'. The present state of the workless poor in Dublin, and the callous apathy with which it is being met, is a blot on civilization and an outrage on the name of Christ.[52]

White's politics had evolved from a desire for a general sense of justice in the country to a specific concern for the suffering endured by those occupying the lowest strata of society.

Learning about the practicalities of counter-hegemonic action from Larkin and Connolly, his activist endeavours were now growing extremely radical. It would be difficult to term them socialist because of his innate resistance to governmental interference; he himself employed the term communist in an abortive election attempt in 1923. Although risking unnecessary pedantry, it is helpful to avail of some shorthand description of the political philosophy he espoused. Probably the most convenient classification was his own statement: A 'Christian Anarchist, which, if I am to have a label at all, and I hate all labels, is the nearest label to fit me', said White in 1937.[53] His original mentor, Tolstoy, described himself similarly.[54]

What is not generally recognised nowadays is that both Larkin and Connolly were described frequently as syndicalists and this political stance would easily have accommodated White's outlook at that time. Although White's description of him as a caveman might lead some to underestimate Connolly, it must be considered that he was the most significant thinker of all the revolutionaries in Ireland at that time. In fact the popular perception (which was perfectly valid) that the British over-reacted in their execution of the 1916 leaders should not be applied to Connolly. Despite the emotive image of a seriously wounded middle-aged man being shot in cold blood, there is a distinct possibility that the authorities were more than aware of the risk they were taking; on the basis of his writings alone, Connolly was one of the most dangerous revolutionaries in Europe at that time.

Chapter 8

James Connolly

Connolly's Thinking

Helga Woggan, the historian, says:

> By the mid 1980s, at least 340 books, articles, pamphlets and newly prefaced editions of his [Connolly's] writings had appeared — mostly of a partisan nature — with more than half of them published after 1966, of which a rapidly growing number were scholarly works.[1]

Conscious of there being almost as many categorisations as commentators on Connolly's views and actions, I am going to confine myself to stating that his support for syndicalism goes a considerable way to explaining his actions.

Although White's posthumous reputation is as an anarchist, and this underpins any analysis applied to his outlook, it is not suggested that anarchism was one of the radical political movements seriously considered by any substantial body of activists in this country. It does postulate, however, that there were considerable aspects to that philosophy that were accepted, in particular among the syndicalists, and this was what attracted White to Connolly.

Syndicalism (*syndicalisme,* French for trade unionism) is a political belief that the means of production should be owned by the workers and that this should be controlled by the trades unions directly involved in that particular industry. However, it does not confine itself to the means of production, believing that eventually all aspects of society, from education and culture to social welfare, would be organised under trade union practises. Although in view of the large rigid bureaucratic unions of today, this would suggest a dystopian nightmare, there was a considerable support for this perspective in Connolly's (and Larkin's) era; the fin-de-siècle 'new unionism' was believed to be free of the nineteenth-century hierarchical structures of the old craft unions; the syndicalists were emphatically opposed to any kind of pyramidic organisation.

This change of ownership would be brought about by the co-operative efforts of the workers, mainly by general strike, but this did not preclude more violent methods. Georges Sorel, the French philosopher with a great regard for the efficacy of proletarian violence, described syndicalism quite simply as a war on capitalism where 'the syndicalists do not propose to reform the State as the men of the eighteenth century did; they want to destroy it'.[2]

It differed from socialism, which would propose that the means of production should be under the control of the community at large and this controlling entity would usually be in the form of a socialist state. Syndicalists, however, believed that a loose federation of trade unions would form the principal unit of organisation in society – these would militate against any hierarchical structure. This is in contrast to anarchism in general, which would propose the commune, a more general collective, as the primary unit. Of course anarcho-syndicalism supports a series of collectives made up of trade unions and is often used interchangeably with syndicalism. Emma Goldman, the firebrand anarchist, for example said that 'syndicalism is, in essence, the economic expression of Anarchism'.[3]

George Woodcock, a Canadian professor of history, in defining syndicalism states that 'it is a method of industrial organization which goes away from all the traditional conceptions of authority and government, of capitalism and the State'. He elaborates: 'While communism, in abolishing individual capitalism, creates a worse monster in its place in the form of the economic state [...] syndicalism [...] sets out to build an organizational form based on the natural needs of men rather than on those of the ruling classes.'[4] Emmet O'Connor, the leading academic authority on left-wing Irish history, if I understand him, would not agree:

> Essentially, syndicalism meant violent opposition to any type of 'servile state', rejecting both capitalism and bureaucratic socialism. Unlike anarchism however, it challenged both systems with a projected workers' state which it proposed to perfect within trade

unions, pending the seizure of power by the masses through the unions.[5]

While this 'projected workers' state' may be specific to some form of Irish syndicalism, it does not correspond to the theorists in England or on the continent, either at the start of the twentieth century or later. They envisaged a loose federation of trades union managing the various sectors of society. This concept is closer to anarchism which supports the idea of a series of inter-connected autonomous communities, self-governing but open to alliance when common interests arise. To an anarchist, and to the continental syndicalists, the idea of any central authority, whether it be state or indeed trade union, would be anathema. This is the fundamental distinction between a socialist outlook and an anarchist-type perspective. This was what caused the split between Marx and Bakunin originally.

Post revolution, Marx believed that a state was required to initiate and regulate the very substantial changes that were about to be brought about. Although he believed that this structure would eventually dissipate under the new equitable conditions that existed, this was too much for Bakunin, the anarchist. Bakunin believed that to approve a new state, regardless of how well intentioned, would eventually lead back to the old repression and injustice. The allure of power would seduce the new leaders into maintaining their authority at all costs and undermine the revolution, resulting in change that was little more than a matter of nomenclature.

Now twentieth-century hindsight would seem to support Bakunin's position, but, on the other hand, serious questions can be raised as to how exactly a stateless society would be run, let alone survive. This, of course, is where the visceral opposition to anarchism lies. Rather than take an extreme position, it probably would be best to summarise by saying that the anarchist believes that regulation tends to abrogate personal responsibility.

George Woodcock, in his book on anarchism, takes pains to elaborate the similarities between it and syndicalism:

> Being governed from below and untainted by the ideas or institutions of authority, the syndicate represents more truly than any other type of organization the will of the workers and the good of society. Its lack of centralization and bureaucracy, of any kind of privilege or vested interest in the present order of society, give it a flexibility of action and a real solidarity [...] After the revolution the syndicates

will form the framework on which the first phase of the free society will be built. Anarchists do not make any plans for the free society in its maturity, as they believe in the open and continual growth of social institutions, and recognize that any hard and fast plan of development will create only a rigid and sterile society. Nevertheless, some kind of social structure should be built [...] This means of organization they find in the syndicate [the trade union].[6]

The Irish 'proposed workers' state' probably originated from the One Big Union (OBU) concept, which Connolly would have encountered in the United States. O'Connor writes that 'American syndicalism developed in response to the growing militancy of emergent monopoly capitalism ... which led to the OBU strategy.'[7] De Leon, the American 'theorist [...] evolved a distinct syndicalist organisational method. The elaboration and refinement of this methodology would become a prime commitment for Connolly' who had no illusions about either the ruthlessness or effectiveness of the British Empire and the necessity to support, with Larkin, any effective political weapon of the workers like the OBU.[8]

The attraction of the OBU was that it gave a strength and a coherence to the trade union effort and greatly facilitated the weapon of the 'sympathetic strike' – a term used almost interchangeably with syndicalism. (Up to that time strikes were generally confined to one particular section of workers – the idea that other trades did not pass picket lines was not universally observed.)

Whatever form the OBU would take, one can be confident that it was never intended to have been the rigid central authoritarian structure rejected not just by anarchists. This was too redolent of the old unionism, which both Larkin and Connolly had experienced and which, apart from the hierarchical, privileged positions of its administrators, was distinctly unsympathetic to their ideals. (O'Connor gives a perfect example: Samuel Gompers, of the American craft union, the AFL, said to the syndicalists, 'Economically you are unsound; socially you are wrong; industrially you are impossible.'[9])

Nowhere, of course, did Connolly himself mention anarchism as something he would support or be sympathetic to. Although not a man to shrink from confrontation either verbal or physical, his reticence was understandable because of the possibility of alienating those he fought for and whose support he needed – the working classes. Apart from its connotations of violence, anarchism was associated with the irrational, the 'vital unreason'.

To propose a revolution was radical enough but to suggest that the existing political and economic structures be replaced with something unimaginably alien, something without any familiar organisation or hierarchy, would be a step too far. To enlist the support of the proletariat, or even the 'locked out' workers, there had to be an understandable objective, a straightforward aim.

Otherwise, desperate though the strikers may have been, there would be no support for a nebulous concept that would have appeared suicidal. O'Casey described the Citizen Army standing to defend 'the fair and just claims of the workers for opportunities to live honest, upright and cleanly lives'.[10] If this straightforward statement betrayed no support for any nationalist aims, it was even more unlikely to be sympathetic to what, at the time, must have appeared to have been wild and unstable notions.

Consequently, syndicalism was a much more familiar idea; take the factories from the owners and let the workers run them. In other words, despite reservations about the 'workers' state' negating syndicalism's anarchist roots, it is suggested that this was anarchism indeed but in a very easily digestible form. Support for this comes from the unlikely source of the *Daily Mail*, whose typically paranoid suspicions may have been much closer to the truth this time:

> A former secretary of the Confederation Generale du Travail [CGT, the original syndicalists] conceded that the principle of Syndicalism was 'anarchy under an *alias*' plotting against the French State by counselling a multitude of dupes to use violence to obtain that which it knows cannot be granted.[11]

Connolly's principal work, *Labour in Irish History*, had been finished around 1910, and it could be read as providing a *raison d'être* for a syndicalist programme of action in Ireland. In Connolly's view,

> As we have again and again pointed out, the Irish question is a social question, the whole age-long fight of the Irish people against their oppressors resolves itself in the last analysis into a *fight for the mastery of the means of life, the sources of production, in Ireland*. Who would own and control the land? The people or the invaders; and if the invaders, which set of them – the most recent swarm of land thieves, or the sons of the thieves of a former generation? [...] for two hundred years at least all political movements ignored this [question] [...] Hence

they accomplished nothing, because *the political remedies proposed were unrelated to the social subjection at the root of the matter.*[12]

The Irish people fighting for 'the mastery of the means of life' were, according to Connolly, the 'Irish working class [who] remain as the incorruptible inheritors of the fight for freedom in Ireland'.[13] Furthermore, Connolly maintained that there existed in medieval times an organisational structure which, if not exactly 'flat', was the very least of hierarchies, with those supposedly in charge, quite literally, trusted servants:

> The Irish chief, although recognised in the courts of France, Spain, and Rome, as the peer of the reigning princes of Europe, in reality held his position upon the sufferance of his people, and as an administrator of the tribal affairs of his people, while the land or territory of the clan was entirely removed from his private jurisdiction.[14]

It would be difficult to find anywhere else such an early example of a kind of syndicalism interwoven with a prescient explanation of his decision to revolt in 1916. At the time of the completion of this work he was still in the United States. Having ended his relationship with Daniel De Leon of the Socialist Labour Party of America, he was working as an organiser for the IWW (The Industrial Workers of the World, otherwise known as the 'Wobblies').[15] Theoretically distinct from the continental brand of syndicalism, the Wobblies' sympathies were, however, very similar in their support for revolution in various forms. In fact, W.K. Anderson, the socialist historian, maintains that they displayed 'a move towards anarcho-syndicalism'.[16] It would be most unlikely if Connolly's experiences there had not made a considerable impact on his thinking in his book.

In passing, it must be mentioned that White, a member of the Anarcho-Syndicalist Union in London after his return to London from Spain in the late thirties,[17] had an association with Mat (sic) Kavanagh (1876–1947), an anarchist who was born in Limerick but who spent most of his life in England.[18] Kevin Doyle, the anarchist writer, states that Albert Meltzer maintained that Kavanagh and White were collaborating in writing a book on Irish labour history from an anarchist perspective;[19] if this is correct, it would have been surprising if Connolly's writing did not have a significant bearing on their work.

The thrust of the narrative of Connolly's *History* suggests a communal society, invaded and radically tyrannised by having a central authoritarianist system imposed on it; it would have been very easy to rewrite this in terms of a Bakuninist anarchism. Anderson, however, is adamantly against the idea that anarchism might have formed any part of Connolly's outlook. In his view,

> Connolly never at any stage had any sympathy for anarchism. Writing in *Justice* in 1893, he referred to anarchists as 'men whose whole philosophy is but an exaggerated form of that Individualism we are in revolt against'. There is not a single instance in any of Connolly's writings or recorded statements which could be used to substantiate a 'charge' of anarchism. For Connolly and for many socialists of his generation, syndicalism was simply the practical application of Marxism.[20]

Anderson's *James Connolly and the Irish Left* is a very fine analysis of radical movements in Ireland but it appears to refuse to entertain the possibility of certain aspects of Connolly's thinking that could be very extreme but, for all that, are still within the framework of rational counter-hegemonic theories.

Connolly's equating of anarchism with individualism displays a misunderstanding, and this is not surprising for a young man of 23 with most of his political study before him; there were anarchist individualists, but most, if they supported any kind of political system, would have conceived of it in some kind of communal form. This is almost a peremptory dismissal by Anderson of the idea that Connolly would have had any support for those beliefs. There appears to be considerable misgivings among historians of that period about entertaining anarchism, in particular as any kind of a valid political theory.

Another eminent commentator on Connolly, C. Desmond Greaves, dismisses two of the principal theoreticians of anarchism – Proudhon and Bakunin – by associating them with Lassalle; this nineteenth-century left-wing activist was actually a dogmatic socialist who, along with Marx, opposed Bakunin's entry into the First International[21]. Anderson describes how the 'outmoded ideas of Lassalle and Bakunin were resurrected through the IWW'[22] and then repeats that their ideas, 'discredited in Europe [...] lingered in America' but nonetheless concedes, puzzlingly, that 'the years 1898 to 1905 saw them flower a second time and bear fruit in syndicalism'.[23] The support for syndicalism lasted at least until the First World War, and this was not just in 'America'; the roots of syndicalism were in France in the 1890s. It existed in England as well, where, in what bordered on a kangaroo trial, the editor of a syndicalist paper, Tom Mann, was sentenced to six months imprisonment in 1912.[24] Anarchism, anarcho-syndicalism and syndicalism are very closely related and all fit within the theoretical opposition to capitalism that Connolly espoused, as, of course, does socialism, communism and Marxism in all their forms.

There is a certain reluctance in the dominant narrative to examine just how radical and uncomfortable Connolly's ideas were and this led to his role becoming encapsulated into a simplistic Catholic nationalism. This formed a popular (and convenient) ideology that left him a reputation as a kind of working man's adjunct to a vastly more glamorous Pearse.

It is not being mooted that Connolly was an anarchist but it is important to examine his writings from a perspective that would have some sympathies with that outlook because it will be argued that there are commonalities between not just syndicalism in general but Connolly's particular brand and the basic tenets of anarchism.

White, long before he declared himself to be an anarchist, had an inherent attraction to and instinct for the fundamental aspects of anarchism. He could never have been described as sympathetic to nationalism; I would argue that it had to be Connolly's syndicalism that White initially found attractive.

Beginnings of the Fight Back: the Irish Citizen Army

The first recorded announcement of a call to raise a volunteer movement came in Jack White's speech in Trinity College Dublin on the night of 18 November 1913. According to White, the call for a specifically Citizen Army came later in Croydon Park, the estate leased by Larkin for the trade union: 'it was at one of these Sunday meetings I first propounded the proposal of the Citizen Army, to the huge enthusiasm and delight of the men themselves'.[25] In attempting to establish exactly when and by whom the actual proposal was made, a considerable number of differing claims surface. The first time the description appears is in the newspaper headlines reporting a concurrent meeting at Beresford Place when Connolly in his speech said, 'he had already referred to the enrolment of a citizen army under the Transport Workers' Union. Every man who handed in his name would be enrolled for drilling and training under capable officers. (Cheers for Captain White)'.[26] On the other hand, William O'Brien, later secretary of the Irish Trade Unions Council and

Labour Party (ITUCLP) and no friend of White's, cites E.A. Aston, a member of the Peace Committee, stating that the

> I.C.A. [was] formed in R.M. Gwynn's room in T.C.D. by Captain White and members of the 'Peace Committee' when that body decided to wind up. Lord Mayor said they could not meet otherwise than as [the] Peace Committee in Mansion House and as too late to go to Hotel [...] they were invited by R.M. [Gwynn] to go to T.C.D.[27]

When White left the College meeting he must have gone straight to Beresford Place. In his own account of the meeting it is not surprising White found himself associating with the more radical movement afterwards. He took what appears to be an instant dislike to Arthur Griffith, both as a man and politician:

> At the time I had never met him and I never came to have more than a nodding acquaintance with him. Even so, I did any nodding there was. I always thought him an unpleasant little man. To me he seemed to emanate the suspicion of the professional Gael towards the foreign or Protestant interloper in the 'movement'.[28]

Rarely did White reveal such a personal animosity in his writings. He went on to relate an unfounded story (which of course he was told on 'the best authority') that Griffith, on being presented with the draft of the Treaty by Lloyd George, 'declared immediately "I'll sign that, Mr Prime Minister, whatever the others do".'[29] This is probably a distortion of George Dangerfield's representation of Lloyd George's wiles and subterfuge; Griffith's goodwill was exploited to persuade him to sign a purportedly innocuous document to co-operate with the Boundary Commission. This, he believed, was to 'quell' a revolt by the Tories on Irish policy; Lloyd George produced it at a later stage to persuade him that he had agreed to something much more significant with regard to the Treaty.[30] White disagreed with Griffith because he 'concentrated on the attainment of fiscal independence', which was probably too prosaic for White. However, his final judgment – that is, that Griffith's espousal of the 1782 Constitution prognosticated 'the crowning work of Griffith's life', the Treaty – hints at a derision in White, indicating that he would not have been on the side of the Free State.[31]

White's own contribution to the meeting was the aforementioned call to raise a movement of volunteers in the face of protests from the crowd. It probably was his affinity for irony that drove him to insist on this being the first call for the (later to be called Citizen) Army at, as he described Trinity as 'the Alma Mater of the British Connection'. It was Connolly, at the later Beresford Place meeting, who laid down the early conditions under which this army was going to operate, and incidentally pointed out that White was not alone: 'we have offers from other officers to do the same'. He said that they intended to

> have a regular establishment – majors, captains, sergeants, and corporals – for we mean to defend our rights as citizens, and any man who means in future to become a member of the Transport Workers' Union must be prepared to enrol himself in our citizen army; so that we will not leave the whole of the work to the Ancient Order of Hibernians or the Orangemen, who, I hear, have ordered a supply of rifles. We have not done so yet. However, we have got the grub, but we want our men to be trained and drilled, so that when it comes to the pinch they will be able to handle a rifle, and when King Carson comes along here we will be able to line our own ditches.[32]

Whatever Connolly may have felt privately about the extravagant claims of buying weaponry when 'grub' itself was seriously scarce, it must have been particularly exhilarating to have even the slightest prospect of a trained army at the disposal of the unions; this was a development that even Sorel would hardly have envisioned. Ireland looked like taking syndicalism a step farther than anything that had been accomplished on the continent, or England, for that matter, but it must be remarked that although this was particularly radical, it was a logical development of the whole theory.

White at that time would certainly not have been privy to notions of this type. In fact, it was only little more than a week before that he had announced to the strikers at a 'surprise' appearance at Liberty Hall that

> it was not quite true to say that he was on the side of the men. His instinctive sympathy was with them, but his reasoned judgment was not, because he had not had the opportunity of studying the position in Dublin.[33]

The words of Æ had affected him, and the incidents concerning the children of the Lockout had greatly upset him. The night following the announcement, there was another meeting, this time in the Antient Concert Rooms under the auspices of the newly-formed Civic League. Roger Casement had sent two telegrams, one of which, to White, said:

> Strongly approve proposed drill and discipline Dublin workers, and will aid that healthy national movement, as I am also prepared to aid wider national movement to drill and discipline Irish National Volunteers throughout Ireland. Please read this at today's meeting.[34]

The other telegram, to Professor Bertram Collingwood of the Civic League,[35] was on similar lines. The Citizen Army as a concept had taken off dramatically in just a day, although it probably had as many interpretations as it had supporters at that time. Casement saw it primarily as an embryonic nationalist movement, while White's idea was, at that time, more basically a workforce trained to defend itself against the police. Casement 'was broadcasting his blessing to the Labour and National drilling alike, although the latter had not yet started'.[36] However, according to one source, White specifically 'gave the assurance that the plan would exclude any idea of military ideas'.[37] Connolly, who spoke at the same meeting, appeared as if he concurred with this notion, but, of course, the Civic League (that is, the erstwhile Peace Committee) was there to be wooed. According to *The Irish Times,*

> Referring to the proposed drilling, he [Connolly] said the Orangeman and others were drilling, and it looked as if they were the only undrilled body. They did not propose to attack the Castle and annex the Bank but they believed that if the men were drilled, not only would they be respected, but what was quite as essential, they would better respect themselves. (Cheers.) If they were drilled the D.M.P. [Dublin Metropolitan Police] and the R.I.C. [Royal Irish Constabulary] would know their places, and they [the workers] would know theirs. (Applause.)[38]

The Civic League members, initially formed as a mediating body between strikers and employers, seemingly unaware of the potential of the Citizen Army, readily agreed with the idea. As White notes:

> it was that innocent civic league which actually passed at my instance the first resolution to drill the Dublin strikers. [...] I sometimes wonder how you sleep o'nights, Robin Gwynn, Æ, Padraic Colum

and Co., knowing the subversive activities to which you lent your august names. Yes! and you thoroughly enjoyed it. We were all mad then, but oh! how much pleasanter it was.[39]

In passing he mentions that 'Professor Houston, of the Dublin College of Science', as chairman of the meeting, became treasurer when he 'received the first cheque to supply with boots and drill staves the Irish Citizen Army'.[40] E.A. Aston, reviewing Fox's *History of the Irish Citizen Army*, reports that it was 'Captain White [who, having] expounded his proposals, backed them with a substantial cheque, which, with other contributions [became…] the first treasure of the Irish Citizen Army.' He then goes to pains to point out (as a participant of that meeting) that the Civic League's name arose from a group who 'thought it well to direct their energies to housing and its allied social problems'.[41]

Even White himself would have been aghast at the time if he had foreseen some of the uses that Connolly had in mind for the Citizen Army. For example, R.M. Fox recorded an incident in November 1915 where a strike picket on the North Wall in Dublin had problems both with clerks who were allegedly 'blacklegging' and 'the police [who] pushed the pickets around outside the shipping office'. Connolly despatched a squad of Citizen Army men to the picket line and, 'fully equipped with rifles and bayonets', they marched up and down: 'It was the first time […] that armed workers carried out picket duty in a trade union dispute.'[42] For that matter, it was probably the first time in Europe such a military attitude was adopted on the part of strikers. It also gives an insight into how cautious the authorities were about inflaming matters among the strikers, that they should allow such a display to take place. Donal Nevin records that the Chief Secretary, Sir Matthew Nathan, 'had opposed demands to seize Liberty Hall, confiscate the weapons of the Irish Citizen Army and deport Connolly to Edinburgh'.[43] An intransigent employer, Edward Watson of the Dublin Steam Packet Company, described as reactionary by Dangerfield, had been regarded in a very poor light by the London Industrial Commissioner and had been denied any support when he refused to settle with strikers. Dangerfield related that a large file on the strike, which lasted from 27 October 1915 up to 15 April 1916, had mysteriously and abruptly ceased with a minute from Nathan to Askwith (the Industrial Commissioner), which stated that 'nothing more can be done for the time being to bring it to an end'. Furthermore, there was almost no coverage from the Irish press and 'on what terms [the strike was settled] is impossible to discover. [...] James Connolly's last industrial dispute has, to some extent, slipped through a hole in history', although Connolly did consider it as 'an opportunity to strengthen the Citizen Army'.[44] All this suggests that events were deliberately played down and probably, in view of the ongoing war, fears of a second lockout would have caused untold disruption. On the other hand, they must have been heady days for Connolly to have a military force to ensure the protection of union members against the inhibitive actions of the State; the ambitions of syndicalism and its appropriation of the factors of production of the economy surely seemed, if not imminent, at least more than theoretical.

William Martin Murphy's outrage at the formation of the Citizen Army, expressed at the Royal Commission on the 1916 Rising, although very hostile, made some very pertinent observations:

> That the authorities allowed a body of lawless and riotous men to be drilled and armed and to provide themselves with an arsenal of weapons and explosives was one of the most amazing things that could happen in any civilised country outside of Mexico. This body was even allowed to hold meetings with uniforms and arms, and to discharge their rifles at night in the streets of Dublin without any attempt to check them or prosecute them. Fortunately the long strike was coming to an end when the Citizen Army commenced to drill. If they had been in existence in the early days of the strike, when the disorders were at their height we should have had a foretaste of the recent fighting in the city.[45]

Initially White's opinion of what the Citizen Army represented was quite different: 'Captain White – in Murphy's version [of their meeting] – spoke of the value of drill and discipline in making the men more amenable to negotiation.'[46] It is highly unlikely that White would have been so amenable to Murphy's wishes but at that stage he still saw it as an expression of his pacifist beliefs. White uses O'Casey's booklet on the Citizen Army, which refers to Francis Sheehy Skeffington as a member of the 'first Citizen Army Council', as 'proof of the pacific purpose of the Citizen Army at the time, for Skeffington was a perfectly consistent pacifist, though, like all really sincere pacifists, the most pugnacious of men'.[47] He also clearly defines his own attitude (and this is likely what made people like Connolly, and indeed, Griffith, cautious of him):

I certainly had no clear goal of violent revolution, national or social. At first I just enjoyed the fun and excitement of the whole thing. There was so much enthusiasm about and such an apparent weight of intellectual sympathy that to my sanguine inexperience a bloodless revolution seemed well within the bounds of possibility. The Citizen Army, after teaching the police manners, could be the nucleus of industrial organization in the new era.[48]

Chapter 9

The Irish Citizen Army

Optimism

Allowing for what could be termed an overblown account by O'Casey of the announcement by Larkin and the subsequent 'enthusiastic and full-throated cheer that shatter[ed] the air', it has to be acknowledged that there surely was a feeling of wild hope that 'this day would be an historic one in the unhappy annals of the Irish Labour Movement'. Up to now there had been nearly three months of continual reverses with the oppression of the police, the blacklegging from imported labour, and an almost universal lack of support for what they were trying to do. Although, as already noted, incidents like the sending of children abroad for sustenance were not anything like as significant as the propagandists on both sides would have it, it must have been particularly disheartening to be condemned by all sectors of society including, most hurtfully of all, their own pastors. Now Larkin told them:

> They must no longer be content to assemble in hopeless, haphazard crowds, in which a man does not know and cannot trust the man that stands next to him, but in all their future assemblies they must be so organised that there will be a special place for every man, and a particular duty for each man to do.[1]

The fact that Captain White, the man who was going to bring this change about, was from the other side, 'an aristocrat and gentleman, and had signified his intention to throw in his lot with his socially humbler brothers', must have made the impact of the news even more pronounced. He was 'ignoring the remonstrances of friends, choosing freely and bravely to stand by the people now in their hour of need'.[2] O'Casey probably came closest to Connolly's idea and the ambition of syndicalism in expressing the thoughts of the strikers at Croydon Park that night:

> This was what was long wanted – a Citizen Army! What could not Labour accomplish with an army trained and disciplined by officers who held the affection and confidence of the workers! Now they would get some of their own back; and vivid visions of 'red-coats and Black-coats flying before them' floated before the imaginative eyes of the Dublin workers [...]. [White's] boyish face was aglow with gratification as he listened to the cheers that seemed to proclaim to him a ready realisation of the schemes he contemplated towards the disciplined consolidation of the lower orders in the battalionised ranks of an Irish Citizen Army. [...] The Irish Citizen Army would fight for Labour and for Ireland. [White asked] all those who intended to second their efforts by joining the army, and training themselves for the fight for Social liberty, to hold up their hands. Almost every hand was silhouetted out against the darkening sky.[3]

White, charged with the same enthusiasm, in a letter to his mother, written at that time, explained his plans. He envisaged a 'scheme of organisation, which is based on a small working unit of eighteen – sixteen men and two NCOs with a loose organization into companies and battalions' for the 3,000 men he fully expected after the fervent demonstration described by O'Casey.

Reality

As often happens, the passions of the night evaporated into the ashen reality of the morning after. Absolutely nobody turned up at the designated hour, White was 'literally alone' and, 'after waiting about an hour some fifteen men had dribbled in in ones and twos'. In an absurdity that could only be real life, the majority of these were 'ardent nationalists of the middle class anxious to instruct me how to organize the nation'.[4] Eventually he began to put together some trained squads, but he was continually frustrated by calls for the men to attend meetings by Connolly and Larkin. They were using the force more as a 'publicity stunt' rather than a trained unit, and there are also reports of it giving rise to various humorous comments.[5] O'Casey, writing about those early days, saw terrible difficulties, but at one with the syndicalists, he still perceived it as a movement where 'men had declared war on their employers'. The greatest tests arose he believed from

> the frequent arrests of the Labour Leaders; the gradual and humiliating weakening of the workers' resistance to the pressure of the employers; the malignant penalising of the Irish Transport Union by the hierarchy of commerce; and the establishment in the Rotunda Rink on 25 October 1914 [sic], of the Irish National Volunteers.[6]

White wrote of his own problems, in his own way:

> I began to feel psychically the collective hostility of the upper and middle classes. I did not get enough psychic support from my adopted crowd to counteract it. I began to know the terrible strain of being in the middle of opposing mass-currents without belonging psychically to either. To keep going I had to depend on what I regard as the spirit, as distinct from the psyche, the mind reaching out to the unborn future founding itself on tendencies, directions of progress rather than any existing actualities. Ahead of me in the future lay a conflagration of 'existing actualities' and the birth of a new state from the ashes.[7]

This combination of religious and psychological analysis is reminiscent of the theories of C.G. Jung, whose speculations on the spiritual nature of the psyche quite often sallied into the mystical. It is very possible that White read Jung, and he occasionally displays what could be his influence.[8] Repeating R.B. McDowell's aside about White on an unrelated matter is particularly pertinent: 'White was in many ways a most unworldly man.'[9] It is very unlikely he was implying that White was credulous, although the man had his childlike side. His eldest son Tony recalls that

> He also had a strange naïvete. I remember during the war my father inviting a Gibraltarian conjurer to dinner. And he did a fairly simple trick: he pulled his thumb in half. My father was fully appreciative – he hadn't a clue how it was done.[10]

McDowell was probably suggesting that White was removed to some extent from the practical considerations of this life; he hardly could be described as a visionary, but some of his decisions and actions indicate someone more concerned with the transcendent than the average person. This aspect of his personality emerges increasingly as he grows older and in particular in the correspondence with his niece at the end of his life. It should be remembered also that as a young man his aforementioned immersion in Tolstoy's writing had a considerable impact (unfortunately this correspondence has not come to light).[11]

Another aspect of his ability to pursue a singular and most personal course at all times is his revelation that at this time, that is, while he was 'drilling the Citizen Army, [he] was actually living at Plunkett House being "vetted" as a possible Plunkettian young man'.[12] In other words he was being considered – and possibly trained – as some kind of executive within the co-operative movement that Horace Plunkett had founded, the Irish Agricultural Organisation Society. White had been influenced by 'George Russell, Æ, the pen and imagination of the IAOS, editor of its organ, the *Irish Homestead,* [who] came out nobly on the side of the strikers at first'.[13] A further possibility that attracted him would possibly be Plunkett's practicality, his belief in the primacy of the economic, and his championing of co-operation, and, of course, he would have been very unlikely to have been discouraged by Plunkett's former role as a Unionist MP (Standish O'Grady, a putative anarchist, was an admirer and supporter of Plunkett.)

Nonetheless it indicates the almost casual approach White had towards the whole socialist campaign; mindful of needing some kind of a career, and aware of his mother's worries for him, he complied with a typical bourgeois set of values by establishing some respectable contacts, seeking, as he said, 'bridges across to the unknown future by milder methods than destiny had in store'.[14] He had a keen awareness of the 'irreconcilables' he was 'trying to combine' and his 'pose to myself and my mother of the self appointed link between minds so different as Jim Larkin and Horace Plunkett, representing such mass interests was pretty thin'.[15]

Training and Displays

Despite White's almost deprecatory remarks about the drilling and training procedures of the Citizen Army in the early stages, it seemed to have captured the interest of the press from the beginning. From this report it would appear that the rather slow start on the Monday night of 24 November 1913, had by Thursday night burgeoned into displays of drilling which, according to the press, must have been impressive:

> The 'Citizen Army' made its first public march last night. Starting from Liberty Hall between 8 and 9 o'clock there was a procession, headed by a fife and drum band, the rendezvous being Croydon Park. The processionists, who were in the charge of Captain White presented quite a martial appearance. […] The police in bodies of about twenty accompanied the procession, but during the outward or return journey no incident of note took place. The tramcars and other vehicular traffic, to a certain extent, were held up while the march was proceeding along the North Strand. About 3,000 men took part in the outing, but outside the ranks of the enrolled men nobody was admitted to the drilling grounds, the entrance to which was guarded by sentries, who demanded 'the password' as each column passed through […] The 'army' at the word of command deployed into line, formed a solid square, and after a short address from Captain White, who passed the words, 'prepare and dismiss', the troops disbanded.[16]

The tenor of *The Irish Times* account, hardly a supporter of such an enterprise, was muted, yet the reporter appears impressed by the display. The article provides no support for White's account of small numbers and inconsistency of attendance, although the fife and drum band and procession along the North Strand point to the influence of propagandists. The whole enterprise appeared to have captured the imagination of the public, and considerable attention was paid in particular to the manoeuvres being carried out.

The employers themselves were watching as well, making a pronouncement on Sunday 30 November on foot of a general muster at Croydon Park, which had been announced in the papers. They declared 'it is untrue to state they are opposed to trade unionism. They urge that trade unions have obligations as well as rights, but are not entitled to use their power to smash capitalism'.[17] Archbishop Walsh, presumably at mass that Sunday morning, 'made another strong appeal for peace', deprecating 'the avidity with which every extreme statement is emphasised, so that one would think the object aimed at […] would make a pacific settlement for ever impossible'.[18] The march that day appears to have been held in conjunction with a demonstration during which a tramcar driver was seriously injured. The marchers were 'opposed by a large force of police' on their way to High Park Reformatory, demonstrated at Mountjoy Prison, and

> subsequently held a meeting in Beresford Place, where addresses were delivered by leaders of the labour movement, and a resolution was passed against the class administration of the law and the forcible feeding of prisoners in Mountjoy.[19]

It appears to have been a particularly important meeting from the organisers' point of view. It was attended by the American syndicalist 'Big' Bill Heywood, who said that 'they were fighting a battle which was engaging the attention of the civilised world'. Adverting to the concept of the One Big Union (OBU), he said, 'it was only by that means they could ever hope to liberate themselves from the iron heel of capitalism'.[20] Connolly, boosted by the performance of the day, boasted that 'the procession showed what a strike looked like when it was fizzling out'. He went on to attack the 'lying capitalist press of Dublin' and referred to a report in the *Evening Telegraph* that 'published a statement [...] which amounted to an announcement that the workers were going to High Park Asylum [where some women strikers were imprisoned] to mob it and to attack the nuns'. He maintained that the aforementioned letter of the Archbishop had actually exonerated the workers when he said that 'the newspapers [...] had been fastening on some statements with the object of putting the workers' position in a wrong light before the public'.[21] Amidst all this triumphalist rhetoric, White's speech must have struck a discordant note. He said:

> he was not a rebel. He had heard things said that were extremely distasteful to him. The police had a perfect right to carry out their instructions, and they were not, one and all, the brutes they were stated to be.[22]

He withdrew this statement in view of later experience, saying, 'I did not know at the time of the amount of extraneous brutality they [the police] were guilty of', but it does demonstrate once again his willingness to go against the popular voice, and again, Connolly, the master of the tactical speech, must have looked askance at this kind of performance and 'took [White] to task for introducing this remonstrant note at the meeting'.[23] Recalling an earlier story recounted by Donal Nevin, this shows why Connolly insisted on White speaking first at a meeting in Belfast some months later, so that he could later undo any harm White might cause.[24] On the other hand, it could be argued that this kind of statement was the admirable intransigence of a man who made up his own mind, even in the teeth of a howling mob, which he would do on more than one occasion in the future.

George Russell and Sheehy Skeffington were also reported as speaking at the meeting, and they all accompanied the workers back to Croydon Park where White, again disdaining any courting of popularity, insisted 'that a football match that was in progress should be stopped'. The import of history was having little effect on some; White 'asked his audience if they realised what they were doing in asking him to drill them at such an epoch-making crisis. If they did they should give up disorder, and be obedient to orders'.[25] Indicative of his willingness to engage with everyone regardless of relevance, he went on to have a discussion with a priest about George Bernard Shaw, who, according to the priest, 'wrote Socialism'. White also informed his listeners that

> he had received an invitation to address an anti-Carsonite meeting in London, but he had replied stating that he looked forward to the day when his force would join that of Sir Edward Carson in the fight of democracy. The result of their drilling would be to bring out the strength, will and determination of all the men –

and then, astonishingly,

'Cheers'.[26]

It appears as if he almost desired to antagonise Connolly and the others, and it is on occasions like this that make understandable the development of his reputation for being, at best, unreliable, and, at worst, mad. He commented himself that 'the greatest vagueness existed as to the aims of either or both', that is the Citizen Army and the still embryonic Volunteers, and then gave an example from his cuttings of an undated, and unreferenced, newspaper report headed, 'Citizen force ready to uphold the authority of the Crown and Government in Ireland'.[27] Certainly the press appeared unsure of how to treat him at this stage. He was a member of the upper classes, and the uncompromising nature of his speeches, although probably confusing, must have lead them to believe that he was some kind of third force. This is exactly what he was, of course, but a force that was never going to gain in acceptance or popularity after this period.

There was continual coverage of the exercises of the Citizen Army for some months after this period, more probably because of the personalities of White and the others than because of any notion that it might represent a very significant threat to law and order. Even the day after the Beresford Place meeting, there was further analysis carried out, although, as the paper conceded, no new developments had taken place. 'The leaders manifested a more conciliatory tone than they have done since the outbreak of the trouble fourteen weeks ago', *The Irish Times* maintained as mentioned earlier. There appeared to have been a focus on White as a new factor in the struggle and consequently a possible voice of reason:

> When the audience heard from Captain White that he was not a rebel, it afforded them much food for thought during their leisure hours yesterday.[28]

It would be quite some time yet before White's stance would alienate him from the elite circles he came from, although he was already a *persona non grata* for some. A series of letters concerning an invitation he had from the Trinity College Historical Society, rescinded by the students, fulfilled his threat to expose what he saw as their pusillanimous behaviour to the public. There is little of interest in the letters, but the newspaper's willingness to air this petty series of differences again demonstrates the public's fascination with White.[29]

Irish Volunteers' Beginning

Meanwhile, during the same week, at the Rotunda Rink in Dublin, 'which holds 7,000 people', the Irish Volunteers were formed. It appeared to have been a far grander affair than the Citizen Army inauguration. Among the speakers were Eoin MacNeill, Padraig Pearse, and Michael Davitt, as well as Jack White:

> Captain White made his way to the platform [...] and was received with cheers from those who recognised him. After a public subscription list was formed, it was announced 'there would be work for the women [...] for a clerical staff, for telegraphists, for cycles, for motor cyclists, for motorists and so on'.[30]

L.J. Kettle, the secretary, a brother of Tom Kettle, 'was boohed by a section of the audience, who were Larkinites',[31] and the chairman said that three fourths of the letters sent to him in support of the movement had been from Protestants. All in all, it appears to have been quite a catholic gathering, with two overflow meetings being held in other locations in the vicinity. Nevertheless, White and Constance Markievicz were the only prominent members of the ICA involved.

White was certainly firing on all cylinders at this time; he also presided over a meeting of the Civic League in his role of elected chairman. This was a protest against the constitution of the police inquiry set up in response to 'Bloody Sunday'. Although the *Star* reported 'a moderate attendance of workingmen', White's interpretation was that the meeting only 'brought about twenty of those belonging to the wealthier classes of Dublin, leaving the rest of the hall to be filled up by those whom he was beginning to think were the only public-spirited citizens in Ireland – the transport workers'. He was still exhibiting a kind of Olympian detachment from the actual politics of the whole struggle. This explains some of his actions, actions that puzzled and exasperated his various allies, who at this stage ranged from the syndicalist Connolly to the pacifist Sheehy Skeffington. He went on to say 'there might come a time when those apathetic folks might have to be given a rude shock'. Complaining that the inquiry represented the concerns of neither 'citizens in general nor of the workers in particular it could not but give rise to the suspicion that it was intended to white wash the conduct both of the police and of the police magistrates'. He said it was alleged that 'in one particular case people in the city were hemmed in like netted rabbits and batoned, without regard to age, sex, or health [...] Photographs were in existence which showed pictures of the actual occurrence'. He then referred to the vested interests which invariably surface in these situations: 'It seemed that they were not to be allowed to investigate the high-handed action of a semi-military police for fear of splitting a party that was supposed to stand for national freedom.'[32] White had no compunction about attacking the Redmondites and the employers who formed a considerable section of that party. In fact, before putting the resolution at the end of the meeting, he indulged in one last sally, referring to the people who did not turn up, for fear that 'they would embarrass the Irish Party' as 'skunks'.[33]

The Irish Worker published a letter of White's at that time which gave his public opinion on Citizen Army manoeuvres. Being neither a professional nor conscript army, the enforcement of discipline – the engine of any military force – presented a problem. White bemoaned the lack of punctuality and regular attendance, but declared himself very satisfied with the 'material' he was working with. Incapable of addressing any situation without assailing some or all sections that he saw opposing him, he once more attacked what he saw as the inert and passive *bourgeoisie*. It would seem to consist, he said, of

> an inert mass of tremulous old women, who, whether Nationalist or Unionist, hold aloof in outraged horror from any attempt to increase in 'common working men' the sense of the dignity of their manhood and deluge me with abusive anonymous letters while their well fed police are deputed in hundreds to accompany the 'Citizen Army' on each of its marches as though it were an assembly of criminals. I would take this opportunity of reminding these superior but timid persons that the workers have as much right to drill for the defence of themselves and their country as any other section of the community and of arousing such of them as are capable of shame to protest against only that section being singled out for police supervision which is thought to threaten their comfortable dividends.[34]

Indicating his awareness of syndicalism, White states that 'the supreme object of Labour at the present day I take to be emancipation from wage slavery and organisation into co-operative industries owned and managed by the workers'. Referring to the extraordinary situation where the English trade union funds were invested in the railways, damaging their own income when they took industrial action, he called the situation in Ireland even more tragic. The strike had reached an impasse over the question of reinstatement:

> in other words, after a prolonged strike labour is obliged to demand that its human capital is admitted back into the capitalist system it wishes to destroy. I am one who believes that labour can never destroy capital, till it ceases to be a commodity to be bought.

However, he did acknowledge (probably from the practicalities of the existing situation, that is, the starvation and the weakening morale of the strikers) that 'it must be a saleable commodity till it employs itself'. This employment would only come about in a system like syndicalism, and he then returned to his recurring theme of discipline: 'To employ itself it must combine for constructive purposes as well as for strikes. To combine it must have discipline; and the simplest teacher of discipline is drill.' Finally, as if some of what Connolly has been saying to him had registered, he included nationalist aims in his aspirations, although with his customary snipe at those whose 'nationalism is all soul and no body'. He exhorted the workers:

> Throw yourselves into this drill like men determined to advance patiently and steadily to a sure goal; whether the first fruit of your labours is the freeing of yourselves or the freeing of your country, time will show. But ultimately Ireland cannot be free without you nor you without Ireland. Strengthen your hand then for the double task.[35]

Differences with Larkin

The press continued to report routinely that 'drilling took place again at Croydon Park' amid accounts of the 'arrival of more free labourers' from English ports and accounts of expectations of returns to work counterpointed by ballots of the workers refusing to do so. On Monday 12 January 1914, the papers headlined as 'a remarkable incident' the occasion when Larkin attacked White at a series of meetings in Sackville Street. White includes almost the entire *Irish Times* report in *Misfit,* but, apart from illustrating the temperamental behaviour of Larkin already noted, it has little of relevance to either the political situation or to White's view of things.

There were two meetings held that Sunday afternoon, the first at three o'clock, protesting once more about the constitution of the commission that was formed to investigate police brutality. The speakers included White, Constance Markievicz, Bulmer Hobson, and 'one or two other ladies identified with the suffrage movement'. A verbal confrontation took place between White and the police that ended with the gathering refusing to move on. One of the suffragists, a Mrs Connery, revealed the anti-Redmondite feeling that underlaid these protests, accentuating the differences among nationalists which were to become evident much later with the split in the Volunteers. Commenting on the 'whitewashing Commission', she said: 'But they were not whitewashing the police; they were whitewashing Castle government and the members of Parliament who had not stood up for the people of Dublin as they should have done.'[36] White gave some facts which he was afraid would not be taken into account in the inquiry, saying that 'solicitors to the Civic league had in their possession over 70 signed statements' testifying to the police brutality. 'In spite of the denials of legal liars', they had photographs which showed police batoning people trying to escape. Then, his innate fairness tempering his rage, he stressed that he 'did not say that all the police were tarred with that shameless brutality'.[37] No such inhibitions affected Markievicz who called it 'a prattling inquiry where everyone could say what he liked, for the evidence was not given on oath'. It was being run by two KCs who were soon to be judges, 'for they belonged to the same trades union as the police'.[38]

It is unlikely the meeting was finished when 'shortly before four o'clock a wagonette drove up from Beresford Place to Nelson's Pillar, followed by a cheering crowd'. Larkin, there for the same purpose as the original meeting, began by acknowledging the presence of White, who had just made his way to the wagonette, all the while also being cheered by the crowd. Larkin said he was the

> son of Sir George White, who defended the British flag at Ladysmith, the dirty flag under which more disease and degradation had been experienced than anything else that he (Mr Larkin) knew of. (At the close of this sentence Captain White rose and hurriedly left the wagonette.)[39]

'I should like to emphasise that what I resented was the attack on the flag in connection with my father, who had died not a year ago', wrote White.[40] As previously discussed, this episode allowed a field day for the press, who were po-faced about White as a dupe for their analysis of Larkin's irascible and unreliable character:

> No sympathy is felt with Captain White in his disagreeable experience with Mr Larkin. There is some curiosity, however, as to the motive which induced Mr Larkin deliberately to insult the flag under which his supporter had served. It is suggested that he may have wished to rid himself of an inconvenient colleague, but the more probable explanation is that there was no premeditation, but that the idea suddenly occurred to him, and Larkin-like, had to come out.[41]

White, experiencing for once what he had visited on others, although hardly as nastily, kept a politician's profile. On Monday night he said:

You ask me will the incident affect my future connection with the Labour Movement? I cannot see why it should. I have certainly been to some extent indebted to facilities which Mr Larkin has courteously given me for getting into touch with the men of his union. These facilities he is not likely to withdraw, from what I know of him, because I resent a portion of his speeches.[42]

Nevertheless, on Tuesday morning *The Irish Times* reported that 'Drilling was carried on again yesterday at Croydon Park. For the first time Captain White was absent from the evolutions of the Citizen Army.'[43] It was not until Thursday that they could report a resumption of the normal service: 'after some days absence, Captain White resumed the work of drilling [...] yesterday morning', and then with all the breathless prose of modern celebrity-chasing, they panted:

> Having put them through their 'facings' and dismissed them, Captain White proceeded towards Liberty Hall. At the entrance stood Mr James Larkin, who was an interested spectator of the manoeuvres. Instead of entering the building, Captain White passed on by Eden quay, without as far as could be observed, exchanging a salutation with the leader of Liberty Hall.[44]

Padraig Yeates relates that White was only one victim among many:

> Unfortunately, facts were never Larkin's strongest suit as a speaker. He must have alienated many by his outbursts that winter [1913/14], and embarrassed his allies. In Sheffield he called Jimmy Thomas 'a double dyed traitor to his class' and accused Havelock Wilson of sending scabs to break the London dock strike of 1912 [...] much of what he said went beyond normal political invective [...] Havelock Wilson and Jimmy Thomas were union leaders who had 'neither a soul to be saved nor a body to be kicked'. The strain of addressing two or three meetings a day, sometimes in venues as far apart as London and Hull, was clearly taking its toll.[45]

As discussed earlier, White was, at this stage, as prominent a figure as any of the other protagonists in this drama, and probably more acceptable to the various interests and organisations that were struggling for position. Later he would say, 'had I known then what I know now, had I been less sensitive to a certain natural suspicion of me on the part of the Labour leaders [...,] I believe I could have brought off a revolution on the Russian model almost on my own'.[46] In view of his popularity at that time, this was not an unrealistic assessment, but whether his temperament, with its volatile Larkin-like side, could ever have settled to the discipline of close-guardedness required for political success is debatable; for all his peace-making and good nature, he was a breaker rather than a builder.

The question about Ireland's social condition being amenable to a Bolshevik revolution is an even more moot topic. However, this did not detract from his analysis, which was now combining a Tolstoyan pacifism with Connolly's brand of socialism and not without a certain theological tinge. In a speech that he gave to the Independent Labour Party of Ireland, on 5 February 1914, reported in the London *Daily Herald*, he said that 'economic and political systems' should be based on 'spiritual and metaphysical ideas'. The theory that 'human nature was intrinsically bad [...] was the basis of ecclesiastical authority, and of half the evils of the educational and economic system'.[47] He is not necessarily taking an essentialist stance here, of the type that has bedevilled anarchism (although nowadays anarchist theory would not accept this, if it ever did; in fact, it maintains that it has a pragmatic approach to humankind rather than positing a benign view). I would suggest that White perceived humankind as neither benign nor malign, or at least, as equally capable of both. He was a pacifist, but a very unorthodox one. His eldest son, Tony, recollects:

> he was never a true pacifist. When there was imminent danger of the Nazis invading Britain and Ireland, my father said that if they came up the avenue to Whitehall, he would take out his shotgun and get a few of them first.[48]

White maintained that, although 'the regeneration of Ireland included co-operation', the Citizen Army was in reserve in case 'the conquest of capitalism could not be achieved by peaceful means'. Although decrying 'sporadic violence', he believed the 'revolution of thought had come; force would be needed to compel legislation'. This is not the stance of a pacifist, but when war was declared he took up ambulance duty, and sometime in 1915 he joined a pacifist organisation, the Fellowship of Reconciliation.[49] A likely explanation for these actions is the influence of Connolly, one of the few socialist, or syndicalist activists, in Europe who did not participate in the war. White is quoted as finishing his speech by saying, 'The ideas and enthusiasm of Socialism and Syndicalism – which were two aspects of the same thing – were dying out because there was no one to translate them into action.'[50] Finally, in a grand gesture, he declared: 'give me twenty thousand men and I will remodel Ireland'.[51] Later he described himself modestly as a 'swollen headed young ass';[52] it was probably more properly applied here, but it must not be forgotten that at this stage he was probably close to having a radical influence on events.

The manoeuvres of the Citizen Army continued to receive considerable publicity in the papers, especially, it seemed, whenever a variation in routine occurred, although at this stage the strike was beginning to collapse and a large number of 'soldiers' began returning to work. Sunday, 25 January, saw a display of 'marching, physical drill to music and skirmishing' in Croydon Park, with White arriving in his motor car. As usual, 'a large force of police [...] accompanied the procession'.[53] An earlier report described the new boots of the participants, 'said to be the gift of Captain White', and the fact that 'the manoeuvres took the form of a sham fight'.[54] White's wry comment was that he had 'expended a pretty big sum out of [his] own pocket for boots for the Citizen Army, a good many of which found their way to the pawnshop'.[55] All this enthusiasm was sadly taking place while the momentum of the strike was gradually collapsing. Shortly after the incident in which Sir George White was insulted, Larkin, at a meeting in Croydon Park, confidentially 'advised his members to go back on the best terms available. His one injunction to them was not to sign the form renouncing the union'.[56]

Chapter 10

Adventures in the Army

Theorising on Structure of State

White's burgeoning radical activism was supported by his developing sophistication in political thinking. This is evident in an earlier article (probably late 1913) which is a typical example of his discursive style; in it he describes a theory he was developing at that time, addressed to sympathisers of radical methods. I would suggest it is as perceptive as anything Gramsci, the Italian radical philosopher, wrote about the concept of hegemony.

His seemingly light-hearted style is misleading and was to a degree unsuccessful because the serious thrust of his argument is lost in what he probably imagined was a populist way of conveying his message, but there is little wrong with his sharpness of analysis. In this case, he maintains that the whole structure of society is under the control of the 'lady typist'.

There are basically three arms of the state: the soldiers who conquer and acquire resources; the police who physically regulate the community; and then, most importantly, the lawyers, who legitimise the hierarchy. Then, he says, 'once down on the lawyers' paper the efforts of centuries, good and bad, humane or destructive of society, continue themselves automatically with the lady typist to circulate them'.[1] White seems to be describing the glue that holds the entire system together, the *sine qua non* of a modern state, something like its grand narrative (or maybe Sorel's myth), which is usually managed, cared for, and disseminated by the administrative classes and their aides, and this he called the 'lady typist'.[2]

This is his allegory for how hegemony is exercised, not by coercion, but by seduction. In other words, misled by the authorities, there arises a tacit acquiescence by the disadvantaged in their oppression, arising mainly out of their reluctance to upset the status quo. This strange inertia in the face of oppression arises from an innate courtesy, or sensitivity, to the equanimity of others.

It was an excellent illustration but one wonders how many of his readers, unintentionally duped by the lightness of his tone, would have missed the point he was making. He describes the prevailing inhibition to question things and the need to overcome it:

> The first step of the social revolution is to steel yourselves to an obstinate unchivalrous refusal to take the lady typist's word for things. 'But the police will insist on our attending to the lady,' you say, 'and after them the soldiers'.[3]

This could be taken as an early example of a kind of discursive formation that is disseminated to buttress the existing hierarchical system. There is, firstly, the social conditioning (the chivalry, for example) that makes one reluctant to question the received wisdom, and then there is quite simply the physical power of the State that will be deployed if one persists. White's response to the question about how one can resist the insistence of the police and the soldiers that one should comply was, 'Oh no, they won't. All they will insist on will be to club you over the head, and put an ounce or two of lead into you'. In other words, they cannot change one's mind for all their violent force; this is coercion, which is not anything as effective as seduction. Therefore, the real obstacle is that 'you are really not sure enough of yourselves to contradict the lady at all'; that is to say, the power of the construct, the hegemony of Gramsci, is such that it is almost impossible to emancipate oneself from it.

As White writes earlier in the article, 'the present capitalists get the fruits of their own and a good deal of the fruits of the workers' labour, *because they know how to keep what they have got* [emphasis added]'. White's remedy for this inability to free oneself and 'contradict the lady' was obscure, and his closet pacifism came to the fore: 'It is a delicate business anyway, but there is not a married man amongst you but knows it can be done – with the right combination of firmness and sweetness.' This argument does not offer a set of specific instructions, but it does articulate the difficulty of resistance by loosely making the point that seduction cannot be counteracted by force, but by something more subtle. One is reminded of Todd May's concept of tactical, as opposed to strategic, resistance in the philosophy of poststructuralist anarchism. Strategic philosophy has a defined alternative to put in place and it resists directly whatever central problematic it perceives. Tactical philosophy attempts to avoid being prescriptive and encourages a resistance indirectly against whatever it opposes; in fact, it encourages resistance wherever it perceives the problem without any overall view, or grand plan. Hence, by its very nature it is nebulous, difficult to articulate, but more importantly, difficult to counteract.[4] A classic example is the 'Occupy' movement, which, to the despair of its opponents, has not in any way defined its aims.

White also commends the qualities of drill, which have 'a considerable effect upon the character, and one most necessary for the workers' purpose'. It is puzzling, in the sense that it is difficult to understand his valorising of what is after all a very mechanical type of exercise. It is possible, of course, that he was supporting a view that saw repetitive, monotonous activity as contributing to some change in consciousness. These ideas were advocated by people like the Russian mystic G.I. Gurdjieff, a contemporary of White's, whose views would be typical of some of the esoteric writing that appealed to White[5]. At least he was looking beyond what the anarchist would see as superficial that is, the notion that regulation under a new regime would change everything; he was aware that the changes needed to be more profound and, most of all, that those changes needed to be in those who took part in the revolution. He informs his readers that, presumably when the revolution comes:

> You would have to have amongst you all [...] the qualities now employed by masters and workers; you would have not only to do your work, market your own produce and pay yourselves your own wages out of the proceeds. That will take discipline.[6]

This appears to be anticipating a period when the workers would acquire the factors of production, but this time the ideas are White's rather than Connolly's. The reaction of the audience/readership to this succinct analysis of the structure of society is unknown.

Meanwhile, White's name was prominent in England as well as in Ireland, particularly in relation to the protests over the constitution of the police inquiry into Bloody Sunday. Francis Sheehy Skeffington and he were 'busy in the lobby of the House of Commons this evening on behalf of the Dublin Civic League. [...] Captain White, while in London will speak on behalf of the Labour candidates in Poplar and Bethnal Green tomorrow'.[7] White believed himself that his popularity took a steep rise shortly afterwards in an event that was reported in great detail in the press on both sides of the Irish Sea.

Butt Bridge

The incident, which took place on Friday 13 March 1914, itself was insignificant and undoubtedly only for the presence of White would probably not have been written up, even in the local press. O'Casey, in *The Story of the Irish Citizen Army,* does not mention it at all, although he generally takes an uncharacteristically benign view of White. However, even *The Times* carried a report of 'a serious disturbance' when a meeting was held 'to protest against the vindictive victimization inflicted on the unemployed by the Dublin employers':

> The crowd, which was headed by between 40 and 50 members of the Citizen Army, carrying long staves, came into conflict with the police, who drew their batons, and in the fight several persons were injured. Among them were two police officers, and Captain J.R. White, DSO, the leader of the procession, who was arrested and charged with assault.[8]

White said that 'by that time the strike had so far collapsed that most of the Citizen Army men, who were nearly all fine hefty chaps, were back in work'. Connolly and he had spoken at the meeting, and White had announced a march to the Mansion House to demand work. He gave staves to what he describes as 'an odd lot of unemployed, who had neither the Citizen Army's discipline nor physique'.[9] Among the 200 or 300 there were, he estimated, four real Citizen Army men in the front rank. So it was a very much under-strength force. A large horse dray of the Royal Mail, on the business of the state, attempted, most probably provocatively, to drive through the ranks while accompanied by the usual force of police. White objected, and a melee ensued which resulted in him being eventually manhandled back to the nearby police barracks and quite badly batoned.[10] Frank Robbins corroborates White's account of being badly undermanned:

> Several members of the Citizen Army taking part in this parade stood by Captain White until they were beaten and overpowered by superior police strength. They were later given medical aid for extensive wounds received from the police batons. The remainder – the non-Citizen Army members – put up little resistance, scattered and fled. It took many months to wear down the sniggering comments about 'the runaway army'. The Dublin press elaborated on this for the purpose of decrying the Irish Citizen Army.[11]

There can be no doubt that White resisted and caused considerable damage to members of the police, aided by stone-throwing from what had become a mob and by 'Madam Markievicz [who, he said] had hung on the flanks of the enemy throughout, darted in and tried to trip up a policeman when possible.' *The Irish Times* reported:

> The crowd followed the police towards the station, and occasionally adopted a menacing attitude. Several times the police formed a solid phalanx to resist a possible onrush [...]. Some six constables took charge of Captain White and pushed ahead, the remainder halting now and again to keep back the crowd.[12]

Several years later, the pacifist Gerard Davies visited Lady Amy, White's mother, in England to comfort her after her son had been jailed for sedition. He was taken aback to find her secretly proud of her son; in particular she mentioned the Butt Bridge incident, telling Davies that it took twelve policemen to get him into the barracks in Dublin.[13] Certainly he had made an impression that was reflected in the charges, which were of 'assaulting the mail van driver, Inspector Purcell, Sergeant Woulfe, and two constables'.[14] Although the treatment of someone who was a celebrity by modern standards exposed the police and their disposition for brutality, White and his circle seemed to regard it as some kind of juvenile escapade: 'My head was a bloody pulp, but my spirit remained exalted from the joy of battle.'[15] Larkin was not amused, still less after the court case when there was what could only be described as an agreement to differ between the police and White. Boyd maintained he again offended White. If he did, Larkin was correct in his view this time: 'working men would not be treated with such consideration. They had been sent to prison for the same offence'.[16] On the other hand, workers also treated the awful confrontations and tensions light-heartedly. White

1. Jack White as a teenager. *(Family photo)*

2. Lady Amy White, Jack White's mother. *(Family painting)*

3. Field Marshal Sir George White, VC. As the 'Hero of Ladysmith' he was a substantial celebrity figure in these islands in 1900. *(Biography of Sir George by Sir Mortimer Durand)*

4. Whitehall, Cooreen, outside Broughshane, Co. Antrim, the White's rather modest family home. *(Family photo)*

5. Sir George, then Governor of Gibraltar, and the Kaiser on his visit to Gibraltar c. 1903.
(Biography of Sir George by Sir Mortimer Durand)

6. Sir George picnicking in Gibraltar with his wife and daughters, c. 1904. *(Family photo)*

7. Jack White as a subaltern in the Gordon Highlanders. *(Family photo)*

8. Jack White c. 1930. *(from Jonathan Cape's original autobiography)*

9. Jack White on Irish Citizen Army manoeuvres with Francis Sheehy Skeffington. *(1913)*

10. Women stick training under the auspices of the Irish Citizen Army. On the right is Jack White with Constance Markievicz and possibly his wife Dollie. All surrounded by a group of admirers. *(Family photo)*

11. Jack White supervising the women stick training with again a substantial number of observers and advisers. *(Family photo)*

12. Jack White supervising the women stick training. *(Family photo)*

13. The happy stick fighters with Constance Markievicz on the far left with hat and Dollie, Jack's wife, on the far right also in hat. *(Family photo)*

14. A newspaper image of Jack White with his bandaged head accompanied by Francis Sheehy Skeffington, March 1914. This was after the incident at Butt Bridge.

15. Jack White, left, with Colonel Maurice Moore, right, and the redoubtable Commander McGlinchey (the man who almost precipitated a Civil War single-handedly). *(Irish Independent)*

16. Jack White in his sixties. *(Family photo)*

17. Pat English (neé Napier) on her wedding day. Jack White's niece, she was his most frequent correspondent in the last few years of his life. *(Family photo)*

recalls that when he struck the police inspector at the outset of hostilities, 'then the band played'. Whether the Citizen Army band was there or not is not reported, but they did play a significant part in the processions and drilling. A speciality of theirs was the tune, 'The Peeler and the Goat', which was played as a provocation to the police who, according to Fox, were hell bent on destroying the instruments.[17]

White's trial was covered by most papers, and White saw it as an opportunity to 'make a huge case of it'. In a publicity drive he had letters 'sent off to all the leading papers in the British Isles, setting forth the devilish apathy of the public [...] about the starving people'.[18] On 8 April 1914, the day of the main hearing, there certainly was entertainment from both sides with 'Laughter' appearing in parentheses frequently in the court report, and this despite White having brought counter-charges of assault against Inspector Purcell and a constable, as well as against the mail van driver for behaving dangerously in his driving. White's counsel was a unionist, because he said the 'Castle Catholic' lawyers were 'all too afraid of the suspicion of pronounced national views interfering with their prospects'. Two witnesses were called on White's behalf who were of the highest calibre: a civil servant whose reluctance to testify made White's defence all the more forceful; and a Mr Verschoyle, a justice of the peace, whose grave demeanour apparently struck a discordant note in the proceedings, and in White's description, which probably conveyed the atmosphere correctly, 'Verschoyle protested against the prosecuting counsel saying "I am quite sure your worship wants a true story" ', while White observed 'the probability is his worship wanted to be amused like everyone else'.[19] On the offer of White's counsel to take no further action against the police, the prosecution entered a *nolle prosequi*, 'with expressions of mutual apology and regret'.

The trial ended with White crossing the courtroom to present the inspector with the blackthorn stick that he had allegedly belaboured him with at Butt Bridge. Bedecked with a green ribbon by 'some wag', it was the sole exhibit for the case.[20] White summed up:

> I was blamed by my own side for weak good nature and waste of the opportunity to score a decisive victory over the police. But then my own side were not shelling out some £10 a day for the case.[21]

This is one of the few places where White's refreshing frankness is missing, and there is no doubt that his love of good-humoured banter and his relishing of the limelight with what he would term members of his own class seduced him into selling out a valuable propaganda point. On the other hand, as mentioned previously, he had spoken about the alienation he suffered when he started drilling the Citizen Army: 'to feel psychically the collective hostility of the upper and middle classes'.[22] It is surely understandable that given the opportunity of returning, albeit briefly, to the fold, he would do so, behaving as he did by basking in the general bonhomie of his old associates for a while. Anyway, as he saw it, he had emerged with honour intact. He said to his mother, 'the general opinion seems to be that I scored a moral triumph' and he also pointed out that 'I don't believe any honest man can keep clear of prison at least once.'[23] He did not miss the opportunity to give his esoteric analysis either, noting his 'views about time, the hidden dimension, showing the inner connection of things, outwardly distinct'.[24]

Larkin, of course, was enraged and, it must be noted, White did not shrink from recording his invective in full:

> If ever a case proved the foulness attached to the administration of the law in this country, Captain White's case surely proved it up to the hilt. [...] [The judge was] a puny place-hunter and carpet bagger [...] who knows on which side his bread is buttered; a judge who would be in the obscurity of a briefless barrister – an obscurity he would well adorn but for the foulness of political life in this unfortunate country.[25]

'Lord Justice Molony, who tried the case, was suave and courteous throughout', according to White.[26] One serious point that counsel for the prosecution made was that White, in his statement, had admitted the very charges against him; in effect he had admitted guilt, which meant his case should have turned merely on mitigating factors before sentencing.[27] Larkin's comments are very pertinent, referring to the case of a man called Daly who 'honestly admitted he had committed a common assault on a scab' and was sentenced to two years imprisonment by the same judge. Undoubtedly he had a point: 'We say [Larkin, that is] because Captain White is Captain White he is allowed to go free.'[28]

White had a final say about the proceedings, publishing a letter in *The Irish Times* alongside the detailed court report of that day. He protested he was represented as 'a person with a natural disinclination towards disorder, whereas the exact reverse is the case', and then went on to diagnose a 'misunderstanding' that 'lies in the current impression that persons of rough dress and unaddicted to regular shaving are of such ferocious disposition that their congregation in any numbers demands additional police'. Calling them gentlemen, he related in what appears to be a condescending manner an incident where 'a crowd of transport workers' allowed 'two unknown and unaccompanied ladies to pass to the front'.[29] This probably was to contrast with the treatment his wife Dollie got from some policemen during the court hearing. John Brennan (penname of Sydney Gifford Czira), reminiscing in 1963, said he met Mrs White at that time: 'a very beautiful woman, dressed in the height of fashion and she was very very angry at the disgrace as she termed it, of her husband being involved in a brawl with the police'. He told her that the DMP were very different to the British police, and he recounts the incident in court in great detail:

> as we walked into the police court, the elegant and lovely Mrs White attracted the eye of one of the force. With an impudent grin, he squeezed her arm, and said 'Hello, Duckey! I like your old French bonnet' – a quotation from a then popular song. Mrs White was naturally furious, and promising that she would report him to Dublin Castle for his impertinence, admitted to me that she *now* understood what I had told her about the Irish police.[30]

Returning to White's letter, the remainder was, in the words of his unsociable Uncle John, 'platitudinous'; he had indulged his taste for the carnival rather than taken the opportunity to demonstrate the endemic brutality of the Dublin Metropolitan Police to the world. In a letter to Thomas Johnson in 1917, he stated that 'I never regretted anything more than as Chairman of the Civic League bowing to Larkin's decision to boycott the police enquiry';[31] this perplexing acquiescence to Larkin's wishes was likely prompted by the justness he perceived in Larkin's criticism in this particular incident. On the other hand, hindsight appeared not to have countered White's naiveté: 'the report, which was presented some five months later, resulted in a complete whitewash of the police'.[32] The far more politically astute Larkin would have been well aware that this was going to happen.

The case gave rise to a series of questions in the House of Commons nearly two weeks later. John G. Butcher, a long-standing Tory MP, addressing Augustine Birrell, the Chief Secretary for Ireland, questioned the 'misunderstandings' that led to the Crown entering a *nolle prosequi*. Birrell said that as 'Captain White had acted as he did under a misunderstanding as to his legal rights [... and] further expressed his regret for what had occurred [... the] Crown, decided with the concurrence of the Attorney General, who was consulted by telephone, to enter a *nolle prosequi.*'[33] Larkin's reaction is not known, but it is unlikely that any of his men, no matter how grave the charges, would have had a hearing that resulted in a telephone call across the Irish Sea. The comportment of the proceedings, and White's exoneration, smacked of expediency and suggested that a closer examination would probably find that there was validity to the more moderate section of Larkin's analysis. Butcher, whose anti-establishment leanings showed even when his party was in power, had the last word. With his scepticism of modern legislative practices, tempered by a mordant wit, he asked Birrell, 'What was the nature of Captain White's misunderstanding as to his legal rights? Did he think he was entitled to assault the constable?'[34]

Disillusionment

White's frustrations with the Citizen Army deepened. O'Casey wrote that White had begun to 'lose hope':

> He seemed to be building on foundations of sand. He had no outlet for his energies. If Labour failed to rise to the opportunity that presented itself, what good purpose could it serve for him to be eternally trying to accomplish the impossible?[35]

Writing to his mother, White said that the 'principal activity I am now engaged in is a campaign to spread the Citizen Army'. He believed then this would result in 'compelling the National Volunteers to cease from their suspicious aloofness from anyone connected with Labour and draw together the Middle Class and Labour National movement'.[36] In 1930 he saw quite clearly that the 'joining together of Labour and National elements in Ireland was not and is not possible'. In an acknowledgment of humankind's acquisitive nature lying at the heart of capitalism he explained:

> A common emotion of patriotism cannot reconcile a concrete and fundamental antagonism of interest and objective. The most pure-souled Nationalists in Ireland, who do not belong to the ranks of Labour, are not freed by their purity of soul from the necessities

of their body. If they live by hiring the labour of others instead of selling their own, they will tend inevitably to hire it as cheap as they can; and the worker who has his labour to sell will tend to do so as dear as he can. The two opposing interests cannot blend. They may combine to kick out foreign interference preparatory to having a straight fight between themselves.[37]

In spite of his attachment to the Labour movement he felt himself drawn to the National Volunteers although, as he said, 'spiritually I had little or nothing in common' with them.[38] O'Casey reported:

> For some months Captain White worked gallantly, trying to do the work of ten men, and making superhuman efforts to organise, drill and equip an army singlehanded, furnished with no help, and receiving very little encouragement. But the inevitable happened; the drills became irregular, the numbers continued to decrease, and, finally, the Captain found himself reduced to the command of one Company of faithful stalwarts, who, in spite of all obstacles, had remained as a sure and trustworthy nucleus of the Irish Citizen Army.[39]

The strike was very much on the wane at this stage. The Butt Bridge incident, as White had noted, did not even have enough Citizen Army members to march because the most stalwart had returned to work.

O'Casey, alert to the dangers of losing White entirely, suggested in a meeting with him that they formalise the army into a 'systematic unit of Labour', and further 'that a Constitution should be drafted [...,] that a Council should be elected [...,] and to generally take steps to improve and strengthen the condition' of the organisation.[40] White was delighted with this idea, and on 22 March 1914 (between White's arrest and arraignment) a general meeting was held and a council was elected with White as chairman. O'Casey was secretary, Markievicz was one of the honorary treasurers, and among the vice-chairmen were Larkin, the Dublin City Councillor William Partridge, and Francis Sheehy Skeffington. As regards the latter, the illusion of a primarily defensive force was being maintained, and of course this was probably essential with regard to the authorities.

'Skeffington', writes White, 'was a perfectly consistent pacifist', and he maintains this is 'proof of the pacific purposes of the Citizen Army at the time'. Noting that Sheehy Skeffington was 'Shot at the whim of a British officer', White goes on to assert that

> In Sheehy Skeffington, and not in Connolly, fell the first martyr to Irish Socialism, for he linked Ireland not only with the little nations struggling for self expression but with the world's humanity struggling for a higher life.[41]

There was no place for Connolly on the council at that time, but the very wording of the first principle of its Constitution left no doubt about his influence: 'That the first and last principle of the Irish Citizen Army is the avowal that the ownership of Ireland, moral and material, is vested of right in the people of Ireland.'[42] The Citizen Army was made 'solid', said O'Casey, 'giving no mercy and receiving none' especially from those similar organisations between which there was 'an impassable gulf of Ideal and Principle'.[43] He reported that White ordered fifty uniforms from Arnott's, and although he makes no mention of it here, O'Casey was horrified at the idea of what was essentially a guerrilla army, as he saw it, being identified so easily in the street fighting that would be its field of operation.[44] Larkin did not agree, probably still aware of the favourable publicity and possibly thinking along syndicalist lines about an army that could wage war, particularly on the state. White's point was that 'without some kind of uniform the men would look slovenly and would feel it'.[45] Larkin, for once, agreed with him, in a politic and possibly conciliatory statement (*pace* his post-trial comments): 'Uniforms would give the men a sound sense of *esprit de corp,* and one of homogeneous unity, encourage the practice of discipline, and instil a pride into the men they couldn't possibly feel in their everyday clothing.'[46] A further controversy arose unexpectedly: William O'Brien, originally a tailor by trade, reported that it was discovered that when the uniforms were 'procured they were made in England and under conditions which Dublin tailors regarded as "unfair" '.[47]

White makes no reference to the meeting as such in his autobiography, and this was probably because of his imminent departure from the Citizen Army. O'Casey, however, reported a revitalised force:

> Two splendid companies of picked men were formed as the nucleus of the City Battalion. [...] In a short time a consignment of haversacks, belts and bayonets arrived. [...] The army was divided into units of

half companies [… and] drills were held twice weekly with White having a cadre of officers now to help him out.[48]

William O'Brien, confidant of Connolly and later to be secretary of the Irish Trade Union Congress and Labour Party (ITUCLP),[49] reports a slightly different picture:

> On Sunday March 29th, 1914 I brought Con Lehane to Croydon Park to see James Larkin and while we were speaking to him Captain J.R. White came in. Lehane asked Captain White how many were in the Irish Citizen Army and White said 'about fifty'. 'Oh', said Larkin 'There are more than that'. 'No', said White 'rather less'.[50]

Recruiting drives were held outside Dublin in what were seen as rural places by the city dwellers: Coolock, Kinsealy, Finglas and Swords. O'Casey records a particular trip that took himself and P.T. Daly, Larkin's lieutenant, to Lucan in White's car along with Markievicz. It seems to have been a particularly pleasant jaunt on a 'happy spring day', and 'after a pleasant tea in a local restaurant' all four spoke to a 'shy and obviously timorous crowd of about five hundred people'. It appears they had a good reception, because twenty names were taken by the secretary and 'these were authorised to hold a subsequent meeting to elect officers and arrange for drills' before the four sped off in the motor car to rousing cheers.

But the 'quietude' of the crowd indicated to O'Casey that the Citizen Army had 'a long and exhausting struggle in front of it before the rural workers would become sufficiently class-conscious to understand the elementary principles of Labour thought and aspiration'.[51] Rather than a paranoid analysis of the threat to his beloved working man, it was a further illustration of the difficulties that lay in a socialist programme in Ireland, despite the successful establishment of a left-wing consciousness in the proletariat in Dublin and the other cities. Although O'Casey's *bête noir* was the National Volunteer force, the Lucan experience indicates a resistance, or at least a lack of support for their plans among the rural community. Fintan Lane, writing about a slightly earlier period (before the Wyndham Act of 1903), quoted Engels as saying that 'A purely socialist movement cannot be expected in Ireland for a considerable time.' Lane maintains that, because of the agrarian nature of the Irish social structure where 'landlordism' exercised a baleful influence, the aspiration of the Irish people was not the alleviation of the lot of the dispossessed but for a 'peasant proprietorship'.[52] It is difficult to gauge how relevant this analysis was by 1914. Just a few years later, according to Conor Kostick, there was 'a movement of Ireland's 200,000 agricultural workers [...] mainly directed at the wealthier farmers over rates of hire'.[53] He recounts these workers joining the Irish Transport and General Workers Union (ITGWU) in 1917 and a number of demonstrations under the banner of the One Big Union (OBU), indicating more than an inchoate socialist consciousness among the rural community.

Lane agrees with O'Casey's suspicion of the Volunteers and the mainstay of their membership, the Irish Parliamentary Party, stating that 'the home rule movement was conservative on social issues and was hostile to manifestations of social radicalism'.[54] Andrew Boyd's perspective goes even further and compares the 'leaders of the Irish Volunteers, [who were] of the middle-class nationalist mentality' with the 'Conservatives in England or the Ulster Unionists in the North'.[55] O'Casey's stance was extreme: the whole struggle was one of class, and he reserved particular contumely for the Volunteers:

> This canting cry of all creeds and all classes is worn to a ghastly shadow: it is the cry of all societies deaf to the appeals of the subject workers of the Nation: it is the long arm that chucks the aristocracy under the chin, who have always been in Ireland a selfish materialistic crew exemplifying in their life that it is indeed a dangerous disease to eat too much cake. These people, whom the Gaelic League and Sinn Fein were, and whom the Volunteers now are afraid to shock, were the weakness and bane of every National movement.[56]

To add to the siege mentality that the workers' leaders must have suffered at that time, a protest was made by British Army officers when they were asked if they would object to marching against the Carsonite forces. This incident, referred to dramatically as the Curragh Mutiny, took place in the same week as the newly revived Citizen Army meeting, the last week of March 1914. Technically it was not a mutiny as the officers did not disobey any order – they were not going to be asked, at least at that stage, to march against anyone – but it led the Irish Labour movement to perceive this as a classic case of one law for the rich, or at least for the middle classes, and another for the poor. The government had appeared to back down. Fox reports that 'there was much industrial unrest in Britain and troops had been moved to various centres for possible use against strikers'. The *Irish Worker* on 28 March 1914 commented:

> As Irish workers we are not concerned with the Officers of the British Army taking the line they have […] but we claim what the Officer may do in pursuance of his political and sectarian convictions, so too may the Private in pursuance of his; and if to-day British Generals [Brigadier General Hubert Gough, General Sir Arthur Paget] and other Staff Officers refuse to fight against the privileged class to which they belong so, too, must the Private Soldier be allowed to exercise his convictions against shooting down his brothers and sisters of the working class when they are fighting for their rights.[57]

Although the officers were mainly unionists and they were only being ordered to prepare to march to Ulster in the event of trouble there, the consideration that was shown them by Asquith's government – calling it an 'honest misunderstanding' – was too much for the Labour commentators. A leading article in the same issue of *The Irish Worker* made the point cogently:

> When our brother Mann published an appeal to our brothers who through economic circumstances were forced to join the army, not to shoot down their fellows fighting on the industrial field […] he was sent to jail for six months.[58]

Fox is incorrect when he says that Tom Mann had just stood trial in London. Mann, 'the well-known leader of the Syndicalist movement', was convicted on 9 May 1912 of 'having incited soldiers to mutiny, and was sentenced to six months imprisonment'. His case was particularly contentious because, although an exponent of syndicalism, he never uttered or wrote a 'seditious' word. The offending article was originally a pamphlet, written by someone else, published in the magazine the *Syndicalist,* which was issued under the supervision of the Industrial Syndicalist Education League, of which Mann was chairman. The judge's summing up and directing of the jury was both notorious and vindictive, seemingly in reaction to Mann's presumption in presenting himself as a lay litigant.[59]

Chapter 11

Departure and Arrival – the National Volunteers

Division

Neither O'Casey nor White refer to the Curragh mutiny, although White had stated controversially at his first talk in Dublin at the invitation of the Peace Committee that if it came to a fight between the British Army and Carson he just might find himself on the side of Carson.[1] O'Casey, probably preoccupied with the dangers that the Volunteers presented, continued to be grateful to White and to tolerate Markievicz because they provided a link between the two paramilitary bodies and quite often assuaged some of the more intolerable insults, as he saw them, delivered by the Volunteers. Long after White had left, O'Casey came to the conclusion that Markievicz's presence was untenable, and after a failed bid to have her ejected, resigned from the Citizen Army rather than, as Larkin suggested, apologise to her. He was a serious loss, not just because of his organisational abilities but, as a true, albeit inflexible, socialist he might have provided the necessary balance and support that Connolly needed when Larkin left[2] (and White for that matter). O'Casey provides an example of the kind of high-handed treatment the Citizen Army was receiving from the Volunteers or their supporters. The following letter was received after several requests by the Citizen Army to use their hall were ignored by Conradh na Gaeilge:

The House Committee, 25 Parnell Square, 12 April 1914.

I received your letter concerning our hall last night. It is engaged now every night, except Saturday, and on this night it is occasionally wanted for a social. The Volunteers use the hall on Tuesday and Sunday nights, and *I don't think* the Committee would give it to *any other organisation* for drill. The caretaker had now a good deal of work to do, and the women, also, who are engaged to keep the hall clean. However, I will put your letter before my Committee at their next meeting, which will not be held till the beginning of next month, - Yours, G. Irvine, Secretary.[3]

The 'silent but relentless antipathy of the official of the National Volunteers'[4] was being countered by frequent efforts 'by Captain White and by the Secretary [O'Casey] to promote co-operation in the use of the hall for drilling purposes, but no concession whatever in this respect would be granted by the Volunteers'.[5] Inevitably it erupted into a row marked by venomous yet pedestrian rhetoric, and, judging by O'Casey's detailed reporting, the fact that he fired the opening salvo at the Volunteers suggests that he was also the chief antagonist behind the whole affair although, as he notes, it was all 'at the suggestion of Jim Larkin'. The missive consisted of a 'challenge' to the 'Executive of the Irish National Volunteers to public debate in which to justify their appeal for the sympathy and support of the Irish working class'.[6] It claimed that the 'ambiguous principles of the Volunteer's Constitution', among other points, had been 'consistently antagonistic to the lawful claims of Labour'.[7] Under the headline, 'Rival Armies – Challenge to Nationalist Volunteers', *The Irish Times* published in full the details of the challenge and pointed out that 'The leaders of the Irish Citizen Army (of which Captain J.R. White, DSO, is stated to be the Chairman of the Army Council), it appears, dislike the Irish National Volunteers.'[8]

Departure from the Citizen Army

This detailed emphasis of White's purported position was intended to flush out some suspicions the paper already had, and the following day a letter was published from White. There can be no doubt that the class resentment behind much of the criticism of the Volunteers was akin to sectarianism in White's mind, and he had had enough:

> I wish to state that I had nothing to with it [the challenge]. In fact I resigned from the chairmanship of the said Council a week ago, doubtful of my power to prevent, and determined not to become involved in such a policy. In my opinion, the all-important point is the speedy formation and equipment of a Volunteer Army implicitly or explicitly determined to achieve the independence and maintain the unity of Ireland, and I will not lift a finger to embarrass anybody likely to work for this end. For an 'Army Council' which has not yet created an appreciable 'army' to issue a challenge to the organisers of a strong and growing movement seems to me little short of absurd. Nevertheless, I believe that for trade unionism to predominate over Unionism is the line of least resistance to the unification of Ireland, and I shall work along that line myself whenever and wherever I get the chance.[9]

Despite the support here for syndicalism, or at least some form of trade unionism, there is a suggestion of the tone of an ambitious young man, leaving a small and backward family firm for a large and exciting national company, and in his own recollections he confirms this. He told Connolly and O'Casey that he was leaving:

> I marched out of the room, a free man, to spread myself with the rapidly spreading Irish National Volunteers; say rather a swollen headed young ass looking for limelight in a movement with which spiritually I had little or nothing in common.[10]

O'Casey was perceptive and surprisingly magnanimous about the departure, but neglects to connect it with the campaign against the Volunteers:

> It is only fair to say that a quiet reflection of past events convinces the writer that Captain White did not obtain the ready and affectionate co-operation his nature craved for. His efforts to understand the mysterious natures of working men were earnest and constant, and were never fully appreciated by those amongst whom he spent his time and a good deal of his money. But we feel sure that he will never be forgotten by those, who knew him, and worked by his side, for many months. He was a gentleman according, as Mitchell says, 'to the British State and Constitution', but he was also a gentleman

according to the kindly and benevolent law of Nature, and those who sat with him on the Council, and differed from him most, now wish to express their sincere affection for one who honestly and unselfishly endeavoured to use his gifts, natural and acquired, to lift the workers to a higher plane of usefulness and comfort.[11]

This is probably the most laudatory piece ever written about Jack White. In a letter written almost thirty years after the event, commenting on a review by a critic called Aston of R.M. Fox's *History of the Citizen Army*, while acknowledging that his intentions were pacifist, White concedes that he was mistaken in 'thinking that the objects I had in mind for the Citizen Army could and would be achieved without bloodshed'. Describing himself as 'its creator' and 'as the primary cause', he calls it 'the first Red Army in Europe [but] it was a Red Army with a difference'. He points out that 'its membership was confined to members of the Trades Union' and that 'its outlook and that of its leaders was first internationally Socialist, and only secondarily became nationally Socialist [...] when the whole anti-war organisation of International Socialism collapsed at the first blast of the trumpet'.[12] He neglects to point out that Connolly was a notable exception to this; George Woodcock also records that the anarchists appeared to have behaved in a similar fashion to the socialists:

> The loudly proclaimed anti-militarism of both anarchists and syndicalists produced no spectacular effects when the testing of war came upon them. Most of the anarchists of military age went to the colours without resistance, and many of their leaders [...] declared their support of the Allies.[13]

The letter addressing Fox's review appears to be the only written evidence of the pacifism which dictated White's thinking about the Citizen Army and incidentally explained his own activities as an ambulance driver during the Great War:

> I hoped to build an instrument [the Citizen Army] to express my own [pacifism], proved by my having thrown up my Commission in the British Army four or five years earlier. The Citizen Army then in my mind was intended to achieve social justice without the shedding of blood, except of course, for a few scalp wounds given and received

in kindly domestic interchange with the police. I faithfully carried this conception into practice, and I honestly believed that when the police by a little domestic discipline, which, with the aid of the Citizen Army, I was prepared to apply, had been subordinated to the Socialist Nation, we could step without further unpleasantness into the Irish Millennium.[14]

He goes on to state that

If Mr Fox's view, endorsed I think by Mr Aston of the pivotal function of the Citizen Army is correct, my would-be pacifist Red Army has largely rectified in deed its creator's pious motive. It saved all Ireland from conscription.[15]

White appears to be arguing that the effect of the Citizen Army was to prevent conscription. This is not a very convincing argument, although it does allow him to convey the aspiration that he was involved in a movement which kept 'alive the fundamental opposition of both Christianity and Socialism to all War'.[16] His impending illness and his isolation in Whitehall at that time may have contributed to a certain vagueness

Although O'Casey's panegyric needs to be taken with a pinch of salt, there still can be no doubt about White devoting his resources and ability to the Citizen Army. That it was originally a pacifist organisation is arguable. White's pacifism was always idiosyncratic; as an advocate of peaceful means he did not abjure the wielding of a big stick. The Citizen Army was certainly defensive, and its primary purpose was the protection of the marchers during the Lockout from the DMP, but both Larkin and Connolly, the real shapers of policy, were syndicalists, although of different persuasions. Connolly's later action in November 1915 in deploying an armed and uniformed force on the picket line must have been hugely symbolic; the syndicalists, for the first time probably anywhere in the world, had their own regular army.

National Volunteers

White joined the National Volunteers immediately after resigning from the Citizen Army, and within a short while he was reported inspecting a battalion of men in Celtic Park in Derry.[17] Sir Roger Casement, as ever, dubious and bordering on the uncharitable about White, saw his reason for leaving the

ICA as a quarrel with Larkin and maintained that the Volunteers originally did not want him but that White

> came to me to try and get him in [...] I persuaded Colonel Moore and Eoin MacNeill to send him to Ulster on an organising visit – as Colonel Moore was our only commissioned officer and we badly needed officers. Here I found him at work in Derry and Tyrone when I visited those places in June. I left him in Tyrone on friendly terms engaged in an effort to start a training ground for the Volunteers.[18]

This account of trying to 'get him in' is flatly contradicted by others. Not alone was White's profile high, but his progress and value in the north was reported very positively in the press along with what appeared to be a flood of enthusiasm for the Volunteers, reflected in the growing number of enrolments.

'Captain' George Berkeley who was appointed chief inspecting officer by Colonel Maurice Moore for the areas of Belfast, Antrim and Down, gives an account of meeting White in Derry when being given an introduction to the Volunteers. (Berkeley, an Englishman, was one of the committee who put together £1,524 to fund the Childers and O'Brien arms shipments to Howth and Kilcoole. He was a staunch Liberal and his raison d'etre may have been as much an opposition to the Conservative Party as a sympathy for Home Rule.)[19] Allowing for Berkeley's generally positive perspective on all the protagonists, it still illustrates the impact that White (and his wife) could create.

> Captain White ... was a man who would have been an exceptional and striking figure in any assemblage at that time. He was six foot two or more; strong; of the Orange man type – yellow hair and a pale skin; but having been brought up in Hampton Court, had acquired there a very attractive manner ... his wife, young and beautiful and always ready to stand by him in any adventure; she was half Spanish, of medium height, dark and graceful ...[20]

Berkeley said White 'was busy organising companies in the neighbouring villages so that they could be brought into the town in case of our being invaded from the outside' and recounted how he went with White and his wife on 'a motor drive through the three northern counties'.

> From village to village we went, and in each one White was welcomed with a joy that was touching [and an eagerness to join the Volunteers]. ... Our tour lasted four or five days [...] we were spinning along the road at about 30 miles an hour – quite reckless in those days.[21]

This was the same car that brought White and his wife to Ballymoney, which he later converted to be employed as an ambulance in Belgium in the early days of the war.

In an interview with the *Irish Independent,* White spoke about his organisational plans, advocating the 'immediate formation of battalions' which would 'entail the grouping of the various companies' and, interestingly, 'Captain White further suggested that representatives from different districts, or delegates from each company [...] should be invited to meet in a central place to approve or amend the suggested scheme.'[22]

This was not quite the conventional military hierarchy of power with a commander-in-chief at the top; it was much closer to governance by consensus, very much akin to the lateral organisation proposed by those opposed to pyramidic bodies of authority. Despite his continued insistence on the value of discipline and drill, which could be seen as a kind of acquiescence with a central authoritarianism, this was, on the contrary, a way of organising affairs that would be of particular benefit to the individual soldier or volunteer rather than the welding of a coherent singular force whose only mind would be that of its commander.

White praised the Irish Volunteer movement in the north, saying that 'from the experience of his tour up to date [...] [there] was strong evidence of the natural military spirit of the Irish people'. Casement joined in the platitudes with 'the hope that a healthy rivalry in military efficiency will [...] [produce] a spirit of camaraderie [...] between the so-called "rival forces" [...] [and] the Volunteers – Orange and Green – will someday combine'.[23] The O'Malley declared in Dublin on 29 May that 'there were 90,000 Volunteers enrolled and it was hoped to make the number 300,000'.[24] On the following day,

> The first public parade and general inspection of the Derry National Volunteers were held in Celtic Park. Thousands of spectators were present [...]. Over two thousand men advanced in review order, commanded by Captain White and gave the salute, and skirmishing,

signalling, company drill and first-aid competitions were effectively conducted.[25]

It must have been a very marked contrast to the days at Croydon Park when White had difficulty getting musters of a hundred mostly malnourished and poverty-stricken souls. Despite Casement's reservations, or at least his qualified support, White, with his military experience, education and intelligence, would have been a formidable force in training, and his leadership must have been of immeasurable benefit to the Volunteers.

He seems to have adopted at this time the identity of the military type, a role he had emphatically abandoned in 1907 when he left the army; this of course was different, like the Citizen Army it was primarily a defensive force. In a speech at Dungannon he protested that 'as a soldier, it was incumbent on him to advise practise rather than make a speech'. Instead, he had 'dealt very largely and completely as to the duty of the new corps, their method and form of drill, imparting many useful and necessary hints'.[26]

This appears to have been the persona that captured the public imagination; one contributor to a local newspaper hoped that 'Captain White, whom so many admire, will continue to develop our military spirit, while leaving the statecraft to the elected leaders.'[27] The private, complicated personality only emerged in moments of stress. His attitude towards the Volunteers was quite ambivalent, torn between his antipathy towards them as the bourgeoisie who supported all that he opposed and, on the other hand, seeing them as an opportunity to give an outlet for the energies of the daemon that drove him. It could be argued that his dilemma was typical of the current *zeitgeist*, uncertainty coupled with a consciousness of possibilities of great moment.

Looking back, White claimed that the Volunteers 'had no definite ideals and no definitive objective', and that 'the movement as a whole proved its lack of solidity of purpose by the evaporation of 95 per cent of it. The remaining 5 per cent made the '16 rising and beat the Black and Tans'.[28] This was a reference to the very large majority that sided with Redmond at the outbreak of the Great War, some of whom went on to fight in the trenches. His figures, although open to question, are only slightly exaggerated. According to George Dangerfield's calculations, 'the new Irish Volunteers were told that, out of a membership of 168,000, it appeared that Redmond had retained about 156,000'.[29] This would actually be ninety-three per cent of the volunteers, leaving 12,000 rebels, just seven per cent (Estimates even on the brink of the Rising in mid-April 1916, never had the figure above

16,000.)[30] White's cry that 'if he were given 20,000 men in Ireland to form a Citizen Army he would remodel Ireland' appeared not to be unrealistic.[31]

White related how hard he worked and with what difficulties:

> In Derry I organised and commanded a brigade of men [around 5,000 men, i.e. two battalions], mostly old soldiers, which I brought to a parade efficiency almost equal to the Brigade of Guards. Derry was a powder mine at the time. Once a week at least I would be called out of bed by an orderly with some report that 'the other sort' (the Orangemen) were mobilizing for a secret attack on the Catholic Quarter [...] I preserved the peace, but I did not make myself popular.[32]

It seems that he was not destined to make close friends in any of his endeavours, despite his being, as noted by O'Casey, someone 'who honestly and unselfishly endeavoured to use his gifts, natural and acquired'.[33] Ironically, if he had stayed in the British Army it would not have been surprising if he had reached the rank of general in spite of his ability to alienate his superiors and colleagues.

Political Instability in the North

White's comment about a 'powder mine' in the north was not confined to the old rivalry of unionists and nationalists; it seems everyone was prone to indiscretions that arose from the paranoia that prevailed at the time. The *Manchester Guardian,* in a wide-ranging article, reported that two British Army companies that went out on manoeuvres with fixed bayonets around Craigavon were the cause of the subsequent mobilising of the Ulster Volunteers to 'keep an eye on the soldiers'.

This was only a few weeks after the extraordinary 'gun-running exploit' at Larne where the Ulster Volunteers commander, reminiscent of some kind of community sporting event, went to great lengths to thank many local businessmen for their co-operation. On the other hand, the Home Rulers and the many other hues of nationalists that went into making up the National Volunteers were described as a 'rapidly growing movement' whose 'promoters' were 'more than surprised at the success which has attended their efforts'.

To add to the confusion of what could be very loosely described as standing armies, the *Guardian* stated that there was an unease among the

'Nationalists of Belfast and Derry' about the ability of Dublin to administer such an enthusiastic force and that 'Northern Nationalists share a good many of the prejudices of the Covenanters, including a prejudice against Dublin.' It uses White to add to this speculation:

> Captain White used to be at the head of the 'Citizens [sic] Army' in Dublin. He believes that Labour holds the key to the Irish question, and for some time he allowed himself to be influenced by Mr Larkin's views that the National Volunteers had anti-democratic and 'Hibernian' tendencies, but the 'Citizens Army' is dwindling in numbers, and the son of the defender of Ladysmith simply could not let his ability go to seed in these stirring times.[34]

It is unlikely White himself would have argued with this report. It was, however, very unlikely, as the journalist suggested, that a mutual alliance would have been formed by both sides against Dublin. What White himself described as the 'atmosphere of neurotic mutual suspicion that might have easily led to open conflict'[35] was so prevalent that the *Manchester Guardian* later devoted another article to the 'circulation of a series of false stories of outrages by the Irish National Volunteers'. These consisted of everything from threatening Sunday school excursions and smashing up band instruments, to carrying out searches of 'respectable' passers-by. A typical example of the potentially explosive mood was when a soldier was supposed to have been assaulted by nationalists and had to be rescued by Carsonites. The truth, according to the paper, was that the soldier had made 'an offensive observation to a young lady which was naturally resented by a Nationalist', and a scuffle developed.[36]

White himself was involved in an incident which was described as 'the silliest story of all'. It is difficult to establish a reliable version of the incident because there is a marked difference between what was reported in the paper, what White wrote in a letter at the time, and what appeared in his autobiography fifteen years later.

Apparently some panic arose in unionist circles because a battalion of National Volunteers were reportedly on their way to reinforce another battalion on manoeuvres outside the city of Derry. The 'reinforcing' battalion was of course hurrying out to join their fellow Volunteers because they believed that they were under threat, and, to add to the tension, a Captain Moore (no relation to the Volunteer commander, Colonel Moore) apparently believed that his land, near where the original manoeuvres were taking place, was under threat by these same Volunteers who intended 'to raid for arms concealed in his demesne'. Moore issued a statement to the 'unfortunate police authorities that he had a force of men armed with carbines and ball and cartridge to protect his contraband treasure'.

The police asked White to stop the second force of nationalists making their way out of the city. In his letter to the paper, White said, 'this I refused to do, after satisfying myself that there was no shadow of foundation for Captain Moore's suspicions'. Blaming the unionists for 'the unfounded fears of that force [which] are the concern of their collective nervous system', he asserted that 'no untoward incident of any sort occurred or was threatened by the Irish [sic] Volunteers'. He also pointed out that he had served with Captain Moore in the Boer War, and '[Moore] will be as ready as I to correct these misinformed mischievous M.P.s who are shameless enough to sow dissension'.[37]

What he did not say until fifteen years later was that he only just managed, with the greatest difficulty, to turn back the second force of Volunteers from what could have been mayhem. According to White's later recollection,

> Commandant McGlinchy, an old regular type sergeant-major, was in command of it. He was a fine type but as obstinate as a mule [...] marching beside him for a few yards, I told him my opinion of his conduct [...] He was more than inclined to be mutinous, but his sense of discipline just held.[38]

He maintained, maybe a little dramatically, that this incident could have had the 'most disastrous consequences to the whole cause of Irish unity and might have set Protestant and Catholic at each other's throats all over Ireland'.[39] Although the event featured all the misunderstandings of a theatrical farce, it also gives an indication of the hothouse climate that prevailed in the northern part of the country at that time. The *Manchester Guardian* reported:

> Of course, every one of the stories was implicitly believed by all of Sir E. Carson's followers, and the feeling of bitterness, previously acute enough in all conscience, had been accentuated just at the time when Unionist leaders, if they were as anxious for peace as they say they are, would have exhausted every means to allay the public excitement. Under ordinary circumstances an Ulster Volunteer who

accepted all these canards as gospel would be a danger to the peace, but he is now doubly so, *having been generously granted permission by his general officer commanding to carry his rifle on the public street,* such permission being countersigned, so to speak, by Mr Birrell, to the astonishment of all who realise the danger.[40]

As with the tolerance shown to the Irish Citizen Army and the incident of their armed picket duty, there seems to have been an extraordinary laxity on the part of authorities to allow this fervour of militarism to fester. The 1916 Royal Commission heavily criticised the complacency of the local authorities towards the private militia that the Irish Volunteers had become, but from the time of the formation of the Ulster Volunteers, Ireland seemed to have become a nursery for military-minded young men.

White had seen action in South Africa and had been at Paardeberg, for example, which was a particularly appalling battle complete with corpse-filled muddy trenches. Although enjoying an almost universal reputation for pugnacity White was a pacifist (of sorts) and, unlike the majority of the bellicose volunteers, he knew what war was in all its awfulness. He must have agonised over his position as the situation in Europe became more unstable.

Differences with Nationalists

White's personal disillusionment had now begun to grow. 'Obviously my authority was being undermined', he observed, in particular about his inability to reprimand McGlinchy, the man who had led out the second battalion from Derry, but more generally about the way his command was being insidiously subverted. He had issued an instruction to reduce Commandant McGlinchy to the ranks by letter to the *Derry Journal*. His orders were published there 'twice or thrice weekly', but this particular one did not appear. On inquiry, he found that 'strong influence had been brought to bear to prevent publication'. An advocate of rule or governance by consensus, White objected to this kind of clandestine activity, which militated against any kind of open organisation.

Secrecy nurtures all kinds of machinations whether political or otherwise; this particular cabal was no exception: 'At last a deputation waited on me and asked me would I fight against my own co-religionists [...]. There were influences in Derry, as there are to this day all over Ireland, that wanted a sectarian victory, not national unity.' His reply was straightforward and simple: 'I would not; that I was there to keep the peace between Irishmen and combine them if I could against the English connection.'[41]

White's workload was such that he performed as the entire staff for four regiments and, in his own words, as the 'storm centre of a delicate and dangerous political situation'. He demolishes any notion of pretentiousness, however, by reporting that Dollie, had left him, again, after first pointing out that he 'was behaving exactly as if [he] was God'. Intriguingly he notes that Dollie also reported having a 'waking vision' of Casement, who visited the headquarters regularly at that time, 'as he sat [...] with a hangman's noose around his neck'.[42]

At this stage, on top of the indiscipline incident, came the spectre of sectarianism that had driven him against Carsonism. Now manifesting itself on the other side, it added to White's burdens. On 9 July the press announced that

> Captain White, Commander of the Derry and Inishowen Brigade of the Irish Volunteers, has handed in his resignation as Commander of the County Board. [...] he declined to state his reasons [...,] [but] another source [said] that Captain White took the step in connection with a question of disciplinary control, the County Board having reinstated an officer whom he had reduced to the ranks. Asked whether his resignation meant the severance of his connection with the Irish volunteer movement, he replied – 'Far from it. I am as eager as ever to place my services at the disposal of the movement, and have now a clearer idea than before of the conditions under which, alone, my services can be of any use to others, and satisfactory to myself.'[43]

As if to support this statement, White is reported, just a few weeks later, as inspecting more than 500 men at Brookeboro, South Fermanagh, where he was 'loudly cheered by large crowds which lined the footway'. Making a speech, he lauded 'the true spirit of patriotism (cheers)', and expressed confidence that 'the Volunteer movement would create a spirit of mutual respect between all classes of Irishmen'. The parish priest who was chairman of the public meeting held after the inspection proposed a vote of thanks to White. This was seconded by the curate who said White was

> a man they could be proud of. He had made the greatest of sacrifices in coming into the Volunteer movement, and he was sure that owing

to the class he belonged to that he had suffered a great deal for having done so. He was a man of the most sterling qualities, well fit to train soldiers and to lead them (cheers).[44]

White continued the inspection and training of the Volunteers, but the outbreak of the Great War crystallised his perspective on the whole movement, and he abandoned a training camp he had planned for Eastern Donegal (de Valera was one of the first applicants for the course, he claimed).[45] He did so because in the struggle for control of the Volunteers the 'constitutionalists' that is, John Redmond, scored a sudden success. Up until then the Volunteers had been controlled by a committee of twenty-five, mostly young rebellious spirits. White called off his camp until the looming split, which he believed would clarify matters, took place.[46]

Disillusionment with the Volunteers

White saw the war as Ireland's opportunity, but in a different light from Connolly or the nationalists. Quite clearly the whole volunteer movement was never going to be a fully professional army; it was basically a weekend outfit staffed with untrained amateurs and a small number of old soldiers.

This was very clear in his account of a training exercise carried out over a weekend in August. He gave a list of the instructions issued to the various companies, indicative of the lack of funds. It was almost a 'bring your own equipment' outing. Discipline, despite his organisation, was quite lax. He 'had some fifteen hundred "mountainy men" out on a mountain side on a wet night', but to get them there he 'had to clear one pub [himself] by brute force'. The following morning when White ordered the men to fall in to parade for Mass, one of the NCOs, with whom he had a difference the night before in the pub objected because, he maintained, it was contrary to Catholic doctrine to work before Mass. White ordered his arrest. There were various mutinous sallies before White's second-in-command managed to organise a compromise by getting the NCO to retire. White ends the account by commenting that although there were serious problems with barrack and camp discipline, he was astounded by the natural military aptitude of the men for field work.[47]

A more universal problem was that the national leadership proved to be wanting, at least by White's standards. He quoted at length from a letter, dated 6 September 1914, from a priest who was sympathetic to White although an 'ardent Sinn Feiner' (possibly Fr Michael O'Flanagan from Roscommon; even though he was writing as late as 1930, White had to guard the letter writer's anonymity):

> From what I can see [the Volunteer movement] is fast falling to pieces. It is impossible to take a bright view at present. [...] its present state proves your statement: a) the utter incompetency of the so-called leaders of the movement, b) the incapacity of National Ireland to organise. That two or three thousand pounds should be spent on the purchase of useless and obsolete rifles while not a penny would be given for the training of officers [...] makes Ireland a laughing stock [...] where such arms were purchased. The Italians [...] must have a fine laugh at the Irish fools that bought rifles dated 1874.[48]

This explains, to some extent, the reference that White made to the Volunteers' equipment when he had announced at Coalisland:

> There was an article in the *Freeman's Journal* telling them that they were past all danger of invasion, as they had sent around 500 rifles, all large blunderbusses, dating between 1875 and 1881, and as far as he knew, there was no ammunition to fit them.[49]

George Dangerfield summarises and contrasts the arms shipments landed by the Carsonites at Larne with those the Volunteers landed at Howth:

> At Larne twenty thousand rifles were unloaded without interference; at Howth nine hundred rifles brought out soldiers and police. At Larne, one UVF messenger died of a heart attack; after Howth four civilians were killed and thirty seven wounded. [...] Larne, all told, had cost £60,000 and Howth and Kilcoole [the other landing place for the Volunteers] £1,500 between them.[50]

Facts like these coupled with his own observations finally convinced White that significant assistance was necessary if the Volunteers were to become a national army of any capability. It is typical of the originality (and foolhardiness, some would say) of the man that he could believe that the source of this help would come from the very force that the Volunteers were originally set up to combat – the British Government.

Chapter 12

Plan for Ireland

White's thinking in 1914, on the advent of war, was that if Britain could be persuaded to treat the Volunteers as a home defence unit, it would provide proper funding for their training, and there would be other possible peripheral benefits, in particular, an inhibition on the introduction of conscription. Most importantly, it would provide Ireland with a professional standing army of its own whenever international hostilities ended. Of course, it must always be borne in mind that there was a nearly universal consensus that the war was not going to last much more than six months, so that, looking back, the plans and decisions arrived at in those days can look quite distorted or even injudicious.

In a circular letter dated 17 August 1914 and sent to various leading figures, White sets out his ideas for the Volunteers. There were a number of points that he maintained were important to start with:

a) The movement had a 'magnificent spirit' and it was all important to preserve this. It would 'evaporate immediately […] if the Volunteers] passed under purely Imperial control'.
b) To maintain this spirit, it was essential 'that they should be trained and officered by Irishmen'. (This was very important, as was the fact that the Volunteers should not be under Imperial control. If that happened they could so easily be ordered to join with the regular forces and fight abroad.)
c) 'The old soldiers and militia men who have now […] been for the most part recalled to the colours, were 95 per cent of them quite unfit for the task of training a Volunteer Force.'

He suggested that 2,000 of the brightest young men, 500 from each province, paid and fed, should be trained for a period of a month: 'The expense of the camps should be borne jointly by the Imperial authorities and the representatives of the Irish people.' The nature of the course would be at the dictate of the regular military, but all discipline would be in the hands of the Volunteers themselves. These cadets on graduating would then form a kind of officer corps and, given fifty men each to command, would establish a force of some substance. He went on to say that the government should provide arms, ammunition, and equipment for 100,000 men which would be 'issued to units as they reached a state of efficiency to satisfy a joint Irish Volunteer and Imperial Inspection Staff'. He concluded that 'the Military authorities will not, I expect, jump at it; but I believe that they will take it if they are given clearly to understand they won't get anything else'.[1]

White was, he said, 'profoundly misunderstood', as a report in *The Irish Times* made clear. The article is dated Wednesday 9 September 1914 but refers to an inspection carried out on the previous Sunday by White and Colonel Moore (Maurice Moore, nominally in command of the whole movement and brother of George Moore, the author).[2] They visited the Coalisland district in County Tyrone and put some 250 Volunteers through their paces:

> Captain White [...] said the world was at war, and Ireland could not possibly sit on the fence. She had to take some line [...]. He thought some time ago that the line for Ireland was to train her own troops to defend her own shores. He did not believe that now. If Ireland wanted to be drilled, the right and patriotic course would be to take the opportunity of learning the art of war now. A few Sundays' training like this would never make them soldiers. He could not see how this Volunteer movement was going to go any further by itself. It was bound to die, unless they got help [...] some of the audience dissented from Captain White's view.[3]

It could be concluded from this that White had suggested the Volunteers should join in the war effort and become trained as real soldiers. He was, he wrote, 'taken to be recruiting for Britain, whereas I was trying to use Britain to put Ireland into a position to enforce her own claims'.[4]

The *Leitrim Observer,* commenting on the same meeting, did nothing to make White's position clearer, repeating that he said, 'let them [the Volunteers] take the chance of learning the art of war now'. The paper did, however, report him as saying that 'he did not believe in appealing to the sympathies of England for what they in Ireland have a right to'. But to confuse matters, when someone in the crowd said that Ireland's interest lay with neither England nor Germany, the paper had White reply, 'that was his opinion up to about a week ago'.[5]

Did White change his mind between the middle of August and the second week of September? It is highly unlikely, as he wrote a letter to one of the three members of the British High Command he was acquainted with, Sir Ian Hamilton, putting forward his original proposals. (The other two were both field marshals: Lord Kitchener and Lord 'Bobs' Roberts.) The letter was dated 19 September, over a week after the date of the newspaper report. Therefore, if the paper was wrong, which it seems to have been, it is a good example of how much White was misunderstood, even when he had explained himself by circulating a letter that surely must have been seen by the press.

Although 'some of the Sinn Fein leaders saw the sense of what [he] was after, and promised [him] support' if he did the 'underground work' and brought it to fruition with British and Irish support, this did not materialise because 'no one would openly face the music'. Most sympathisers with the idea were 'not ready to court suspicion of being pro-war and pro-British, by a scheme which involved the co-operation of the British authorities'. He then said, 'I can see now they were probably right.'[6]

White's letter to Sir Ian Hamilton, which he quotes in full, sets out the ideas mentioned already for the Volunteers, emphasising the need to recruit officers from within the ranks. The overall plan was summarised by Hamilton himself as 'a big force of Irish Volunteers exactly on the lines of our own Territorial force, i.e. without any obligation to go abroad or do military work beyond the defence of Ireland'.

White made several more important points. He said he believed he was more in touch with feelings in Ireland than the Redmondites; in fact, he believed that the Redmondites were 'suspect in the minds of many [...] of having desired and still desiring the destruction of an organisation which might predominate over their own'.[7] He used the letter from the anonymous priest to inform Hamilton that 'the Provisional Committee supposed to be responsible [for the Volunteers] is universally discredited [...] at the last meeting the members actually drew revolvers at one another'. Because of this fragmentation in leadership, he forecast that the situation would become critical unless radical steps were taken, and that it was now becoming 'a question of Ireland actively loyal or disloyal'. He believed that the Redmond carrot of a Home Rule settlement was illusory, 'as they [the nationalists in general] realize that Carson will be in a far stronger position than ever to nullify it at the end of the war'.[8] He stressed that now was the time for Britain to act so that

> The men who trade in bitterness of the past for the gratification of their own vanity can be silenced once and for all now by care and judgment. Once allow them to get a seeming modern instance of England's treachery, and repression of their propaganda or themselves would only fan the flames of suspicion and discontent.[9]

A similar but shorter letter was sent to Field Marshal Lord Kitchener. This was described by White as not entirely sincere because he 'was seeking a practical guarantee against England defrauding Ireland of all she had promised her'. Certainly, if he had succeeded, a standing, trained army of up to 100,000 men would have been more than acceptably persuasive. The proposal received short shrift from Kitchener: 'it is impossible to give official sanction to what you suggest'. White discovered later that Kitchener had 'declared he would not trust one single Irishman with a rifle in his hand one single yard, and that he made no exception in the case of Redmond or anyone else'.[10]

Hamilton, on the other hand, was sympathetic to the idea and actually approached Asquith with it. Whether the Prime Minister's reply of '*Hors la loi*' applied to the idea or maybe to White himself is not made clear. White saw Hamilton as having imagination beyond the common cast of the soldier and reported finding a copy of *The Pilgrim's Progress* in Hamilton's coat one day, remarking wittily that 'Bunyan I had thought at the time was incompatible with the more callous bunions of the military mind.'[11] Although Kitchener's reputation for a dull, ruthless efficiency was well publicised with his brutal 'scorched earth' policy against the Boers after 1900, it is unlikely he fell under the 'bunion' classification. In an acknowledgment of the impracticality of White's plan for the Volunteers, he appears to defer to him: 'the blunter intelligence of a great Figure saved me from prostituting mine'. Hamilton, for all his 'imagination', had a considerable number of questions to answer about his own performances: he was the overall commander at the Dardanelles disaster, apparently acting rashly without sufficient military intelligence as to the composition of the Turkish forces opposing them.

White's Individualism

Although the plan White proposed had many flaws and, because of the entrenchment of almost all parties, had little possibility of succeeding even on a limited scale, he once more displayed a willingness to put aside grievances, to ignore the hostility that he would arouse, and all in a spirit of reconciliation beyond the distrust and antipathy that had festered for centuries. The grand narratives of nationalism and imperialism, the banners that he saw people needlessly sacrificing themselves for, never presented any attractions for him. Earlier he had attempted a similar approach in a humanitarian bid to alleviate the suffering of the strikers when he approached William Martin Murphy in either late 1913 or early 1914. Murphy dismissed him:

> [White] called one day to my office for the purpose, as he said, of settling the strike, I told him there were a great many candidates for the office he was seeking. He then explained to me that his method was to drill the strikers. I pointed out to him that it was difficult enough for the police to keep any kind of order in the city when dealing with an undrilled mob, but if they were all drilled and possessed fire-arms, it would be quite impossible for any force of police to deal with them. He said he had not thought of that, but it would be all right, because when they were drilled they would be disciplined, and it would raise their moral tone, and then they would be no longer guilty of outrages.[12]

Despite the unsympathetic portrayal (and an unlikely one, with its unfamiliarly timid White), Murphy reveals an unwillingness on White's part to occupy an entrenched position. This flexibility in White's approach may have earned serious disapproval from Larkin and even Connolly, but he was steadfastly his own man, and if there had been any receptivity on Murphy's part at all, there might have been an outcome other than the appalling hardship endured during and after the Lockout. This avoidance of intransigence, arising from an awareness of how it develops from taking a fixed position whether politically or socially, was again a harbinger of the enlightened poststructuralism that recognises how fatuous, and dangerous it can be to steadfastly stick to a rigid and absolutist position.

Another way of looking at it is to see it as a pragmatic common-sense approach. That is, to analyse the positions on both sides of a debate or dispute and to conclude that an unyielding upholding of the values on either side will inhibit any hope of a resolution. Murphy would have imagined he had some principle to uphold that was more important than any compassion towards the strikers; the workers, on the other hand, would have believed that White was selling them out by depicting them as orderly, disciplined, and more easily exploited. Similarly, White was willing to risk contumely from the nationalists when he approached the British authorities and requested their assistance in training. The lack of support on the part of the Volunteers for White's attempt at securing this kind of cooperation suggests they would have perceived such rapprochements as parleying with the enemy, even as possibly treasonous.

It has to be acknowledged that White himself did not make it easy for anyone who might be so disposed to be persuaded by him. And it must have always been difficult for his listeners to categorise him, as happened in a meeting which occurred around the time of the split in the Volunteers. Professor Eoin MacNeill, first Chief of Staff of the Irish National Volunteers, delivered a lecture entitled, 'The Irish Volunteers in Their Relation to the Language Movement and Irish Nationality' on Thursday, 1 October 1914, under the auspices of the Gaelic League. Judging by the applause MacNeill received, his audience seemed to consist of the residue of the Volunteers after the majority had left with Redmond – nationalists of one hue or another. He said anyone who said they were not pro-Irish but anti-English and pro-German was a liar, and although 'they heard a great deal now about fighting in the cause of civilisation', he questioned the motives of Britain which 'deliberately implanted the seeds of hatred, fratricidal strife, murder and civil war' in this country. Protesting that 'he was not going to say one word about the controversies that had been going on for some time past', but that it now appeared that 'all the powers of the earth were arrayed against the nobodies [his term for the (nationalist) Irish Volunteers]', and as the 'nobodies' were not afraid of the task before them in the past, 'they were not afraid of the task before them today [...] [because] they had all that was true to Irish nationality at their back. (Applause)'.[13]

Lord Ashbourne then spoke, asserting that he stood with Redmond, and this precipitated a departure of The O'Malley and others in protest from the room, because 'a gentleman connected with the present recruiting campaign [had been allowed] to address the meeting'. It was then that White spoke up. As the report went, he 'asked "Is this in the interest of the Gaelic League?" and their being cries in the negative, most of the audience resumed their seats'. White then addressed the meeting. He said that there was

> a lamentable split in a moment of crisis in the fortunes of the Irish people. England's extremity might be Ireland's opportunity in exactly the reverse sense in which the phrase was generally used. It might be Ireland's opportunity to get England to help to train and discipline her manhood if she could not do so herself. But if England

was to help Ireland she must do so for Ireland's permanent benefit, as well as for her own temporary benefit. The great point was that in Ireland there was a deficiency in the quality of leadership; the scum was on top. In so far as Professor MacNeill's revolt was a revolt against the political machine, he would back him to the last breath; but so far as it was a failure to recognise the present limitations of the Irish people, then he would say 'God give him wisdom'.[14]

Apart from the 'scum' comment, it was a reasoned speech but totally against the tenor of the meeting. It was highly unlikely that there was going to be any support, at least overtly, from what was basically a gathering of the embryonic revolutionaries of 1916. White's openness about his plans before a crowd including MacNeill, whose interests hardly paralleled his own, once more reveal either a naïveté or a courageousness born of desperation, or most likely a combination of both.

Redmond

White had a readiness to put aside differences on a personal basis, and there is little evidence of him holding a continuing antagonism towards those he encountered in his political travails; MacNeill rates little or no mention in his available writings. However, along with Griffith, as previously mentioned, Redmond was someone White had considerable antipathy towards, surprisingly, when White, of all people, should have identified with Redmond's position as a well-meaning if misunderstood figure. The fact that Redmond had 'a profound reluctance to endorse physical force even under the greatest provocation or despair' should have tallied closely with White's pacifism.[15] However, there were limits to White's tolerance of the 'steady, sensible, practical businessmen' that Redmond envisioned at the helm of Ireland's economy after Home Rule was established.[16] According to Casement, the antipathy was mutual. Writing to Alice Stopford Green in early 1914, Casement observed, 'As to my seeing Redmond, he would no more discuss Home Rule with me than, say Jack White. He probably looks upon us both in the same light.'[17]

Redmond's behaviour during the Lockout left more than a little to be desired, even in the eyes of some of his supporters. Redmond broke his silence on the Lockout in 'a public speech on 28 September 1913 when he [...] avoided the subject'.[18] Dillon was the Irish Parliamentary Party politician who 'finally handled the question directly on 19 October [and] said, "We cannot succeed [...] in achieving for the working classes of Ireland as we have done for the farmers until we get National self- government".'[19] As Joseph Finnan says, 'no one ever explained why Irish workers had to wait for serious reform while Irish farmers did not'.[20]

White did not appear on the scene until the night of 6 November 1913 when he first heard Dillon making clear his indifference to the situation of the strikers. The infamous slums, which had left a deep impression on White, were under the remit of Dublin Corporation which was dominated by the Irish Party for more than ten years. That conditions there would be improved radically under Home Rule was questionable, if not exactly risible.

White also believed the Volunteers were practically hijacked by the Redmondites. According to him and his unnamed clerical correspondent of 1930, they were insistent on monopolising the nationalist movement at all costs and, in their concern to be involved, paid little heed to the logistics required, resulting in an inefficiency that permeated the entire organisation.[21] (Of course, his concerns about the Volunteers were not confined to the Redmondites, for he had little sympathy with the other side who eventually became the Irish Volunteers after the split; he saw them, correctly as it transpired afterwards, as in a minority.)

White had an additional reason to take issue with Redmond and that was not so much his judgment that England had to be supported in its difficulty, but the deleterious effect Redmond and his forces had on White's own offer. If the British Army Command had the offer of nearly 200,000 Volunteers from Redmond, White's suggestion had little to recommend it. In his letter to Hamilton, White wrote:

> I may exaggerate the tendencies I have observed in Ireland in the interval between Redmond's speech in offering Irish Volunteers and the present. They have taken no shape but they might. The reception of Redmond's manifesto will show how things are going but if there is a hitch, I hope you will take steps to make the views expressed in this letter known in the right quarters.[22]

White refers here to the offer of 3 August 1914 in the House of Commons when Redmond

> brought the Unionist benches cheering to their feet [when he said] we offer to the Government of the day that they may take their troops

away and that, if it is allowed to us, in comradeship with our brethren in the North, we will ourselves defend the coasts of our country.[23]

White's letter, dated 19 September 1914, although allowing that he might be exaggerating the unrest, was tentatively suggesting the British might look to alternatives (more specifically, his own proposal).

The letter proved prescient; the split in the Volunteers was only days away (24 September), and although only a minority dissented, it was still from that determined group that eventually emerged the main body of the 1916 rebellion. Dangerfield also notes that Redmond's House of Commons speech was 'followed by a subtle deterioration in his own prestige and that of the moderate nationalism which he represented'.[24] White was suggesting an outlet for the military mindedness of those not participating in the war effort. He believed this would have formed a very substantial figure before the split, and in a way he was right because the figures for the National Volunteers fell considerably short of the expected enlistment figures:

> In November and December [1914], the Redmondite Volunteers were said to be untrained, poorly armed, and losing numbers. In December, the police consensus was that Mr Redmond's recruiting appeal had little effect. The enlistment figures up to 15 December [...] of National Volunteers [was] 7,819 [...] the whole of the following year [...] 10,794 were National Volunteers.[25]

This totalled fewer than 19,000 men out of an original force of about 160,000 and supported White's predictions. Of course the greatest damage done to White's suggestion was the almost simultaneous offer by Redmond (20 September, the day after White's letter of offer) to increase the Volunteers' role in the war. According to Redmond:

> The interests of Ireland [...] are at stake in this war. This war is undertaken in defence of the highest principles of religion and morality and right, and it would be a disgrace for ever to our country and a reproach to the manhood [...] if young Ireland confined their efforts to remaining at home to defend the shores of Ireland from an unlikely invasion.[26]

The import of Redmond's statement, that is, that the Volunteers would actively participate in the war rather than act just as a home guard, may not have yet reached Hamilton when considering White's proposal, or he may quite simply not have believed that Redmond could deliver, but he seems to have taken White seriously.

White believed afterwards that the authorities were calculating and cautious: 'I see now that the risks and results of the '16 Rising were preferable to this British trained force.' He explains why Hamilton was interested, and admits that Hamilton, unfortunately, was right, that 'trained and equipped with British help they would have "come over to complete their training" and no doubt volunteered for service',[27] in the war itself, thus defeating the whole purpose of White's plan.

It could be said that what White was really suggesting was that if Redmond had not volunteered his force, the authorities would have considered White's proposal, but only as another method of getting around whatever conscription difficulties they might have. This becomes clearer when he describes his effort to persuade Lord 'Bobs' Roberts, an old campaigner with his father but still a military figure of enormous influence:

> Bobs was certainly attracted by the idea [...] It only carried him a step further in a project he had already envisaged of *going over personally and carrying on a big recruiting campaign.* Now he seemed almost prepared to consider whether he might not undertake the whole supervision of recruiting equipment and training of a great Irish Volunteer Army.[28]

Roberts was really only interested in drafting as many Irishmen as possible for the war effort. He wrote to White's mother on 31 October 1914 saying that he would have responded to White's idea if he felt it would do any good.

White's mother, at least to some extent, supported what White described to her as 'the last chance for the real welding of Ireland and England together'. Whether Roberts ever actually ever subscribed to that idea is a moot point, but it once more illustrates White's access to the corridors of power that such a letter could be elicited from Roberts, who died just two weeks later at the age of 82. Nevertheless, for all his contacts, or more probably because of them, White believed, unlike Redmond, that Britain had little intention of letting go of Ireland. He spelt it out: 'I saw the British military and political powers were incapable of conceiving the idea of Irish independence, let alone of giving it practical recognition in their treatment of the Volunteers.'[29]

White's difficulties with Redmond included Redmond's conservatism, his disregard for the suffering in the Lockout, his proprietorial attitude to the Volunteers that inhibited proper training, and finally the decisions he took on the war. There were three strands to the latter. Redmond did not seem to realise, contrary to evidence like the Curragh mutiny or the contrasts between the Larne and Howth arms shipments, that Carson had substantial support from the British Government. 'Carson will be in a far stronger position than ever to nullify it [Home Rule] at the end of the war',[30] White said about the illusion that Britain's promises would prove to be.

The British would resist Home Rule settlement because they 'were incapable of conceiving the idea of Irish Independence'.[31] Ireland was the weakest link in the British Empire and socialists, from Marx to Lenin, believed that the overthrow of British rule was necessary before the social revolution proper took place. Lenin, for one, had said, 'A blow delivered against the English imperialist bourgeoisie by a rebellion in Ireland is a hundred times more significant politically than a blow of equal force delivered in Asia or Africa.'[32] It would follow that resistance to any kind of breakaway by Ireland would be of paramount importance to the Empire.

Redmond's belief that 'making common cause in the war provided an unprecedented opportunity to solve the intractable Irish question' was a chimera.[33] Further, his supporters who argued that 'to desert England at her first opportunity [...] "would be unquestionably a gross act of treachery and bad faith"' were simply wrong. [34]

White detested war, but whether he believed that Redmond was foolish to imagine that this was a war to protect small nations as opposed to a great imperial struggle is not recorded. He did believe, however, that Redmond was gulled by the British authorities, and this was due as much to the cultural differences that separated the two islands as to any political astuteness, or lack of it, on the part of either of the protagonists. White may, by heritage and breeding, have been an Irishman, but by birth, education, and conditioning he spoke the same language as the imperialists, that is, he understood their values; he had an entrée to their inner plans and motives. He knew them for what they were and, quite simply, Redmond did not.

Departure from Volunteers

White, his ideas for resolving the Irish question dismissed, must have felt that he had no further part to play in the Volunteers. The war had been continuing since August and although one report has him called up for service – 'It is understood that Captain White DSO, who is now in command of the Irish Volunteers of County Tyrone has been recalled to his regiment by the War Office'[35] – there is no evidence either from White or elsewhere about what difficulties this caused him.

Certainly it must have been resolved because Earl Roberts's letter, some months later, sends his good wishes: 'I trust Jack will get on well now in the work which I understand he has undertaken on the Continent.'[36] This seems to be a reference to the ambulance duty he took up at the battle front. His little-mentioned pacifism becomes very clear when he quotes Freud about war in a passage that has heavy overtones of Weber in its view of the state:

> The individual in any given nation has in this War a terrible opportunity to convince himself of what would occasionally strike him in peace time, that the state has forbidden to the individual the practice of wrong doing, not because it desired to abolish it, but because it desires to monopolize it, like salt and tobacco. The warring state permits itself every such misdeed, every such act of violence as would disgrace the individual man.[37]

White goes on to reveal:

> My real vision of the future Ireland was – dare I say *is?* – a state that shall rise above the monopoly of wrong-doing to become the organic collective expression of free individuals.[38]

Although a state is how he sees the embodiment of this ideal, it is one like none previously, and comes closest to his later expressed anarchism. He refers once more to pacifism, recalling Sheehy Skeffington, his murder, and O'Casey's words about him: 'He was the living antithesis of the Easter insurrection: a spirit of peace enveloped in the flame and rage and hatred of the contending elements, absolutely free from all its terrifying madness.'[39]

In a spirit probably inspired by Sheehy Skeffington, but in keeping with his Tolstoyan influences, White converted his 'Ford two-seater', which had been the source of comment at Ballymoney, into an ambulance and headed for Belgium. This seemed the best compromise between his Connolly-inspired socialism and what could be described as the call of his heritage and training to support the Empire in its hour of need. It was there, in Dunkirk, that he said:

> I saw enough to intensify my instinctive loathing of the whole filthy mechanical slaughter – yes, and my contempt for the mentality that could accept it as all in the day's work. I wanted to get outside, above it all, get behind the roots of the filthy thing in the human mind and soul.[40]

Probably for the first time, no doubt fostered in the fevered emotions and suspicions of wartime, White began to be aware that his previously unquestioned entrée to the inner circles of empire was being regarded suspiciously. He learned that 'his position' was, in that sinister phrase, 'causing comment'. A conflation of his position with Casement's, who was in Germany at that stage, his involvement with 'rebel armies', and the notion that he might be a spy eventually led to him abandoning his pacifist, or possibly conscientious objector activities.

He left the front and with Dollie, who had accompanied him as a nurse in his ambulance duties, spent some time in Paris. She, as in Derry previously, spent little time with him before leaving again, this time to her mother in Gibraltar.[41]

It would appear from the various remarks made by White that marriage was an institution he found difficult, in both theory and practise. There are lengthy questions in his correspondence in later life on the institution. He describes it, for example, with more than a hint of subjectivity, as 'a very frequent field for the surrender or suffocation of the soul, a kind of psychic cannibalism, in which one of the parties devours the other, or the cannibalism may be mutual'.[42]

In a final polemical flourish, in his autobiography he writes that 'God ordained the family' but that this is the 'kind of platitude by which dignitaries of Church and State disguised their bankruptcy of any vision or creative imagination'.[43] If the family is not operating properly then its eminent position in society would have to be re-examined. In other words, true to his form, the received wisdom, regardless of what its authority might be, has to be questioned.

White's experience in Belgium had increased his horror of war and this led him to join the Fellowship of Reconciliation at their office in London some time in 1915. George M.L. Davies, a pacifist and conscientious objector, was the secretary, and he and White had a number of conversations about the Irish Citizen Army and White's concerns about what was being planned in Ireland. Davies seemed to believe, in his recollection, that White was aware of some plans for rebellion. Later, when news of the Rising broke, they met at Davies's home in London. Davies remembered White agonising over what action he should take:

> I remember pacing the quiet road with him late at night trying to dissuade him from following his impulse to throw in his lot with the rebels and finish fighting, though, intellectually at any rate, he felt its futility and immorality.[44]

Chapter 13

1916 Arrest and Imprisonment

White decided not to join the rebellion, but the executions, Sheehy Skeffington's wanton murder, and the news of Casement's arrest during the week of the Rising probably left him believing that some drastic action would have to be taken to bring the authorities to their senses. He travelled to the South Wales coalfield 'to get the miners out on strike. Why? [he asks] to save Jim Connolly being shot for his share in the Easter Rising in command of the Citizen Army'. He had finally taken the irrevocable step away from his own side: 'Things have gone with a run the other way, and I, as an Irishman first have definitely gone with them.'[1] The subsequent court case makes this very clear when the statements he intended to deliver were read out. On a sheet of paper, which he had torn up in the police station but which had been put together again, he appealed to the workers:

> You are fast being led into industrial slavery. You know it, and I am apprehensive and angry, but too bewildered to move. To rob you of your right over your own poor bodies is the work of tyrants. To rob you of your sovereign power, of your own will, is the work of devils. Awake, brothers, before your liberty is dead. Arm yourselves against your real enemies. Say to the tyrants and their agents: 'The first man who lays hands on me against my will dies'.[2]

The report said that he had attempted to induce the miners to come out on strike 'in order to compel the Government to show leniency to the leaders of the rebellious outbreak in Ireland'.[3] He was actually hoping to disrupt the coal supply in the war effort, in particular to the naval war ships. ('Had I succeeded I would have crippled the coal supply for the British Fleet.')[4]

When told he should be fighting for his country, his understandable, but unfortunate response was 'that he would rather be placed with his back to a wall and riddled with bullets'. He said that he was present at an interview between his father, Sir George, and the Kaiser, when the latter said 'that he could never understand England, and had never been able to secure her friendship'. Most probably the mention of the now demonised Kaiser precipitated his arrest and probably constituted part of the charge, against him, 'making a statement likely to cause disaffection to his Majesty'. A further charge of 'having in his possession documents the publication of which would be likely to prejudice the administration of the forces' arose from there being found on him a 'manuscript of a speech to working men expressing hatred of the army and its discipline, and urging his hearers not to enlist'. The defence consisted of his argument that

> the rebellion had been brought about by Ireland being goaded by the officials of the British Government in Dublin [...] he [White] denied that he wanted Germany to win the war. Whilst Casement went to Germany, White did not, although given the same opportunity [...]. [He] had always shown great sympathy for the downtrodden, and [...] the Welsh being Celts, he thought he could arouse their sympathies.[5]

Both his mother and Dollie spoke for him, saying, 'he was not disloyal but felt keenly on the Irish situation'.[6] The stipendiary magistrate sentenced him to three months. The day he was arrested, 12 May 1916, was the day Connolly was executed, and when White was transferred to Pentonville, a week prior to his release, he maintained he was 'placed in the prison hospital which was fifty yards from the hanging shed' where Casement was executed around about the same time.[7] The syndicalist and the Protestant radical, the two revolutionaries, probably the only two who ever quietened him, from two opposite ends of the political and social spectrum, had completed their course, almost together. As previously mentioned, Lady Amy was visited by Davies, the pacifist, shortly after White's imprisonment at her home in Hampton Court. She was 'distressed and scandalised', but when Davies told her about his conversations with her son, she demonstrated the ebullience that White had inherited: 'Jack was always on the side of the oppressed. When he led the procession of the unemployed in Dublin he kept twelve policemen at bay with his stick.'[8]

Questions were raised regarding the difference between the treatment White had received and the sentence of three years' penal servitude handed down to John MacLean, the Scottish socialist, for what appeared to be a series of similar transgressions. According to one report, 'Some eighteen police officers gave evidence that on various occasions they had heard John MacLean urge the Clyde munition workers to "down tools", as a protest against conscription.'[9] It was probably another example of the establishment looking after its own even *in extremis,* although the authorities' severity could be explained by the fear of another 'Connolly', but closer to home. Such were the protests that MacLean was given an early release anyway.

Confinement to England

Shortly after White's release, he was reported as appealing as a conscientious objector before

> Finchley Military Tribunal [...]. He did not attend, but a representative produced a telegram from him stating that he had proved that he was domiciled in Ireland, and that, therefore, he did not come under the Military Service Act. The case was adjourned.[10]

It would appear that the authorities, or the more bloody-minded of them, had decided White was now a target to be harried. He had, with the approval of Earl Roberts, carried out pacifist duties on the battle front and, as already mentioned, had registered with the Fellowship of Reconciliation, an international support group for conscientious objectors.

Andrew Boyd states that when White was released, he was 'immediately banned, by order of Henry E. Duke, Chief Secretary at Dublin Castle, from returning to Ireland'.[11] This is corroborated by 'Our London Letter' in the *Irish Independent* on 11 July 1917: 'on his release [White] had to give a pledge not to attempt to go to Ireland, in opposition to the veto of the authorities, as the only means of securing liberty of movement in England'.[12] White had written to Duke, the *Irish Independent* said, on 20 June, maintaining that the general amnesty which had been given to the Irish rebels should apply to him as well. With the practiced obfuscation of bureaucracy and the suspicious whiff of personal spite, Duke's private secretary had replied that 'he was "transmitting the Captain's communication to the Chief Secretary, who was in Ireland." Since then Captain White had heard nothing more on the matter […] it is surely time [to] let him know how he stands'.[13]

White was meanwhile active in several matters; according to the *Irish Independent*: '[he] is at present working for the Vacant Land Cultivation Society and he is trying to start a scheme for a National Union of Allotment Holders'.[14] He had also been badgering the authorities for the release of Constance Markievicz, 'the sole Irish prisoner to be denied the recently granted privilege of association with comrades'.[15] True to his mother's spirit he had not allowed establishment sanctions to get him down: Anne Marreco reports Markievicz, on her release from prison on 17 June 1917, being treated to strawberries and cream on 'the terrace of the House of Commons, with Eva [Gore Booth, her sister], an Esther Roper, Mr [Alfred] Byrne [later Mayor of Dublin] and Captain Jimmy White resplendent in top hat and spats'.[16]

It is doubtful if the sybaritic life held much attraction for White. His work with the agricultural proposals had earlier included yet another proposal to avert conscription in Ireland. This was explained in a programme he put together which involved increasing greatly the number of people working on the land in Ireland and thus boosting production that would be of benefit to both countries. In promoting this, White, thanks mainly to Stephen Gwynn, secured a meeting on 21 December 1916 with Henry Duke. Writing to Thomas Johnson he explained that he was unaware that 'Duke had caused resentment by refusing temporarily at any rate to receive a deputation.' Apparently this deputation was from the 'Trades Congress Food Prices Council' held earlier that month in Dublin on 16 December. When Duke offered to let White go to Dublin, temporarily lifting his 'embargo', to form a deputation of his 'friends', Johnson and the other Labour leaders would not take part because of the original refusal to Congress. White, in his letter to Johnson, dated 17 January 1917, did his best to persuade him to change his mind:

> I sympathise and agree with your objection to accept unconditionally an offer through me of something refused to you direct. But at the same time you should, I think, recognize that I passed on the offer to you because I felt it was absolutely necessary that you should know of it and probably to your interest to accept it, and that your complete disregard of an offer made through me weakens my position, and I believe also weakens yours.[17]

Louie Bennett, the women's labour leader, although suspicious of White, seemed to be supportive of a meeting in some guise, when she wrote to Johnson on 26 December:

> If he [White] omitted all references to food produce as a substitute for conscription and made no question of a bargain, do you think Labour Party would join in a deputation? I'm not satisfied that Captain White is the man to organise such a combined deputation and yet he seems to have the ear of some sections in all three parties he wants to combine.[18]

Boyd also relates that White 'accused the unions of doing nothing to get Henry Duke's exclusion order [...] revoked'.[19] In his letter to Johnson, White complains:

> On personal grounds, to say what I mean quite frankly, I think Irish labour might spare a little attention for my personal feelings who should have earned some consideration from you all by raising the Citizen Army, exposing the Police brutality on the map of my own skull and being imprisoned as the only man in England who raised a finger to save Conolly [sic]. I am doubly obnoxious to all the narrow, i.e., the most powerful element in my own 'class' because they regard me as a traitor to its ideals and interests, and may soon find myself obliged to lay myself open to their vengeance by resisting some fresh form of compulsion – military or industrial.[20]

White had already informed Johnson on 6 December that 'if there is a general election I want to stand for an Irish constituency primarily on this programme [the land development and increased food production]', but when he wrote again on 7 October 1918, this time asking to be included as a Labour candidate, he was refused. Johnson, always the devotee to the minutiae of regulations (and not just when it suited him), replied:

> 'candidates must be and remain members in good standing of a Labour organisation, eligible for affiliation to this Congress', and as I understand you are not a member of any such Union you could not be adopted as a parliamentary candidate. In any case you would need to be nominated by one or more affiliated bodies, who would undertake financial responsibility for your candidature.[21]

Of course, it must be recalled that Connolly on at least one occasion deliberately spoke after White in order to repair potential damage. This might indicate that as much as White admired Connolly, the feeling might not have been reciprocated, at least to the extent that he would have trusted White as a Labour candidate. However, it has to be suggested that if it was refused in such a manner as Johnson's, it would have contained at least a tincture of irony.

When exactly White did get back to Ireland has not been established. Boyd writes about his socialising with D.H. Lawrence and his circle of friends in 1917. John Cowper Powys, who had an extensive correspondence with White over ten years up to his death, relates that the other Lawrence (T.E. of Arabia fame) acted as 'midwife' to *Misfit*. Powys also recalls in his diary how White told him he had 'kicked Lawrence in the arse' (D.H. that is!), and Powys fears similar treatment himself, reporting receipt of

> a letter from White of White in anger accusing me of being lazy, 'superior'; false and smug; like all the English! And saying he was angry with me & felt contempt for my character & would like to kick me in the BALLS.[22]

White appears to have cultivated those writers he felt might share some of his more esoteric views. Powys, although in robust dispute with him over many matters, described White as his most exciting correspondent and was very well disposed towards him.[23]

The character based on White in D.H. Lawrence's novel, *Aaron's Rod*, was called Jim Bricknell, a highly strung, impulsive character, given to talking about experiencing transcendent feelings in his chest.[24] The novelist had little sympathy with White's political views and did not understand that White may have been terribly frustrated at not being able to take part in the revolutionary rumblings in Ireland, but for all that there is a truthfulness to the portrayal which resonates as correct.

Bricknell is described as having a fine military bearing, slim and six feet tall with thinning red hair and is 38 years old, which is pretty accurate; although reputedly six-foot-two White would have been exactly that age when he met Lawrence in 1917. Rawdon Lilly, the principal character, apparently an autobiographical portrait of Lawrence, behaves in a rather deprecatory manner to Bricknell and gets punched in the stomach in a chapter titled 'A Punch in the Wind'; ironically they had been arguing over 'Christly Love'. This incident is related to have occurred in real life in Lawrence's country cottage when White was staying with him and his wife Frieda. Professor Mark Kinkead-Weekes believes that Lawrence behaved in a provocative and irritating manner, which was reported honestly in the novel. If this is so there can be little doubt that an attraction existed between Frieda and White also – Lilly is described as undergoing several private rages against both of them during the stay and at one stage attempts to get Bricknell to leave in spite of Tanny's (Frieda's) objections[25].

Although the portrait is not flattering, it must be remembered that Lawrence's novels are replete with people who took offence at his portrayals – the phrase 'a breach of hospitality', first used by a wealthy family Lawrence stayed with in Turin, seems to have accompanied him through his life. Richard Aldington, who knew Lawrence well and is also one of those featuring in several scenes with Bricknell as Robert Cunningham, describes how in the first part of *Aaron's Rod* 'everyone who did anything to help him [in late 1917] is mercilessly satirised'[26] and goes on to describe 'a cold letter from his agent' about *Aaron's Rod* describing it as 'full of libellous matter'.[27] Although constantly at odds with what he perceived to be the *canaille* or even the *canaglia*, as Kinkead-Weekes has pointed out, Lawrence's integrity as a writer did not allow him to evade his own initiation of the bad behaviour of others, so White did have some justification in punching him – either in the stomach or the chest[28]. Aldington also bears out that this incident did occur.

White also featured in another book, Mary Manning's *Mount Venus*, a much later work featuring a revolutionary family in Dublin in the late thirties.[29] Although suffering by comparison with Lawrence's, it is a witty intelligent work that gives an idea of how White was viewed socially. A particularly interesting aspect is that White's character speaks about experiencing a transcendent feeling in his chest as well. However, it does lack the devastating realism of *Aaron's Rod*.

Mount Venus is located in Dublin in the late thirties and again, Manning's character, Bob Considine, is featured accurately as a middle-aged man – White was 60 in 1939. Although the novel is not exactly the light frothy entertainment the blurbs on the dust jacket might suggest ('the gayest, oddest family you've ever met in fiction') there is a humour and pace to it that reads well even today. Unfortunately White is drawn somewhat two dimensionally and appears as a buffoon; his soubriquet is Captain Cock Eye, indicating someone of an unbalanced temperament. The principal character, Caroline d'Acosta, mostly referred to as the Doña (a take on Maude Gonne McBride) describes him as 'a fool but a very honest man'.[30]

His role, more considerable than in *Aaron's Rod,* has him acting as a kind of foil to a revolutionary family as an ever-present inflammatory radical, ever willing to tilt at windmills. Although the author almost definitely knew White[31] and probably regarded him with a certain wary affection it could be confidently ventured that she had little insight into his character.

Possibly the ebullience of his demeanour could overwhelm people, but in this particular work he is more than overdrawn. At one stage he has been introduced to a professor and Mrs Windpacker, Americans on a fact-finding tour about Ireland and he spends his time 'breathing heavily and passionately into Mrs Windpacker's face'. The couple on leaving rather hurriedly are heard to discuss him:

… Mrs Windpacker …to her husband 'I've never had such an experience in my life, Forris, do you know he pinched me?'

'Obviously a psychopathic,' said the professor, 'of the manic-depressive type. Did you notice the unnatural elation? Some day he'll kill someone.' He added with conviction, 'If he doesn't kill himself first.'[32]

A considerable debate occurred after the book was sent to the publishers Jonathan Cape (also White's publisher for *Misfit*).[33]

The company's lawyers were concerned there might be a risk of libel because of the nature of the topic of the book – basically the activities of a radical collection of people in the censorious 1930s of Dublin and its environs. It was believed that some of the characters could be easily identified and they were particularly concerned about the possibility of three individuals seeking legal redress because of how they were portrayed – Maude Gonne McBride, Eoin O'Duffy and Jack White. (It is an indication of those times that the chief concern about Madame McBride was a suggestion that her character, the Doña, had lived with someone when a young woman.)

Mount Venus was originally published in the United States in 1938. Although Cape had contracted to publish it on this side of the Atlantic it never appeared here. Despite Denis Johnston, the playwright and barrister, approving the changes that were made, the caution of Cape's lawyers appeared to have prevailed (although the impending war may have also had an impact).

Analysis of Sinn Féin

White was certainly back in Ireland in 1918, and, despite his reservations about Griffith, he appears to have thrown his weight behind the Sinn Féin election campaign. *The Manchester Guardian* reported him as rendering assistance, in the form of appearing on platforms, along with people like Colonel Maurice Moore (brother of the writer George Moore).[34] Around this time he wrote a pamphlet called *The Significance of Sinn Féin: Psychological, Political, and Economic*. It was published by Martin Lester of Dublin and sold for the not inconsiderable sum of one shilling.[35] It was quite critically reviewed in the *Irish Independent*, almost definitely by Sean O'Casey, who took exception to the political role that White claimed for the Citizen Army: 'It does not serve matters to state that the Labour Citizen Army was the driving force of the rising, and that the menace of conscription was defeated by a strike of Irish labour.' He also attacked White's idea that an alliance, or at least assistance, was available from the Labour Party in England: they 'seem to be hiding their light under a bushel when Ireland's name is mentioned', and he finishes with a barb at the psychological section of the essay which seemed 'at the least to be fanciful'.[36]

Written immediately after the December 1918 General Election, the pamphlet appeared to be an attempt to reconcile White's own ideology with the Irish *zeitgeist* after Sinn Féin's overwhelming victory. The Irish Labour Party had no candidates, and although some would see substance in Joseph Lee's charge that Thomas Johnson and William O'Brien had 'shirked facing the electorate',[37] the party had a reasoned approach for their withdrawal, which was explained at a meeting in the Mansion House in November. 'The unexpected call for an armistice' changed the whole international tenor of the situation, said Johnson, so that

> In light of the new circumstance, the National Executive recommended the withdrawal of all Labour candidates at the coming election. They did so in the hope that the democratic demand for self-determination, to which the Irish Labour Party gave their unqualified adherence, would therefore obtain the freest chance of expression at the polls.[38]

Whether Connolly would ever have assented to this decision is a moot point, and certainly Johnson's own approach seems to have been very conservative in its vision of the future: 'It was the object of the Executive to prepare the way for an active and possibly a dominant Labour Party in Ireland in the future.'[39]

However, at least a considerable amount of thought had gone into the future. Lee reveals that 'a draft "Democratic Programme" had been prepared by the leaders of the Labour Party [...] [which] contained too much of Pearse, not to mention Connolly, for the socially conservative elements in the Dail'.[40] The document was later presented in a modified form by Sean T. O'Kelly and adopted as the 'Democratic Programme of Dail Eireann'.

White's pamphlet is a response to all of this and is a singularly impressive tract, reasoned and prescient in its analysis. It recalls the syndicalist ideals of Connolly and promotes its more radical ambitions, while at the same time taking cognisance of the new dominant ideologues, de Valera and Griffith. White's dislike of Griffith has already been discussed, and he makes no mention of de Valera, but he must have done some considerable refashioning of his thinking to accommodate their substantially different agendas. The pamphlet is divided into three parts, as the title suggests: psychological, political and economic.

Although O'Casey peremptorily dismissed the psychological section, and today it does seem outdated, it is worth recounting the basic points if only because it illuminates White's later politico-economic analysis and his attempt at a synthesis of nationalism and socialism, that hoary old question of Irish politics.

White saw two struggles in Ireland, one of race and the other of class. Race he associates with the unconscious, the inner, the emotional, even the soul, and this he believed was manifested in Sinn Féin. Class is the conscious, the outer, the intellectual, the body and is represented by Labour (whether that of the Labour Party of Johnson and O'Brien is another question). A coalescing is required of the spirit of the emotional, that is, the soul, with the rational intellect of the body.[41]

In other words, Sinn Féin, with its thinking on a higher plain, needs the pragmatic intellect of Labour for it to develop, as much as Labour needs the motivating dynamic of the emotions of Sinn Féin to propel it.

Political analysis: White's political analysis began with the fact that even Lloyd George saw a need for a 'fundamental reconstruction' after the war, but White's concept of this is far more radical than any of the ideas of the elected representatives. He described as Parliamentarianism the political movements that had a 'tacit acceptance of the continuance of the basis of government which we are at present familiar'. This 'is as obsolete as a wooden plough', and he bluntly asserts that 'a true self-determination of a whole people cannot be achieved under the forms of Government that have heretofore passed for democracy'.[42]

O'Casey's review, puzzlingly, seemed to see him as in some way complying with Parliamentarianism. He writes, 'if [White] means to suggest that Ireland should join one of the hostile camps into which he tells us that England is separating at present, very few will consider his advice as being worth much'.[43]

Admittedly White's arguments were quite often not the clearest but it was also possible that O'Casey paid little attention to the pamphlet, believing there was not much substance to White's thinking. (This I would suggest is another example of what bedevilled White; there was a very substantial depth to his thinking, but, whatever demeanour he presented seems to have militated against him being fully appreciated.) O'Casey's antipathy towards what he believed to be Connolly's embracing of nationalism makes it all the more surprising that he lacks any sympathy for the points White's pamphlet makes.

Reminiscent of Marx's critique of capitalism and its boom and bust cycle, White argues the 'instability of the whole world order' has been caused by the present economic system. This realisation was unfortunately only at the intellectual level among the 'International Socialists', so that they had succumbed to 'bellicose nationalism' at the 'first blast of the trumpet'. The 'power of emotion was on the side of race', and so the socialist doctrine, 'not yet ingrained in the subconsciousness', was cast aside and men fell once more for the old narratives of king and country.[44]

However, Ireland did not partake in the war, because its 'race emotion' caused it to be against imperialism (at once the father and the child of capitalism), according to White, and it actually, almost unknown to itself, fought the socialist good fight instead, that fight being the 1916 rebellion. O'Casey cavils at this, and it must be conceded that a considerable number of the Volunteers, including Pearse (despite his sympathies), would have been aghast to imagine they were involved in a socialist rebellion.

On the other hand, Connolly's whole *raison d'être* was more or less as White represented it. It should also be noted that as early as this, just two and a half years after the Rising, when there would have been plenty of participants to challenge the statement, White adamantly maintained that 'the driving force [of the Rising] was the Labour Citizen Army'.[45] This directly contradicts the conventional chronicle of a nationalist rebellion for the glory of Caitlín Ní hUalIacháin, with Connolly as a lieutenant of Pearse's, purportedy having demoted the cause of the working class.

Returning to White's argument, he believed that although Sinn Féin now represented this force for revolution (the electorate having rejected the Irish Parliamentary Party), it was unlikely to succeed alone and had to ally itself with Labour. There were powerful forces ranged against it, not just Britain with its '80,000 troops in Ireland', but the international order intent on maintaining the status quo:

> Glancing abroad we find Mr Daniels [US Secretary of Navy, 1913–1921] proclaiming the need of a supreme American navy, M. Clemenceau [French Prime Minister, 1917–1920] declaring himself a realist and planning that the war to end war shall in no way disturb the old game of military preparedness [...]. Any League of Nations under the patronage of Capitalistic Governments can only be a league of exploiting rulers against exploited peoples, from which Ireland can expect nothing but a reinforced coercion, for, to quote Connolly again, the cause of oppressed nations and oppressed classes is one and the same.[46]

This was borne out, not surprisingly, when Sean T. O'Kelly, the first Ceann Comhairle, 'was sent to Paris, where he knocked persistently upon many doors, but was never admitted to the Peace Conference'.[47]

There is also what White calls the problem of 'the two racially distinct sections of Ireland', simplistically, the 'Scotch Protestants' and the Celtic nationalists. Liberation depends 'on the explanation of the two Socialists, Connolly and Marx' and will only arise from the emancipation of the Irish workers, that is, as was believed in '98: 'national emancipation arising out of human emancipation' (the antithesis of Johnson's reason for withdrawing Labour from the general election, and, for that matter, the laying waste of the achievements of the feminist movement). In Ireland, borrowing almost directly from Connolly's *Labour in Irish History,* White wrote:

> in any subject nation, the owning and employing classes are forced by economic pressure to make terms with the oppressor with whom and whose system they become linked by a hundred golden threads of investment and the like. Thus the onus of the struggle is thrown more and more on the working class.

In Ulster, according to White, where 'the ascendancy caste [...] are the fortified outposts of England's rule in Ireland', there was 'a profiteer's paradise', aided and abetted by an 'unorganised labour' that has dammed itself off 'from the twentieth century by their concentration on damning the Pope'. It was clear to him that the overthrow of this system, and subsequent unification of Ireland, had to come from the proletariat. Sinn Féin was the working class, he said, 'in the widest sense of the term', or at least it had to join with the proletarian movement to be successful.

White concluded the pamphlet's political section by stating that 'Ireland herself is the scene of the exposure of [the British] democracy's deep rooted fraudulence.' Taking examples like the Larne gun-running, the Curragh 'mutiny', and the 'wholesale arrest of Sinn Féin leaders', he believed that they were evidence of how 'the gang possessing economic and political control abrogate democracy as soon as they see their control threatened':

> We thank, therefore, both Sinn Féin for separating Ireland from the form of Parliamentarianism which has hitherto blessed us, and the British Government for its determination to prevent us saddling ourselves with a native version of the same blessing.[48]

Economic: The final part of his pamphlet is the economic section, and here White cautions Sinn Féin that peace is far more inimical to their plans than war. The 'League of Allied Nations' is able to collectively 'defend and continue the Capitalistic system', whereas during wartime they are separated into hostile camps and unable to pursue the 'camouflage' of their intentions and the subsequent 'stupefaction' of the people, and, of course, the proletariat will also prove fractious by enquiring about constructs like 'the causes for which they are asked to die'.

White repeats that England is not 'the sole enemy', although Sinn Féin is correct to blame them for what Ireland suffered in the past. Again he quotes almost directly from Connolly's *History*: Economically the English disrupted the existing system 'by the superimposition of the feudal system of land tenure on the Irish clan system of communal ownership, the land passed in to the hands of the few and with it the basis of all the means of subsistence'.[49] Certainly the Land War 'pulled out the roots of the feudal system', but White cautions that this is only a partial victory because there is a real danger that 'the comparative prosperity of the farmers [might] tend to make them unite to enforce the status quo on the labourers'.

In one sense, this prescience is a concern that a co-optation of some of the workers could occur; that is, those who were previously tenant farmers would lose their revolutionary credentials and behave just as exploitatively as the previous land owners. This has bedevilled Marxism and is probably a constitutive factor in the development of Stalinism. White's solution was to aspire to the transcendent; he believed that 'material prosperity can militate against spiritual freedom [...] [that] the spiritual life of a nation is not something apart from its material welfare'.

He maintained Sinn Féin was mistaken in looking towards the USA, that this 'Capitalist Republic' was part of the worldwide cartel of oppression, and that emancipation lay with the growing proletariat movement. Witness a 'leader in *The Times* headed "Bolshevik Imperialism"', this was proof that 'that authority is steadily extending', he said. It was a class war and there are three main points that must be addressed:

The factors of production must pass from private hands to the workers.

Income from any such property to private people must be abolished.

The proper organisation of the workers and their education out of 'false consciousness' must be carried out.

In other words, they needed to be made aware of their enthralment to the meta-narratives or their unconscious acquiescence with ideologies that could support social structures that worked to their disadvantage.

The workers, 'sufficiently awake', could 'assume control', but their success was inhibited by the clerical and administrative classes who, for some reason, 'throw in their lot with the owners and employers'. White seemed to equate a substantial portion of Sinn Féin members with these clerical and official classes and believed he was now persuading them to change allegiance.

He used the Joint Industrial Councils, 'the Whitley Councils', in England to make his point. These attempts by the government to improve industrial relations after the war involved all kinds of discussions on employment conditions but did not, as White perceptively points out, admit the workers into the 'counting house side of the business'. Furthermore these talks resulted in 'a sapping of class loyalty in exactly the same manner as has already been notorious among Trades Union officials' – a classic case of the dangers of parleying with the enemy and being subsumed into the dominant discourse. Unless the workers gain access to all aspects of production, they will only 'assist in riveting the chains of wage-slavery on themselves'. Therefore Sinn Féin was absolutely correct 'in rejecting the principle of the Whitley Councils as applied to Anglo Irish relations' and refusing to sit around the table with the British government.

He finishes by stressing that Ireland's independence must rest on the overthrow of capitalism. Apart from his continual leaning towards a kind of ecclesiastical eloquence, there is a considerable change in his political analysis in comparison with his debut speech on Ireland, printed in the *Irish Review*, delivered in late 1912 in London. It must have been disappointing to him that his old comrade, O'Casey, did not treat the document more seriously.[50]

This pamphlet is a very clear picture of White's philosophy and depicts, I would suggest, more or less his mature perspective on Ireland and all its interests. After his confinement (the first of many) and his enforced stay in England he probably had time for a lot of reflection. Although making several offers to the Irish Labour Party and suggesting various strategies for advancement, White appears to have been firmly ignored. His previous value as a high-profile member of the British elite had little relevance in the battles that lay ahead. It was unlikely he would ever side with Sinn Féin. He would never take up arms in the struggle for independence, and his politics were too extreme and revolutionary for the luminaries of the Labour Party.

It is worth attempting to summarise his argument:

Politically White believed that 'parliamentarianism', his word for government 'with which we are presently familiar', was a system that had proved to be defunct; even Lloyd George talked about a 'fundamental reconstruction'. Britain's fraudulent behaviour in Ireland showed how 'the gang possessing economic and political control abrogate democracy' to protect their interests. Even the 'League of Nations was a league of exploiting rulers'.

The proletariat were duped by 'bellicose nationalism' to take part in the war. This type of nationalism was clearly in his mind when he addressed the role of Sinn Féin, now the dominant political party in Ireland after the election. It is doubtful if White welcomed this. Both the conservative economic policies of Griffith and the party's exclusionary nationalist outlook militated against the kind of social revolution he supported. *The Significance of Sinn Féin* suggests a course of political action which that party was unlikely to take; rather, it is a tract stating his ideas which, although bearing traces of the influence of Connolly and Marx, include a number of inchoate anarchist theories.

Threaded through the pamphlet is an attempt to envisage a role for Sinn Féin in his image of the future, as he had to acknowledge their overwhelming success in the election of 1918. White saw two irreconcilable cultures in Ireland – the 'Celtic' nationalists and the 'Scotch' unionists. Emotion of one kind or another was what provided the driving force of a revolution. However, in Ireland's case, the 'emotion on the side of race' was not going to provide any cohesion; there could not be unity with two such disparate sides.

He believed the only recourse was through labour, the working classes, and quoted Connolly: 'the cause of oppressed nations is the cause of oppressed classes'. Socialism provides the only possibility of a synthesis and it has to be adopted by Sinn Féin, who he imagined were, if not quite working class, at least sympathetic to labour, unlike in England where the clerical and administrative workers primarily sided with the Conservatives.

He said that 'the really instructed International Socialist is the best and only practical Nationalist'. He declared that there would have to be an entirely new form of government, 'new wine would be spoilt in old bottles'. He suggested the best form this government would take would be those of soviets, and proposed three guiding principles: there should be neither private property nor private possession of the factors of production; private income from rent, interest, as well as income from these factors of production should not be allowed; and, finally, the 'false consciousness' of the workers should be eliminated.

These requirements could be encompassed within socialist principles but White's conclusion that there was a 'pressing need' to organise 'Ireland on an alternative economic base' suggests that, although he does not clarify what this might be, he was envisaging, or at least amenable to, something vastly more radical.

Chapter 14

War of Independence

By 1920 Jack White's political perspective could be basically defined as Marxian in the sense that he had become quite opposed to capitalism and believed a new socio-economic structure should lie in the hands of the working classes. His scepticism about nationalism remained and was growing, although he did believe it provided the necessary impetus to initiate a revolution. In fact he saw Ireland as a cockpit, 'as the detonator of the world revolution', where the struggle was beginning.

Rarely mentioned by him, however, was his fundamental opposition to the Catholic Church. Although later in life he maintained he was a Presbyterian, White under Tolstoy's influence, was opposed to organised religion. Tolstoy who, as mentioned earlier, refrained from using the term 'anarchy' (probably because of its pejorative connotations), could be very polemical in his writings:

> The churches as churches, as bodies which assert their own infallibility, are institutions opposed to Christianity ... Not only have churches never bound men together in unity; they have always been one of the principal causes of division between men, of their hatred of one another, of wars, battles, inquisitions, massacres of Saint Bartholomew, and so on.[1]

He was equally scathing about government –

> Government authority, even if it does suppress private violence, always introduces into the life of men fresh forms of violence, which tend to become greater and greater in proportion to the duration

and strength of government. So that although the violence of power is less noticeable in government ... because it finds expression in submission, and not in strife, it nevertheless exists, and often to a greater degree than in former days.[2]

In spite of all this contumely it must be remembered that Tolstoy's profound spirituality was the acknowledged inspiration for Mohandas Gandhi and his embracing of 'whomsoever smite thee on thy right cheek, turn to him the other also' – an aspiration that White, for all his innate belligerence, espoused.

On 30 March 1920 Jack White 'preached the communist doctrine in a lecture on "the Future of Labour" in the Town Hall, Galway [...] under the auspices of the Irish Automobile Drivers and Mechanics' Union' (ADU).[3] This union had 'struck in November [1919] in protest at the introduction of compulsory permits for vehicle drivers; a move by the authorities designed to assist the monitoring of transport'.[4] Six months after the nine-day strike in Limerick (the Limerick Soviet), the ADU's action was the harbinger of a number of tactical industrial strikes taken by workers essential to the British military operation in Ireland. Emmet O'Connor writes that

> Dockers, and then railwaymen, commenced a seven-month selective stoppage in May 1920, refusing to handle or convey British munitions. In all cases, the [Labour] Congress executive intervened to snaffle these actions, indicating no greater enthusiasm than Sinn Féin for distinct class participation in the national struggle. However, the push/pull of direct action and the consolidation of the Republican consensus brought Labour into unofficial, but open, alliance with Sinn Féin.[5]

This association with nationalism compounded White's difficulty in his relationship with Labour. Snubbed, at least once, by Thomas Johnson (see Chapter 13), he must have been particularly perturbed by the conciliatory stance taken by both Johnson and William O'Brien. Neither, of course, would have been the type of potential comrade that White would have endorsed. O'Connor gives a thumbnail sketch of Johnson: 'an intellectual' who 'invariably beavered away quietly to moderate radical impulses; a duplicity that infuriated his radical critics in the 1920s'.[6] O'Brien, on the other hand, 'had vision and grasped the need of de-anglicisation'. However, despite his 'almost filial devotion to Connolly',[7] in a speech in August 1918, reported by Conor Kostick, he displayed a remarkable indifference to either Connolly's antipathy to bureaucratic old-style unionism or indeed the ideals of syndicalism:

> You know how [the employers] have fully equipped offices, able and trained staffs, experts and specialists to advise in every department, great palatial buildings, all the agents, machinery and material necessary for a great undertaking, and you know how far-reaching and effective all these are. *So also must the labour movement and the unions, if they are to do the work for which they are designed, and to do it effectively and successfully.* [...] For the conduct of our movement is, to a certain degree, a great business and *we must have it managed on big business lines.*[8]

There is no evidence that White was aware of what could be argued to be a fundamental shift in Labour's position in 1918. *The Irish Times* reported that, at a special session of the Irish Labour Party and Trade Union Congress (ILPTUC) to adopt a new constitution, a resolution was proposed by a Mr J. T. O'Farrell, of the Railway Clerks Union, to delete

> certain paragraphs dealing with the recovery for the nation of complete possession of all the natural physical sources of wealth of the country; the winning for the workers of the ownership and control of the whole produce of their labour, and the securing of the democratic management and control of all industries and services by the whole body of workers in the interest of the nation, *and subject to the supreme authority of the national government.*[9]

These were to be replaced with

> a paragraph to secure for the workers the full fruits of their industry, and the most equitable distribution thereof that may be possible, *on the principle of the common ownership of the means of production*, and the popular administration and control of each industry or service.[10]

This amendment, which was a clear call to syndicalism and did not include submission to any government, was defeated; only two delegates voted for it.

Interestingly, Johnson was quite frank about his opposition to it. According to *The Irish Times,* 'Mr Johnston [sic] said they were asking the Congress to subscribe to James Connolly and George Russell rather than to Sydney Webb and Arthur Henderson.'[11] Admittedly this statement is ambiguous and could be read as Johnson disingenuously suggesting O'Farrell's proposal meant subscribing to Webb. However, the proposal is insisting on 'the common ownership of the means of production', which is quite clearly far more radical and more in keeping with Connolly's syndicalism rather than any concept remotely connected with Webb's socialism. Connolly was dead only eighteen months; the ILPTUC, for all its revolutionary rhetoric in the *Voice of Labour* and its successor, the *Watchword of Labour,* was being led by a much more moderate set of trade union officials.

Nevertheless, Labour still had White's allegiance. On the other hand, although not opposed to de-anglicisation, rather seeing it as a distraction, his concerns about Sinn Féin became more evident in his Galway speech. In many aspects it reprised his article discussed in the previous chapter. 'A Sinn Féin Republic was not sufficient; they wanted an independent Worker's Republic', he said. There was no indication of the number of people who attended, but as a replacement speaker for 'Mr Eamonn McAlpine (late editor of the "Voice of Labour")', he could hardly have been regarded as a figure of the first order of importance. However, his lecture was original; he placed an emphasis on the 1916 Rising that must have struck some of his apparently enthusiastic audience as a little overstated. Nevertheless, they applauded his references to the Irish Citizen Army (ICA), to Connolly and Larkin, and even his assertion that this army, this group of 'loyal and determined men [...] was really perhaps the actual cause of the Rising'. Warming to this theme, he said the Rising was concerned about a much wider issue than even the 'freedom of Ireland herself. I want to show you Ireland as the focus of world forces – as the detonator of the world revolution, as I believe she will be – of the world revolution as it effects Western Europe'. To pursue this point he enlisted the memory of another Irishman who had a profound influence on him. According to the *Connaught Tribune*:

> He always felt that Sir Roger [Casement] and himself had a finer grasp than any other man he had come across of the position of Ireland as a sort of vital sensitive spot in a great world crisis – not Ireland fighting for its own freedom, but Ireland as a vital spot in which the freedom of the whole world depended. But Casement

saw the thing in what he (Captain White) termed the capitalistic sense.[12]

White believed that Casement's idea was for Ireland to hold the balance of power between Germany and England with an armed neutrality; this was not anything as radical as White believed the solution to be. An uprising of a syndicalist nature with the workers taking control of the factors of production was required. In passing, it has to be remarked that White's interpretation of Casement's thinking had to be largely conjectural; Casement did not confide in him. In fact Casement did not reciprocate the regard White had for him at all. Commenting on White's defence against sedition in Wales in 1916, Casement had said, 'Capt White knew as much of my plans or ideas as Biggar's dog "Seamus".'[13] White had to be aware of this attitude, and it is a further example of his refusal to allow personal differences to colour his perception.

In any case White's political perspective had hardened into a radical socialism, which at that time he believed to be an anti-statist communism. Even in his description of the 'Russian Soviet system' there is a marked emphasis on communal governance at the expense of any form of state. He said that the 'members of [a soviet's government] could be recalled from power by the people at any moment' thus (theoretically) militating against the formation of rigid hierarchical authorities. Again, apropos of Connolly's *Labour in Irish History*, he uses an Alice Stopford Green-type perspective on early Ireland as a model to aspire to:

> In Ireland people would have to go back to the communal system which existed before Cromwell came, under which the land and industries were owned by all the people, in clans or septs. [...] Pearse and his comrades stood for taking them back to the past when that system obtained; Connolly stood for bringing them forward to it.[14]

Sinn Féin, 'in spite of itself', he warily suggests, 'know they are out to do away with English domination', but beyond that he believed that they did not have a definite plan to accomplish what was needed to be done. Dividing the world into communism and capitalism, he argues:

> Ireland is trying to be on neither side trying to make it appear that her national freedom is something which only concerns herself and

does not concern the rest of the world. But so spiritual are its forces, they are based on the bedrock of humanity and extend to the rest of humanity, and until Ireland realises that her freedom is something bigger she will have to wait for it.[15]

He believed the 'seven centuries experience of what capitalistic oppression means' and of 'robbery with the veneer of legality about it' had given the Irish a 'revolutionary spirit'; like Marx's proletariat, they had nothing to lose but their chains. He cautioned against what he termed a 'mere racial Sinn Féin revolution'; the workers should organise 'both militarily and industrially' and he

> suggested organising working committees in every trade's union so as to get to know how to run the industries when the present masters were out of it. They should have social committees to organise food supplies in revolutionary areas. He believed the Citizen Army should be extended to fight on a definite industrial basis.[16]

It was a speech, not only in accord with the syndicalism of Connolly, but cautiously critical of the nationalism of Sinn Féin and that of Casement as well. It was a speech against English capitalism, but it additionally charged the English workmen with 'apathy and cowardice' in not allying with their Irish counterparts in what White saw as the inevitable class war.

The evening concluded with Fr Fidelis, OFM, the chairman, expressing views as uncompromisingly radical as White's when he concluded that the 'fundamental remedy was to have the workers themselves become owners and that, he thought, was the real solution of the Labour question'. He proposed that they 'would have to bring about a system that would enable the ninety seven per cent [unpropertied] to partake, also as owners, of the wealth of the world'.[17] A stance as revolutionary as this, taken by a cleric in a location like the Town Hall in Galway, suggests that the tenor of the times was far more amenable to ideas expounded by White and other left-wing activists than hindsight would conventionally allow.

Within a fortnight, on 12 April 1920, White was arrested outside Mountjoy Jail. While voicing his support for 100 prisoners who were on hunger strike he 'was removed by the military'.[18] There had been continual turmoil because the plight of the prisoners, locked up without trial, had captured the public imagination and the authorities were taking matters very seriously:

Processions of workers passed through the streets and the constant throng of people before Mountjoy Prison until nightfall was kept back by a barricade behind which was a strong force of military and police. No tanks were employed, but searchlights played over the city for the first time.[19]

The ILPTUC had called for a 'general stoppage of all work throughout the country to-morrow (Tuesday), April 13', [20] in support. They had been on hunger strike for eight days, and White promptly joined them. Thomas Johnson was acting secretary in place of William O'Brien, who had been imprisoned in England. In an interview with the *Manchester Guardian,* Johnson had indicated the power of the unions: 'out of 650,000 organisable workers in Ireland, including Ulster, there were almost 350,000 trade unionists' and Johnson had given his 'imprimatur' to the manifesto which instructed:

> You are called upon to act swiftly and suddenly to save a hundred dauntless men at this hour. Their lives are hanging by a thread in a bastille. These men, for the greater part our fellow-workers and comrades in our trade unions, have been forcibly taken from their homes and their families and imprisoned without charge, or, if charged, tried under exceptional laws for alleged offences of a political character in outrageous defiance of every canon of justice.[21]

A precedent had been set on 23 April 1918 when a similar strike was called 'with a paralysing effect everywhere, except in Belfast'.[22] At that particular time it had been a protest against the possibility of conscription coming into force in Ireland. It had been a 'token' strike, but this time the strike had a definite aim and succeeded. By 17 April, the press was reporting that all hunger-strikers were now released, although pertinently an aside noted that 'A few prisoners remain to be dealt with. Captain White is still detained.'[23] There seemed to be considerable confusion about the settlement, and some prisoners, 'who were "exempted" by their fellows from the original strike', had now started to fast. White had joined these along with Cathal O'Shannon, although it is difficult to see what involvement he had with the others. In any case, he was released into the Mater Hospital the following day.[24] There can be no doubt that this was an extraordinary success for Labour, or more accurately, for the working classes. It was a complete climb-down by the authorities (the prisoners had even refused to sign forms guaranteeing their future behaviour), so much so that the *Freeman's Journal* reported that Lord French, the viceroy, was about to resign in protest at the turn-about in policy of the 'Irish government'.[25]

Sometimes it is difficult to establish the point White wishes to make, but it could be argued that this strike settlement confirmed his faith in the potential of the proletariat to bring about radical change. However, he believed that this was not in any way being realised by the relevant organisations that should have harnessed this dynamic. The reservations he had about the official ILPTUC, and in particular Johnson and possibly O'Brien, were further aggravated by his lack of enthusiasm for Sinn Féin and its brand of nationalism, as well as for his old *bête noire,* Arthur Griffith. In an article in *The Watchword of Labour,* official organ of both the ITGWU and the Labour Party, he repeats his Galway declaration that the 'battle is between Communism and Capitalism. No man and no country can be on both sides without despising the one and serving the other'. He questions the commitment of the British workers who are 'disunited, hesitant', and suggests that the Irish can give a lead, at least in enthusiasm. He introduces the notion of the symbol as motivator for revolution: 'If principle [...] is a force and the imagination [is] the medium of its operation, then symbols influencing the imagination are the greatest power for good and evil.'[26] 'Symbol' as a motivating factor, suggest an acquaintance with Sorel and his theory of the myth.[27]

White refers to the need 'for a meeting place for Labour and Sinn Féin'. As in Galway, he is being careful not to offend Sinn Féin, seeing it as supporting the 'race-experience' of the Irish people, as opposed to the socialist, or more prosaic aspirations of the Labour Party. He then utilises a very radical article by Willie Gallacher, who was later to become one of only three Communist MPs in Britain. Gallacher, in describing the Communist movement, maintains it is hampered by the equivocation of those who are merely 'reformists' rather than wholehearted communists, and says that 'their inclusion in a Communist Party would sooner or later spell disaster'. In opposition to these, he maintains there are a considerable number 'who are opposed entirely to any sort of Parliamentary activity'. These individuals, possibly anarchists of some kind, are acceptable to Gallacher, although of course he himself did get involved in 'Parliamentary activity'. However, possibly the main reason why White cites Gallacher is his statement that 'each Communist candidate would take an oath of loyalty to his class, *and refuse to submit to the authority of the Labour Party,* the Monarch, or the Constitution [emphasis added]'. White is now expressing not only his unease with Sinn Féin, but also (and on the front page of *The Watchword*, no less) he questions the attitude of the Irish Labour Party. There had to come a point when he would openly disagree with O'Brien and Johnson.

White concludes his article with a further acknowledgement of Sinn Féin's motivation by 'race-experience' but warns more will be required: 'the brain will have to say more and the blood less'. The supplementary irregular British Army forces had been arriving in Ireland for a couple of months previously and White's very accurate prediction of what was to come was based on hard experience:

> Ireland is going to be subjected to Boer war methods. Let no one think this is an empty threat. The British Empire will be faithful even unto death to its master, Beelzebub. I was through the Boer war and I know that the blockhouse methods can and will go one better than the guerrilla tactics heretofore so successful. God forgive me, I helped hunt Boers who fought like lions and rode like Centaurs, to their inevitable surrender in a country which was one great partitioned cage. And they made it all a cage, 3,000 miles of it by 1,500.[28]

From the time he returned from England, White was active in protests and speeches, but there is no evidence to indicate that he was aligned with any particular political party, although Andrew Boyd states that he 'was implicated, but not directly, in the formation of the first Communist party in Ireland'.[29] In December 1920 White was arrested again at his residence in Dublin by those same practitioners of the 'blockhouse methods' he predicted. The 'auxiliary police', the *Nenagh Guardian* termed them. It was also noted that 'a pathetic feature of his removal from his wife is that it had been arranged that a serious operation would be performed on his child at noon on Sunday'.[30] The child was a little girl called Ave, whom the Whites had adopted.

He appeared, early in the following year at Edinburgh Sheriff Court, charged with 'uttering a sedition at an unemployed demonstration there on Sunday, April 10th'.[31] Despite submitting that the 'words used were every day rhetorical utterances usually found when feeling ran high in industrial crises, the Sheriff repelled the objection'.[32] Whatever influence White may have had with the British authorities seems to have dissolved, or indeed whatever tolerance they may have shown him as one of their own; he was sent to prison, on what appears to be almost a trifling matter, for two months on 29 April 1921.[33]

Politics and Personalities

It is not unlikely that when White first appeared on the political scene in Ireland in 1913 there might have been a perception of him as a kind of 'third way' figure. Neither nationalist nor unionist; by birthright and war record acceptable to the British; by religion and family to the Protestant collective and by his sterling support for the poor and indigent – in all, an Irishman. The dominant milieu prevailing at the time would, despite Carson et al., have seen an inevitability of Home Rule, but almost certainly closely connected with the British Empire.[34] White would have articulated the compromise that all sections might have been able to agree to. As already described, the extraordinary coverage in the media, and even something as insignificant as the Butt Bridge incident meriting mention in Westminster, would have supported the idea that White was the man of the moment.

Whether he could, or would, ever have fulfilled that role is very doubtful. For all his sophistication of analysis and his obvious intellect, White did not have the necessary equipment to be a politician. I would suggest there was a naiveté about his perspective on humankind which appeared to believe that if the folly of people was pointed out to them, then it would be readily accepted and acted on, to the general concordance and contentment of all. The fact that people would primarily be concerned about their own interests before dealing with the greater good never appeared to have complicated his prognostications.

In any case, the perception of him as a potential resolution to Ireland's problems was short-lived, and certainly by the time he was arrested in Cardiff in the vain attempt to rescue Connolly, his reputation among the authorities, and indeed among quite a number of his fellow activists, would have been, at best, as an incorrigible troublemaker.

In July, 1921, not long after leaving prison in Scotland, a truce was declared in Ireland. White's scepticism of Sinn Féin became clearer. In a pamphlet, titled *Ulster's Opportunity*, written shortly after the Treaty was signed less than six months later, he saw their *raison d'être* as a political party disappearing. Their 'unswerving fidelity to principle can no longer be sustained'; he believed they had sold out with their acceptance of partition. Now, his dismissal of that party was not because of his disappointment at the loss of a sovereign thirty-two counties, rather, if one examines this pamphlet, it appears to be a concern that the new 'Free State' would become a bastion of narrow fundamentalist Catholicism. (He also stated, later admittedly, that this was a prediction that the republicans themselves would find unacceptable and take violent action.)

He acknowledged that he had 'worked for political and economic freedom in Catholic Ireland, and is proud of having done so; [but] he has always realised that till Southern Ireland is freed from the enslaving elements of Roman Catholicism she cannot gain independence'. Now, he maintained that Ulster had the opportunity of taking the political initiative in Ireland. He believed there were three choices – 'Bolshevistic licence; Roman tyranny, working through the alliance of a Catholic Free State and a casuistic Empire; or ordered freedom, evolving from a purified Protestantism'. The type of Protestantism this appears to be is a pragmatic, down-to-earth kind that will 'realise the Christian emotions in a reborn Society'.[35]

What is surprising about this perspective is not his advocacy of Protestantism (that was always latent in his thinking) but his use of the word 'licence' for what I can only presume he means communism. Certainly in those years he was a supporter of communism but, as always, his support was always qualified by his own very definite notions. I think it would be difficult to deny that, as with his mentor Tolstoy, all his political beliefs, no matter how radical at times, were underlined by very firm 'Christian' principles. This was later to burgeon into something almost eschatological, probably as his despair for the world political situation deepened.

Around the same time that *Ulster's Opportunity* was published an article appeared in *The Irish Times*, where details were given about various documents relating to the activities of the Dáil, including the draft of a proposed treaty 'between the Russian Socialist Federal Soviet Republic and the Republic of Ireland, together with copies of observations thereon by the President, Mr De Valera'. White himself had turned his gaze to the Russian Revolution and saw there a possible answer to the question of a synthesis between socialism and nationalism:

> There was also seized during a raid by Crown forces on the IRA headquarters, and published in the *Morning Post,* a long communication from Captain White, DSO, addressed to the Minister of Defence (Cathal Brugha) detailing a trip to Russia by Messrs Connolly (son of James Connolly) and McAlpine, who had interviews with and 'were warmly received by Lenin and the heads of the Bolshevist Government'. Captain White says: 'The Mission was laid before

the Irish Republic by Ernest Blythe but appears to have little consideration and no realisation of the vital importance of the issue involved.' These and a few other similar British disclosures were virtually the only sidelights on the doings of the Dail during the period of its suppression. Captain White [...] stated that he had 'no delusion that an Irish Republic was possible in a capitalistic world'.[36]

Andrew Boyd stated that White funded what must have been the above mentioned trip to Moscow of Roddy Connolly and Eamon McAlpine in July 1920. These two represented the 'Socialist Party of Ireland [SPI] at the Second World Congress of the Communist International'. The trip resulted in the SPI becoming the Communist Party of Ireland (CPI), and although White 'was implicated, but not directly, in the formation' of the CPI, he had now become a very radical socialist.[37] Nevertheless, he seemed to have continued to have formed alliances with any of the counter hegemonic movements whose actions at a particular time he would have agreed with. Like Connolly, he supported anyone whom he believed might further his cause.

On 23 June 1922, a serious incident took place in Cushendall, County Antrim. According to the first report in *The Irish Times*, issued by 'The Ministry of Home Affairs of the Northern Parliament', 'Crown forces' were fired upon by 'a group of fifteen to twenty men standing near the corner [in the village of Cushendall] and also by other men on the high hill behind the tower'. Fire was returned and four men were shot dead; there were two others wounded and these were deemed to be victims of 'stray bullets'. Remarkably, 'there were no casualties to the Crown forces'.

Positioned underneath this account was another from the paper's 'Ballycastle Correspondent'. This directly contradicted practically everything in the quasi-official report. It said that the forces had opened fire without warning on a group of young men gathered in the village square. When they ran away they were followed, and one, on being 'asked if he was a Catholic' and replying 'in the affirmative', was shot dead, 'the body being riddled with bullets'. The other three men were murdered in a similar fashion. Ironically, 'only for the intervention of the Cushendall police the death roll would have been larger'.[38]

The White family owned property in Cushendun, a few miles from Cushendall, and Jack would have been very familiar with the area. He raised some very strenuous protests about the murders and as a result fell foul of some of the authorities, in particular an 'officer of specials' called Anderson.

Such was the level of harassment that he wrote to Sir James Craig, the Northern Ireland premier. Apart from his complaint he made some interesting observations about himself: he said the only organisation he ever belonged to in Ireland was the Citizen Army; that for at least two years now he had condemned 'not only the policy of assassination but of physical force at all on the Republican side both in public and private, in speech and in writing', and, most pertinently, he wrote, 'I have recanted publicly all belief in permanent social change except preceded by a change in man's inner consciousness.'[39]

Although, the afore-mentioned naivéte is evident in appealing to the esoteric spiritual values (and 'the inner consciousness') of a man like Craig, there is nothing either obsequious or self serving about the letter; he quite bluntly states that if his attempted intimidation is deliberate then he will resist it 'by every means in my power'. In an effort to get his voice heard he appealed to Colonel Moore-Irvine, the commanding officer of the area, for a reference; some of the colonel's remarks are worth recording:

> In a couple of hours talk with him and impressed by his ability and breadth of view I came to the conclusion, contrary to the general idea, that he is neither mad nor vicious. He is a thinker, a philosopher, and a metaphysician, but an idealist and a visionary of the extremist type, altogether impractical and lacking in constructive force. As I told him, while agreeing with his ideals as necessarily the grand aim of all thinking and Christian men, yet the world was totally unready and would take probably hundreds of years of travail to reach the goal. He is living spiritually on the mountain top and thinks it is possible for all humanity to reach that pinnacle by one step or bound.[40]

The Secretary to the Northern Ireland cabinet, William B. Spender, responded for Craig, almost unilaterally, one feels, as if he sympathised with White's plight and wanted to give him support. Spender was also an old Wykehamite and a friendship of sorts begun. Of sorts, because Spender who was quite obviously a decent man had taken on a job that required high levels of tact and diplomacy, and these traits were not alone alien to White but seemed almost to bait him to extremes of behaviour. White responded almost immediately, grateful for Spender's interest but also pointing out that on the very morning he received an acknowledgment of receipt of his letter (4 August) his accommodation at Cushendun was again raided; apparently the authorities knew nothing about this 'unofficial' enterprise. Nevertheless, he favoured Spender with a résumé of his analysis of the state of the country, similar to his *Ulster's Opportunity* pamphlet but a little more candid. He wrote:

> Moral issues must ultimately govern political and Ireland is at present in the grip of moral rogues and moral cowards. By the former I refer to the Free State leaders who have perjured themselves once and will do so again as soon as it is safe to do so. [He obviously was referring to the Treaty signing which he saw as an apostasy of republicanism].
>
> England will desert Ulster by natural affinity of moral corruption with the Free State. Therefore the only course for Ulster is to join hands with the Republicans, when their nobility of aim is purged of hysteria and their party of the rag tag and bobtail which has joined them for sensation of loot. If the Northern Government has the moral courage to take the initiative in this, it will save Ireland from a cataclysm, which is otherwise inevitable.

In a kind of postscript which was handwritten on the back of his typed letter he reveals a particularly anti-Catholic stance. It has to be conceded that in the context of the time, and in light of his own experience, there is a validity to it (at least from the perspective of someone of White's background):

> I realise that to speak of Free State leaders as 'moral rogues' may be sweeping. There is however a tendency to double dealing and deceit in all Catholics and especially the Irish. The fierce fidelity to principle of the true Republicans is the correction of this and has much more in common with the open directness of Ulster Protestants.[41]

Of course, when one considers the revelations of strategic honesty (termed mental reservations) adopted by the Catholic Church, this statement acquires a certain validity. On the other hand it should be borne in mind about this rare burst of bigotry that White, despite his often enlightened stance could hardly keep himself unsmirched in a society that fostered a superior 'planter' mentality towards the indigenous breed. Joe Lee's comments on the racism of the Ulster Protestant are worth recalling –

> Ulster Protestants fashioned an elaborate set of images to sustain their sense of identity. One portrait enumerated in a loving degree

of arithmetical precision the characteristics of the 'Belfast man' as 'determination 98, business capacity 94, courage 91, trustworthiness 90, self-esteem 84, mental vigour 78, hospitality 70, general culture 55, artistic tastes 48, social graces 44'.[42]

This self-indulgent, narcissistic nonsense of the 'settler race' was contrasted with their stereotyping of the Irish Catholic as 'lazy, dirty, improvident, irresolute, feckless, made menacing only by their numbers and by their doltish allegiance to a sinister and subversive religion'.[43]

Spender informed White that Craig had initiated an inquiry into the Cushendall incidents on 12 August 1922, headed by a Barrington Ward, KC. On 13 September, Major General Flood, Military Adviser to the Northern Government wrote to Spender informing him that 'Captain Anderson, [White's persecutor] gave evidence in front of Mr Barrington Ward … and satisfied him as to the bona fide of all action which he took in the matter.' There is no record of White's reaction, but it would be placing an exceptional demand on his naiveté if he had been surprised at this outcome. In any case, it would not have been uppermost in his mind at that time; he was incarcerated in Wellington Barracks, in Dublin, having fallen foul of the authorities on the other side of the border.

Chapter 15

Reality, Theory and Jail

Realities

White had been arrested by the Provisional Government, on 22 August 1922, while visiting Sean Beaumont, 'an Inspector of Irish in the Department of Agriculture and Technical Instruction'.[1] While they were confined in the barracks there was an application for 'a writ of *habeas corpus* for the production of Mr Beaumont and Mr White, and to show by what authority they were detained'. There was neither a warrant for their arrest nor had they been charged with anything. In a hearing, illustrative of the instability that prevailed in those times, Justice Dodd was told by Mr Nolan-Whelan, counsel for White and Beaumont, that the Provisional Government was not the 'King's forces'. Dodd could only conclude that

> there is nothing but chaos in Ireland; [...] the King has gone and nothing has come [...]. Are our lives and our property to be subject to any people who take it on themselves to say that the authority of arms is the only authority in Ireland?[2]

However, the Provisional Government's argument prevailed that a 'state of war and rebellion does exist which justifies the application of martial law'; White and Beaumont were further detained.[3] It has not been established how long he spent in prison on this occasion, but probably not more than a few weeks. Certainly Beaumont was free on 27 November 1922 to attend a 'sitting of the Committee appointed by the Corporation of Dublin to inquire into the treatment of political prisoners', where he gave evidence about the 'insufficient accommodation and poor sanitary arrangements in Wellington Barracks'.[4]

White himself had written at an earlier time (20 October) to W.B. Spender for whom he appeared to have developed a liking. It is unlikely he would have written this while in jail. It is difficult to imagine what threat White presented that he should have been incarcerated at that time; his inflexible opposition to injustice, as he saw it, found him continually occupying positions that courted no popularity but hardly merited the reaction of the Provisional Government.

An interesting aside is the peripatetic existence of White at this time; in the space of six months there are as many addresses used by him on his correspondence – Dublin, Belfast, Broughshane, Cushendun, Carnlough and Letterkenny. It may be an indication of the pressure he was under, and certainly he must have been tremendously disappointed at how politics were developing both north and south. This may have been what prompted him to write as he did now. It's a brief note but worth recording in full:

Dear Colonel Spender,

You wrote to me so nicely in reply to my letter to the Prime Minister that I write to ask you, if I may come and see [you] on the 30th. Oct. for choice as I expect to be in Belfast that day. A day or so later would do equally well. I want to ask you to help me. I have come to realise that I have wasted my time and energy in movements I had far better have left alone, and if I am not too hopelessly committed, I would like a job and would be willing to serve a humble apprenticeship, Yours sincerely,

J.R. White.

Spender treated this request in a courteous and considerate manner; in fact his sensitivity to what must have been an extremely difficult letter for White to write is a mark of the man. He pointed out that

> we are absolutely overwhelmed with applications in our Civil Service, and have been obliged to decline the offers of a very large number of people, including a Brigadier General, who have done most excellent service in the Ulster Division.

White met him anyway although stressing that he 'could not take anything of a military nature even if they'd have me, but something in the line of education … some day'.⁵ This mild flirtation with a meek deferral to conventional authority cannot have lasted very long. Even his burgeoning friendship with Spender was to be severely strained at a later date; possibly as he got older, his irritability and short temper increased, and this was to fracture his relationships with a lot of people who would at least have sympathised with his viewpoint.

His active participation on the periphery of politics both north and south was to continue. He was invited to stand as a candidate 'in the interests of the Workers' Republic' at the next election by the workers from East Tirconaill at a meeting in Raphoe, Co. Donegal.⁶ Anton McCabe writes that White 'would have been known personally to some in the area because, in the summer of 1914 he had drilled volunteers' in that area.⁷ White confirms this:

> On investigation I found that the moving spirit behind the issue of the invitation was one Boyle, stationmaster at Raphoe, who had been a member of the deputation of Derry Volunteers, to which I had given an uncompromising reply. Boyle had respected me for my straightness, and in the interval had come to realize the true patriotism of my motives.⁸

That was 4 June 1923; ten days later he was to accept that offer but not before generating his almost inevitable controversy:

> At a public meeting in the Mansion House – which resolved to demand the immediate release of the prisoners – Captain White, one of the speakers, condemned the use of arms by Republicans in the recent trouble. He aroused the ire of a section of the gathering, and many of his remarks were drowned in an uproar of catcalls, jeering, and hissing. […] Captain White in supporting the proposal [the immediate release of prisoners] said that he would sooner the prisoners North and South remained in confinement, unless they came out determined that the holy cause of Christian Ireland should be sought by Christian means only. He was about the first man in Ireland to get up to dissociate himself definitely from physical forces by Republican or any other body. He thought that it was a fatal mistake that led Republicans to adopt physical force from the start. From this point the interruptions were general and at times Captain White could not be heard because of the uproar.⁹

Turned down by Johnson when he asked to stand as a candidate for Labour in the 1918 general election, White had an opportunity with the Tirconaill Workers' Council to go into parliament with those whose political aims he had more in common. He might have been more diplomatic in how he dealt with them, but as he said, 'Alas! I had to disappoint him [Boyle] again.' He explains himself:

> I myself had come to realize that the only way to overcome the deep-seated damage done to the national life by the sectarian issue in Ireland was to strike at the theological root. Common labour ideals and common economic interests represented in the slogan 'Workers' Republic' were not in themselves alone strong enough to bridge the religious division. That division could only be healed by the healing influence of the reconciling and incarnating spirit of Christ, superseding the destructive dichotomy of the warring creeds.[10]

Having, as he said, 'condemned the whole Republican physical force movement as morally and politically unsound', White announced that he would stand 'not as a Workers' Republican, but openly as a Christian Communist'.

White also declared that the 'Free State was so morally unsound that it would have perished of its own moral rottenness, had it not been strengthened and given a false sanction as the government of Law and Order in the panic induced by the civil war'.[11] This was possibly made very evident to him when Justice Dodd raised the question of who had authority in White's earlier *habeas corpus* application. The statement at that time by the Provisional Government bears repeating: 'a state of war and rebellion does exist which justifies the application of martial law'; White saw this as stating that all power rested with those who were armed – in other words, the rule of the gun.[12] His additional call, that as a 'Christian Communist' he would tend 'to unite the workers north and south not only in an economic interest, but in a common and individual Christianity', would not have been perceived by the Catholic majority as acceptable.[13] There would have been too much suspicion of, even antipathy towards, what was a very Protestant-sounding aspiration. In any case, it is not surprising that the chairman of the eventual meeting in Letterkenny, James Gibbons, said that 'any views expressed by Captain White were in no way to be considered the adopted policy of Labour in Tirconaill'.[14]

White believed that the changes that were occurring as a result of the new Provisional Government were superficial; the same inequitable systems were prevailing but now merely under a different authority. Consistent with his *Ulster's Opportunity* pamphlet, and indeed with what he wrote to Craig, White indicated that he was looking for something more profound, claiming that

> society was founded on an entirely false foundation – animal rather than human – and that a change of the whole principle of the social structure with true Christianity was essential if a great calamity was to be avoided. The only real cure was a combination between the farmers and the labourers to change the system at the root and introduce communal ownership. This demanded more than an economic change; it demanded a change in human nature itself. Foolish people had, he said, asked him was he out to destroy the Catholic Church. Far from it. Without the help of the Churches in remoulding human nature to believe and apply Christianity, what he sought could not be achieved.[15]

This was moving beyond a materialist analysis to the question that had bedevilled politics from prescriptive philosophy to Lenin. The question is how the people would maintain sufficient revolutionary fervour to carry out the profound changes required for a new society. White's answer seemed to lie in the transcendent where the people would embrace an 'individual Christianity' . There are those like Marx who examined the current socio-economic structure for its faults (inevitable in any system). The fundamental question was whether the change initiated by the inequilibrium would manifest itself as a radical overturning or merely an adjustment. Marx used the Hegelian 'dialectic' to describe this inherent dynamic. Like Hegel he believed that a recognition of the problems (mainly the inequities within the structure) was what provided the initial momentum to the dialectic.

White, on the other hand, supported what could be described as a Messianic perspective. The faults within a system remained obdurate and immutable unless directly addressed by humankind with the aid and approval of some kind of higher power. This is not as religiously extreme as may first appear; one would suggest that it forms almost part of conventional human belief. As Circe said to a prevaricating Odysseus, 'Step your mast, set sail and trust in the gods!'

Where White may have erred, as I have pointed out already, was in his rather unworldly confidence that humankind, on the error of its ways being pointed out, would immediately take corrective action, instead of, in reality, taking all possible measures to defend its position. What was admirable was his fortitude in maintaining his message of non-violence, and his condemning of all parties regardless of how sympathetic he may have felt to their aims.

Boyd said that the 'Donegal Workers' Council was not in the least interested in Christian Communism'.[16] Within a week White resigned as a candidate and explained that his 'invitation to contest Tirconaill in the workers' interest issued only from a small group with no claim to represent the district as a whole'.[17] McCabe comments, maybe a little unreasonably, that 'while personally a dedicated socialist, White, the man, was erratic in the extreme', and this, he believed, was supported by his report that White proclaimed 'his refusal to take the oath which was required to sit in the Dáil [and] [...] appealed for co-operation from the churches in implementing communism'.[18] Refusal to take the 'Oath of Allegiance', as it was termed by the anti-treatyites, was possibly seen as tacit support for them by White, but the truth is that regardless of any political affiliations he would have difficulty with an oath of fealty. His repugnance dated back as far as at least 1908 when he was swearing in the new recruits to 'my liege Edward' who, it might be recalled, did not remotely measure up to being entitled to a fidelity of this sort. However, expecting the churches to promote communism would leave White open to the charge of being erratic, or at least impractical. On the other hand, it should not detract from the fact that White's solution at least went beyond the conventional remedies that ultimately depended on the maintenance of some kind of forceful coercion.

Jack White continued to appear in the news from time to time, but the halcyon days of 1913/14 were never to be revisited. He was invariably taking a stance on situations that, although requiring to be addressed, were usually passed over by more conventional activists. He represented the refugees who had fled to the south when the 'Northern Government' began interning those believed to be political malcontents. At a meeting in the Mansion House on 18 October 1923 a resolution was passed, yet again, calling for the release of all political prisoners in Ireland. White 'made a statement on the negotiations that he had last June with the representatives of the Northern government' and presented a report by the 'Secretary of the Northern Parliament of that interview' where he had asked:

on behalf of a number of refugees from Ulster, that they should be allowed to return to their homes in Ulster on giving a pledge to abstain from all unconstitutional actions either in the Free State or in the six counties and the Northern Government on its part should not demand from them any oath against their conscience as a condition of their return. Captain White also suggested that the same basis should apply to the interned persons from whom guarantees of good faith to abide by any agreement they might freely enter into could be given by those making representations on their behalf. The Northern Government decided that they could not entertain the proposal at present. The same offer was made on August 10th and was rejected.[19]

It is a typical stance for White, perfectly reasonable, but, again possibly too trusting in human nature; not only would the northern government be unlikely to take such a position, but it would be surprising if any but a very few refugees would make such a commitment. But there have been others who appreciated what White was about. Peter Delargy, writing to *The Irish Times* in 1978, said that 'White had been approached by Sean Murray, an IRA man from Cushendall, Co. Antrim (and later founder of the Communist Party Ireland) who was acting as spokesman' probably for the refugees referred to above. They were 'Northern republicans who were seeking a guarantee of a safe passage to their homes from the Stormont Government, now that the war appeared to be lost'.[20] White again contacted Spender, Secretary to the Northern Cabinet, who put him in touch with Sir Dawson Bates, Northern Minister for Home Affairs. 'White who had been initially optimistic, was disappointed to find Bates cautious and unimaginative', according to Delargy, who goes on to observe: 'had the first Stormont Government contained men of the quality of White and Spender, rather than the blinkered Bates, the course of history might have been altered'.[21]

Mother's View

White, at this stage had formed quite a respect for William Spender, so much so that he asked him to intervene with his mother Lady Amy in the matter of his inheritance – Whitehall, the family home at Broughshane. He appeared to believe that his mother, who had tenure on the home for her lifetime despite living in England, did not trust him; that she believed that either he would get into trouble with elements in the North, or (more likely) fritter away whatever resources came under his control. What he asks Spender to say to Lady Amy is of interest because it gives an indication of how he saw himself, or at least how he hoped someone like Spender might perceive him. Once again his voice displays an unbounded confidence:

> She does not I think realise in the least how much my desire to continue and enhance a family tradition is bound up with the efforts I have been making and how my exclusion from the place in the next few years may deprive me of the right setting to complete a work which so far has been all kicks and misunderstandings and no ha'pence.
>
> I think you have some inkling of the insight which almost exclusive concentration on one subject has given me. You may not believe, as I do, that that insight will be valuable to the Northern Government when events develop a little further, on the other hand it is just conceivable that you may. Anyhow I don't want to throw away for lack of asking for it the great influence which I feel sure a letter from you would have on my mother, if you could, (i) make her realise something of the difficulty and delicacy of what I have been attempting to do and my persistence in attempting it. (ii) if you can truthfully do so persuade her of the likelihood of some fruition of my efforts [being] of real use to the country, or at any rate its possibility.

Spender drafted a letter for White's approval, almost by return (15 February 1924) in which he clearly indicates his opposition to White but demonstrates his feelings of goodwill nevertheless:

> ...I have been brought into touch with your son, with whose views I, of course, profoundly disagree [...] In our conversations, however, I am bound to say I have been convinced of your son's single-mindedness and sincerity, and although I must admit that he thinks that the policy of the Nth. Govt. is likely to produce very serious consequences, he has assured me that he will never be a party to any violent steps in advocating his aims.

After some attempts by White to fine-tune Spender's letter it eventually was sent to Lady White in essence unchanged from the above. Even a sentence added which said that Spender 'did not anticipate that [White's] residence in

N.I. is likely to lead to ill consequences' was hardly a ringing endorsement and it was not surprising that Lady Amy, albeit graciously, refused to reconsider her decision. She acknowledged to Spender that it was a 'comfort' to her that 'he has been working persistently for peace'; then she gave what appears to be a reasoned account of her decision and not without evidence of a motherly affection –

> It is not alone, on account of his political views that I do not wish to hand over Whitehall to him during my lifetime. He has not the money to live there, nor do I think from my former experience of him, is he likely to stick to the life he would have to lead there and make it pay. I wish I could think so for I should love him to be there, but I am just afraid of telling him to make the attempt, as I fear it would end in disaster. It is so good for Jack to have a friend like you – and I do hope you will continue to keep in touch with him. As you can imagine it has been a very great trouble to me, that my only son has taken the line he has done, since he has gone against the traditions of his family, yet, I cannot help feeling he is in many ways nobler than most of us and is certainly a very lovable dear fellow.[22]

Although Spender's assistance was in vain, White expressed his gratitude – 'you couldn't have said fairer from your point of view'. This did not inhibit White from castigating him a short few months later; he was continuing to believe in the possibility of a united Ireland, but one that certainly must have proved unacceptable to those in the south and probably inconceivable to those in the north – he still imagined the leadership would be formed primarily from Ulster Protestants. Ulster in isolation might be forced by the 'unscrupulousness' of Lloyd George to take the 'lead in an evolutionary looking Ireland'. He believed failure in unification would result in a civil war between north and south. In a letter addressing the press in October 1924 he referred to the massing of troops from the Free State and Ulster on 'their respective borders' because of the Boundary Commission – the people deputed to draw up the division between the two states. He wrote:

> The state of things under which two bodies of decent human beings regard each other through a curtain of superstitious ignorance and fear lightened by hardly a ray of understanding is a damnable one. Its existence is the fruit of English policy in the past.

And now he believed the delineation of the border was irreversibly hardening the divisions. He attacked his only remaining sympathiser in power:

> My dear Spender,
>
> ... I challenge you ... to resign your position [presumably as Secretary to the Cabinet] and say what you know, that every avenue of peace had not been explored ... this horrible pandering to the crowd on the part of the leaders who thereby become sustained to its worst passions is the source of more evil that all the positive crimes on earth. (16 Oct. 1924)

He then, a week later, crystallised his position and once again lashed out at the unfortunate Spender:

> Ulster can be the pivot of class war or of realised Christianity. For the latter she must blend her practical qualities with Celtic imagination at its finest and most ideal. Every word you write assumes that the British Empire is the last word in 'civilisation' and that the Celt had nothing to contribute. You drive them out unless he will accept your culture and deny his own. When your Government refused my offer and you continued to serve it, you stultified any power you might have to secure liberty to all classes and all religious provided they do not attempt to introduce violent methods, for the rejection was a deliberate preference of violence to peace. Your conscience as an official swamped your conscience as a Christian. You stood between Dawson Bates and his cronies. (21 Oct. 1924).

White had been continually harassing Spender and whoever else would listen to him in the North to release the internees. In his eventual reply to White, Spender seems to have chosen to ignore what he probably saw as the wilder, almost eschatological side of White's thinking:

> I am not going to refer to the Elections, but will deal only with ... our Government here [that] is very anxious to continue its former policy of releasing the internees gradually and continuously, but honestly Mr de Valera's action has made things very difficult in this respect.[23]

I would suggest that despite almost completely ignoring the content of White's letters Spender still had sufficient regard for him to continue correspondence. Referring back to Moore-Irvine's note to Craig and even further back to O'Casey, there is a continual strand of appreciation of White by people, who although often in opposition, perceived a deep integrity to his thinking.

Social Revolution?

In the South, White's outlook as manifest in his speeches and writings had now little or no resonance with any of the nationalist movements and his socialism could be described as very radical. Boyd writes that he was an 'active member of the Irish Workers League (IWL)' founded by Larkin, which Moscow hoped would prove more reliable than the CPI, but Boyd goes on to say that most commentators have rejected it as 'a political party of any sort and have portrayed it more as "a social organisation" '.[24] For all that, White's politics were not as isolated as might first appear; there were significant strands among members of the ILPTUC that would have had a similar outlook, and this is clear in Emmett O'Connor's analysis of Labour thinking in 1921–23. O'Connor reports that a general strike, on the lines of the 1918 and 1920 successes, was being mooted in what appears to be an apocalyptic atmosphere among some of the workers, including the president of the ILPTUC, Thomas Foran. This was caused by several factors, including, probably most importantly, the general slump that occurred at that time, which initiated a round of wage cuts. O'Connor explains Sorel's idea that syndicalism 'cultivated a sense of catastrophe as a revolutionary state of mind, a crystallised vision of the final combat, predicated on pessimism'.[25] This pessimism was the 'more accurate and authentic expression of life as it voiced the misery of mankind'; it countered the 'bourgeois concept of progress' and it was what 'led Connolly towards Easter Week'.[26] Sorel's concept of the myth, which encouraged the proletariat to act, had to have integrity to it for it to be effective. He believed that pessimism was 'a metaphysics of morals rather than a theory of the world';[27] the pessimistic radical was without illusion and practical about the task ahead. Robert Young's description of Connolly, comparing him to Fanon, the anti-colonialist revolutionary and thinker, suggests the same idea:

> [Connolly] was altogether more historicized and pragmatic than Fanon, shorn of any existential glorification, a position that he was

perhaps able to take because socialism had already provided him with self-respect and the moral advantage.[28]

Sorel also believed that pessimism encapsulated 'a conception of a march towards deliverance'; that is, the pessimistic outlook provided the dynamic that would have maintained an enthusiasm among the strikers (or revolutionaries) during the long struggle ahead. These notions correspond to White's; he believed anarchism allowed for an 'elemental vitality' which was essential to motivate the workers.[29] His insistence on Christian principles dictating these actions appears to be similar to Sorel's idea of integrity in action to the extent that I would argue that he must have read Sorel. (In the interests of accuracy, it is important to emphasise that Sorel was not a supporter of Christian beliefs; his admiration was for the Church's employment of scripture as a motivating 'myth'.)

Whether there was sufficient support for such action – that is, an all out general strike at that time – is debatable. The fact, as O'Connor states, that the 'conclusion of the Anglo-Irish war in July 1921 modified the political instability from which workers had formerly derived considerable freedom of action', must have inhibited any industrial action.[30] Furthermore, in a comment on the thinking of the most influential labour leaders of the time O'Connor observes that

> Surprisingly, the success of Connolly's pessimism in 1916 had no influence on Labour thinking. Despite some comparison between Labour imagery and republican mythology, the separatist view of history as a cyclical pattern of struggle made no impact on the Congress leadership. Indeed, the two most influential leaders, O'Brien and Johnson, were convinced optimists. [...] In the midst of pessimism, they put their trust in progress.[31]

Whether White would have subscribed to this explanation is not known but certainly his scepticism about nationalism was probably strengthened by the general lack of sympathy for what he saw as social justice in either the Provisional Government or the anti-Treatyite forces. O'Brien – 'a natural bureaucrat'[32] – and O'Brien's close ally Johnson ensured White would have no part to play in conventional Labour politics, although there was mention of the possibility of him standing in Liverpool as an unofficial Labour candidate in the 1924 general election. The *Manchester Guardian* reported, 'there is promised an introduction of several candidates by the Irish Nationalists between whom and the Labour Party there is friction'.[33] If the dissatisfied Labour members had been looking for someone controversial, then White would have admirably fitted the bill. Apart from his earlier mentioned letter to the press there is little to substantiate him being seriously considered.

Middle Years

White became involved in peripheral movements whose idealism was inversely proportional to their pragmatism. Arthur Mitchell describes the scene:

> The socialist left in the mid- and late 1920s was a desolate place. In addition to Larkin there was only the short-lived Workers Party of Ireland, launched in the spring of 1926 by Roddy Connolly and his sister Nora, Tom Lyng, a member of their father's original party, Captain Jack White of Citizen Army fame and P.T. Daly, who was then seeking new allies. The party announced that its objective was a 'Workers' State', with sweeping nationalization and workers' control of industry.[34]

While sharing in these aspirations on the very edge of the community, White continued to maintain his position as a prominent member of whatever represented high society in Ireland. His attendance at a garden party in Templeogue for the Dublin Gate Theatre is reported shortly after *Misfit* was published.[35] On the other hand there is a glimpse of the kind of penury he was enduring; unsuccessful in employing Spender to release his mother's grip on his inheritance, he is reduced to a dependence on her and the others in the family. A letter to his youngest sister, Georgina, reveals a man not exactly overflowing with *joie de vivre*. Although it must be said that to have to write to one's small sister about money, who did not exactly approve of him anyway, surely gave emphasis to the morose prognosis of the job he spoke about:

> My dear Georgie
>
> First let me acknowledge your letter and the cheque you sent as well as the one mother sent in her letter for the week beginning Nov. 10th.[prob. 1930] …

> I started work yesterday at £3 a week organising the [Irish] Workers Voice. While that lasts you can tell mother she need not send me anything.
>
> I can't say whether it will last or no. I do not think I am likely to lose the job for lack of my own energy, for it is right on the main thread of my own efforts and I am chosen for the job to energize them and create a circulation which at present is below 2000. But with one exception my comrades and paymasters have the usual Irish mentality in addition to that, *if I do succeed, as I expect I shall, in making the paper a living force, it will ipso facto become a menace to the government and probably be suppressed and myself arrested.* So it is no good pretending that I have entered the ranks of secure and respectable wage earners.[36]

His penchant for controversy was not confined to politics. A few years before that the *Irish News* described how

> A sensation was created in Kingstown, County Dublin, on Wednesday when it was reported that a man who had gone out in a boat had not returned. He had hired a boat from a boatman, and the last the latter saw of the craft was in rough water halfway towards Howth. Subsequent inquiries by the police gave rise to the belief that the missing man was Captain JR White, DSO, son of the defender of Ladysmith. This turned out to be correct, but fortunately, the fears for his safety have been dispelled, as he has turned up again at the Marine Hotel, Kingstown. It is stated that Captain White took the boat for the purpose of taking a short cut to Howth, and returned by the circuitous land route through Dublin, leaving the boat behind at Howth.[37]

The *Manchester Guardian* stated that White told the man he hired the boat from that he only wanted to go for an hour's rowing, and 'it was not supposed that he intended to go outside the harbour, as the sea was altogether too rough for a rowing boat'.[38] *The Irish Times* even carried an interview with him, in which White stated that the first 'information of his decease was when [he] saw a hotel porter packing [his] bag' after his return to the hotel the following night. 'I always take the shortest route', he said, but 'when I got to the other side the water was rough and I could not find a landing place', so he had to row around until eventually he found a 'little creek'. It had taken him three and a half hours of what must have been very hard pulling.[39] One is left wondering whether the whole incident was as innocuous as White would have it.

Imprisonment Once More

Among the revolutionary workers groups was an association called the Irish National Unemployed Movement. This was the body that White was involved with in a 'hunger march' in Belfast in 1931 when, according to the reminiscences of James Kelly, the newspaper reporter, it proved very difficult to get an accompanying band that could play non-sectarian songs. Eventually a band was found with a rather limited repertoire and the protest marched to the singularly inappropriate tune, 'Yes, we have no bananas'.[40]

In possibly the same procession, although both *The Irish Times* and the *Manchester Guardian* identify it as being organised by the Revolutionary Workers Party, there were some serious disturbances, and White along with three others were charged with disorderly conduct calculated to lead to a breach of the peace. White was at the head of the procession and, according to police evidence, had refused to go back when instructed to do so by the officer in charge. It was alleged that he shouted, 'Come on, we will rush the police.' On being 'pushed back by a policeman', White assaulted him 'by striking him with a stick he carried'.[41] White, appearing in court with a bandaged head, defended himself, giving 'what he described as the antecedents of the trouble'. A fortnight earlier White's group had first attempted to hold a meeting and this was prevented after a number of Orangemen had drummed for three hours resulting in the police dispersing the meeting. 'The police showed shameless partisanship [a fortnight ago and again last night]'[42] when a 'deliberate breach of the peace by Orangemen [was] protected by the police'.[43] White admitted that he had called for the marchers to go forward, but 'his honour was at stake to protect free speech'.[44] He then went on to say:

> I was set on with the utmost brutality by at least six policemen at once, and was hammered over the head and arms. Look at my condition with blood from my head. When the men whom I am bound to say seemed ashamed of their work, stopped it I heard non-

commissioned officers call to them: 'Beat him up'. The constable's statement that I assaulted him is utterly untrue and is deliberate perjury. I did not strike a single blow or use an insulting word.[45]

Of the other three defendants, two pleaded that they had been unwittingly caught up in the whole drama; one, Johnston, was on his way to the pictures, and the other, Davidson, 'the son of respectable parents', was an Oxford student, whose nineteenth birthday occurred on that day. The third man, Thomas Watters, a member of the Irish Revolutionary Workers' Party, claimed that 'the police were there in sufficient force to protect the procession to the place of the meeting, but instead they made a vicious attack on the workers behind'. The case against Johnston the picture-goer was dismissed, but the other three were fined forty shillings or, in default, one month's imprisonment. Additionally, White was fined £5 for assaulting the police constable or, in default, two months' imprisonment. All three were ordered to 'find bail for twelve months'. White refused to do so and was taken to the cells where he was joined by Watters.[46]

Reading the entire report in the *Irish News* (the account corresponds closely to the other papers but has more detail), there appears to have been a complete lack of tolerance by the police to the protest and certainly White was targeted. When he cross-examined Constable Seay, the policeman White was alleged to have assaulted, Seay acknowledged he had 'no marks as a result of the blows'.[47] Ironically this incident was an example of what Connolly had aspired to; a sectarian-free class protest, knowing no borders. In fact one of the leaders of the Revolutionary Party, Thomas Geehan, said that the Northern Ireland authorities were merely following 'the example of their friends in the Free State and [making] the place hot for militant workers'.[48] The image of the two political entities, inimical in almost everything but their opposition to the plight of the unemployed, is interesting.

James Kelly (the journalist) again, goes into detail about the whole incident:

> Sir Dawson Bates, Minister of Home Affairs who controlled the Royal Ulster Constabulary and the 'B' Specials as if they were the private army of the Unionist Party, was quick to sense the political menace of this historic turning point – 'the October Revolution of 1931' some optimists of the Left dubbed it. He ordered police baton charges when the pathetic, shabbily-dressed half-starved legions of unemployed from the Shankill and Falls attempted one night to

march along Royal Avenue. They were dispersed brutally and among those arrested was Captain Jack White, son of a British General of the Boer War, who had come up from Dublin to show his Socialist solidarity with the Belfast workless. The following morning I saw this distinguished looking man standing in the dock of the Belfast Custody Court with a blood-stained bandage around his head.[49]

Both Watters and White served one month. The Irish Labour Defence League planned a reception for them on the evening of their planned release, Saturday, 17 October 1931. At a meeting of the Irish Workers Revolutionary Party held on the Sunday previous to discuss this, a secret RUC report gave an account of the speakers maintaining that 'Capitalism all over the world faced an acute crisis.' In a reminder that little changes in times of economic turmoil, the speaker, James Kernaghan, said that 'Germany was cutting down the period of unemployment benefit in an effort to balance her Budget, just as Great Britain had done.' Further comments were made about the Free State pursuing similar policies with the 'Emergency Powers Bill' which was introduced 'for the purpose of suppressing certain organisations in Southern Ireland'.[50]

A handwritten comment on the secret document suggests that White and Watters should be released early to avoid possible disturbances, and this was approved because a further note reports that they were released at 9am on the Friday morning.

Chapter 16

Spain, War and the End

Exclusion

The Northern Ireland authorities, or at least Sir Dawson Bates, Minister for Home Affairs, had enough of Jack White. He was not going to be given another opportunity to get involved in counter hegemonic activities in the six counties and was immediately served with an order under the Civil Authorities (Special Powers) Act of 1922. It stated –

> Whereas CAPTAIN JAMES ROBERT WHITE, D.S.O., of Dublin, is suspected of being about to act in a manner prejudicial to the preservation of the peace and the maintenance of order in Northern Ireland: AND WHEREAS it appears to me that it is desirable that the said Captain White should be prohibited from residing in or entering the area hereinafter specified ... I HEREBY ORDER that the aforesaid shall leave the area ... forthwith.[1]

The area specified was the entire area under the jurisdiction of the Northern Ireland government with the exception, for some reason, of the town of Limavady in County Derry. Apart from the questionable constitutionality of an Act that had been 'rushed through Parliament when disorder was rife' almost ten years before that (and for an entirely different purpose – its thrust was mainly anti-republican), this was also an excessive and unjustified proscription by Bates. (The purpose of allowing White to live in Limavady was possibly to counteract any legal move to declare the order invalid. It could also be employed as a kind of house arrest, although White had no known connections with the place.) Although born in England, White's ancestral home was Whitehall, in Broughshane, County Antrim; he was a citizen of the United Kingdom and never at any time saw himself as part of the Irish Free State, although he always considered himself Irish.

It was a step as drastic as the equally unconstitutional action of the de Valera government which deported Jimmy Gralton from the Free State in 1933 to the US. Gralton, born and reared in County Leitrim, was also a member of the Revolutionary Workers' Party. One is minded of Joyce's claim to the Nobel Peace Prize because of his unification of so many factions (from the British empire to the Catholic nationalists) in their opposition to *Ulysses* – Communism and its allies succeeded where Christianity had singularly failed in uniting both ends of the bitter political divide of this small island.

White was supposed to have left for England the night after his release from prison. In spite of various negotiations he felt unable to sign a commitment that Bates required if he was to reconsider revoking the order. He did, however, offer to 'undertake ... not to take any further part in public life while the exclusion order is in operation'.[2] This was not sufficient for the authorities. What they actually looked for is not known as there is no record of the actual undertaking that Bates required him to sign; in fact Bates's voice during this and the following period of appeals does not appear at all, except as a signature on the legal pronouncements.

White, according to his various appeals, kept to the requirements of the order; there is however, a record by police of him being in Belfast until 5 April 1932. It is generally acknowledged that he complied with the exclusion order after that time. Several requests were made; Sam Kyle, the trade union leader, who appears to have known Bates, made representations in 1934. A similar approach was made by Harry Midgeley a Labour member, who tabled some questions in the Northern Parliament. There was no response from the government except for a puzzling comment by Mr Rowley Elliott, that Clogher in South Tyrone (which he represented) was no place for undesirables like Captain J.R. White who 'was dumped into his constituency'.[3]

Even the reports by the authorities seemed to have become more sympathetic. One civil servant wrote that White was an 'unfortunate gentleman [who] is not naturally vicious, but is unbalanced and cannot I fear be relied on to keep quiet in any position likely to excite him. He has a certain amount of personality and when worked up can be a dangerous agitator'. Seeping smugness, he noted that White 'has been quite out of the limelight since he got his medicine here', but he was 'inclined to recommend giving him another chance'.[4]

Dawson Bates remained obdurate, however; in a reply to Sam Kyle, a Major Harris from the Ministry of Home Affairs wrote that the minister [Bates] regretted that he 'is unable to acquiesce in any departure from the arrangements which were made and the conditions which were laid down in 1931'.[5]

The same smug adviser to the minister seemed to have changed his position on receipt of the various appeals and commented a year later that 'there is really not much in what Captain White seeks ... if [he] should start any agitation it should be just as easy to make out a fresh exclusion order'. There may have been a pragmatic stance taken to all this because White had changed his attitude, literally overnight. (His mother, Lady Amy, had died.) On 28 April he had written once again to Bates, looking to meet and discuss the fact that he had now finally come into his inheritance Whitehall; Bates had refused. The following day White wrote again:

> I have observed my pledge for three and a half years. I now feel that I am entitled to the sympathetic consideration you promised. I have no intention of making trouble, and, were I to do so, I could be proceeded against like anybody else. But I can no longer be a party, especially now I am a tax and rate payer of Northern Ireland, to the abrogation of my own political rights. I therefore withdraw my pledge, and unless I hear to the contrary from you, I shall assume that I am free to return to Northern Ireland and reside there in the exercise of my normal citizen's rights, so long as I do not contravert [sic] the established law.[6]

There is no record of what Bates's reply was, but it did not please White at all. In a very angry letter, dated 13 May, he accused Bates of employing 'dishonourable methods':

> You trapped me in 1931 into giving you a pledge by a promise of most sympathetic consideration of any representations I made about my position in the future; that promise you shamefully broke ... if you choose to issue a fresh deportation order against me after having cancelled the old one rather than own your breach of faith in the past and your misrepresentation of my words in my letters of 28th. and 29th. you must do so. I have acted honourably, you have not.

Without Bates's comments it is impossible to make a judgment but taking what White said in his letter of 29 April and bearing in mind the autocratic nature of that government, it is likely that Bates, recognising the inevitable, had dressed the narrative to suit his own taste. In any case, on 16 May 1935, Dawson Bates signed a revocation of the exclusion order.

On the other hand, it must be acknowledged that White gave Bates ample reason to be cautious of him. One of Bates's aides describes him as 'a stormy petrel' who 'cannot resist the impulse to join in any fight that is going'.[7] It is not difficult to see how this view developed. An undated anonymous and typically malicious block-lettered missive states, 'he has been in touch with the communist parties of England and Germany also with the soviet union in Moscow. His intentions are to raise hell … he has financial backing from the above parties …'.[8]

White's appetite for intrigue extended to India. He met Phillip Rupasangha Gunawardena, a Ceylonese activist on 16 November 1931 in England. Gunawardena was a member of the Indian Freedom League and what he discussed with White is not recorded, but White was leaving for Liverpool immediately after their meeting 'to engage in revolutionary activity among Irishmen'.[9] On 22 November that same year, just released from prison, he 'presided at a meeting against Imperialism held in Canning Town Public Hall, London'. Puzzlingly (because of the exclusion order and his purported adherence to it), the RUC have him attending 'a Communist meeting held at Library Street, Belfast, on 22 March 1932'.[10]

White's imprisonment in Belfast meant he had now served prison terms in all four jurisdictions on these islands – Wales and England in 1916, Scotland in 1921, and the Free State in September 1922. He had also crossed swords, or was about to, with most political forces, whether on the side of the authorities or no. He had employed his stick (as a peaceful defensive weapon, he would have it) against such diverse bodies as the old DMP, the RUC, the various British police forces and the Orange Order; he was shortly to come to blows with the IRA and, a little later, the Blueshirts. His position as a radical left-wing activist was now firmly established; he would have qualified this himself by protesting his adherence to Christian principles which explained his pacifism – although, as in his own description of Sheehy Skeffington, it would be the sorry opponent who conflated this ideal with passivity.

Marriage and Family

A number of factors leading to a domestication of sorts may have influenced White's pressing need to return to Northern Ireland. As mentioned, his mother's death brought him to the family home, Whitehall, at Broughshane outside Ballymena. In 1933, or earlier, he had met Noreen Shanahan, whom he married in 1938 and, although in his late fifties, he started a family.[11] Patricia Wheeler, niece of Noreen, described the Shanahans as 'staunch Parnellites'. Noreen's grandfather was John Joseph Clancy, an Irish Parliamentary Party MP, who was one of the nine 'members who continued to support him after the Kitty O'Shea scandal. He lost his seat in 1918 to the Sinn Fein'.[12]

White was not popular with the Shanahans, 'for being so aggressively anti-Catholic and, worst of all, quarrelling with Noreen's father, George Shanahan, a most peaceable man by all accounts and, incidentally, himself a Protestant'.[13] Derrick, White's son, wrote that 'though a devout Catholic my mother married my father in a registry office and my older brother Tony was born technically illegitimate'.[14] Although a tolerant and open-minded family, the Shanahans would probably have had difficulty with what would have been regarded as unconventional extramarital behaviour at that time. White's attitude was typically irreverent; he referred to a vicar's wife not calling to Whitehall because she had 'some scruples about Noreen and I having anticipated the normal sequence of wedlock and childbirth'.[15]

T.J. McElligott, the journalist, reported vociferous rows and numerous difficulties in the marriage.[16] This is corroborated by both Tony and Alan who would have been old enough to be aware of what was going on: Tony recounts that his father's 'relationship with my mother was an uneven one, sometimes very stormy',[17] and Alan writes about 'subliminal memories of occasional raised voices and tears which vaguely depressed me'.[18] Coupled with the fact that Noreen was undoubtedly a devout Catholic, a member of the Catholic Evidence Guild, and probably concerned for the spiritual welfare of her children, White's opposition to the Catholic Church provided plenty of grounds for tension. Alan writes that

> after JRW's death our mother embraced a sort of manic Catholicism motivated in part, I suspect, by a need to expiate what she may have felt were the gigantic sins of having her first son out of wedlock and

two others within a marriage not recognised by the catholic church, epitomized in that uncompromising era by the likes, God help us, of Archbishop John Charles McQuaid. Did you know for example that Derrick and I (Tony too probably) were re-baptized in case, as Derrick once put it, the Presbyterian version didn't take?[19]

On the other hand, the stereotype of the intimidated and misled woman is not accurate in this case. Tony writes that 'apart from religion, they got on very well'.[20]

Noreen was a woman of determination and spirit; White would not have been attracted to her otherwise, according to his grandniece Katy English.[21] Noreen's niece, Patricia Wheeler, said that she worked as a secretary, 'not of the nail polishing type', but rather of the managerial class, administering whatever business she was employed in – a first mate to the chief executive or captain of the ship of state, as she would have it.[22] Most impressively, Alan remembers her addressing 'unsympathetic hecklers at Hyde Park's Speakers' Corner each Sunday for several years'.[23] A considerable amount of her letters to White are extant from 1934 when their relationship was beginning. There is a consummate style to her letters, revealing not just a highly intelligent woman torn between her allegiance to her religion and her affection for White, but an artistry to her writing that leaves one disappointed that she has left no formal works behind. Even in the most casual of notes she manages to delight with passages like the following – her reference to a woman she obviously did not like: 'She has the wandering lacklustre eye of the born gossip, becoming animated only when she is [about to speak herself].'[24]

White referred to her continually in his correspondence with his niece Pat Napier; usually it was in what could be described as a wry manner, but with an undoubted underlying affection. The arguments, referred to by all, could in a way be part of not a match made in heaven but a real world human partnership with all the emotional weals and warts that complement a couple's togetherness. Referring to one of their ongoing differences, he wrote that Noreen:

> preferred Protestant baptism to none and as I well knew, would not prove her Catholicism (which doesn't exist in either form or substance) by giving us two children and a husband she happens to love for the pleasure of baptising and working for no little 'Pope'.

So her complete inconsistency is really clear to herself and I give it about another year before she is done with the grosser superstition altogether. We will then be divinely happy. We have been getting steadily happier and happier and as my rational certainty that her religion is, at best, ignorant vulgar nonsense, and at worse, devil worship increases, I have been less and less upset.[25]

It is not surprising that his youngest son Derrick expressed his irritation with White's 'overwhelming self-assurance'. Reviewing his father's account of his relationship with his first wife Dollie, he wondered at the self-centredness of the man: 'No mention is made of their conversations, not a word about joy, passion, tears, embraces and all the emotional baggage that is part and parcel of being in love.'[26] In mitigation, describing his father as an anti-Catholic who paradoxically marries two (his two mortal sins, as White liked to say), he wrote that White was 'devoid of pettiness or grudges' and his correspondence 'often shows a profound and sometimes touching self-doubt'.[27] Although he must have been an exceedingly difficult man to live with, Derrick is possibly being a little unfair to him; for White and his ilk, emotions like passion would have been almost alien to write about except in a very deprecatory, even embarrassed way.

Further Protests, Spain

Meanwhile White continued his individual campaign in the Free State. Boyd reports that he joined the Republican Congress in 1934 and 'was chairman of one of the six branches of the congress in Dublin'.[28] According to Alan Mac Simóin, a journalist and historian with anarchist sympathies, this was 'a movement based on workers and small farmers, that was well to the left of the IRA'. The branch White chaired was a contingent of British ex-servicemen, and in 1934 on the annual march to Bodenstown for the Wolfe Tone commemoration they were attacked by 'Sean McBride's IRA men'.[29] Two years later, at Easter 1936, they were attacked at Bodenstown again, this time by 'blueshirt gangs all along the route'. White was 'badly injured by a blow of an iron cross ripped from a grave'.[30] He reported himself that 'the pious hooligans actually came inside the cemetery and tore up the grave rails to attack us'.[31]

Just a few months later, in October 1936, White went to Spain. His visit there made an important impact on his political life as evidenced by his writings that survive. It is generally believed that what he saw in Barcelona, along with conversations with Emma Goldman, crystallised his thinking and led him to believe that anarchism best expressed his political philosophy. However, Albert Meltzer, the anarchist, in his autobiography, claims that White was a member of the Anarcho-Syndicalist Union (ASU) and this would appear to be some time before he went to Spain.[32] In his autobiography Meltzer states that White had a 'running quarrel with his estranged Roman Catholic wife and her ecclesiastic advisers who periodically kidnapped his daughter'.[33] If Meltzer is correct, it would suggest that White was involved with an anarchist movement before 1935 when Dollie sued for divorce. Meltzer describes White as someone who did not fit the conventional description of an anarchist, whatever that might be, but was a 'very sincere' and 'excellent speaker'.[34]

Well aware of his profile among the various security forces in all of these islands, White would have had to keep a low profile on his way to Catalonia. He was reported to be a member of the Spanish Medical Aid Committee, a British group who sent out units of doctors and nurses to the battlefront; this would have facilitated his passage.[35] However, it is unlikely he was not involved militarily in some way. Mac Simóin provides an account (probably gleaned from Meltzer) of White with the Connolly Column, training militia members. He also reports, which is more likely because of White's putative pacifism, that he coached women in the villages in the use of the pistol for defence.[36]

White's involvement with the militia is doubly doubtful; Emmet O'Connor states that 'The James Connolly Centuria was in the International Brigades, who, as communists, would not have been involved with the Militias.'[37] White himself confirmed that he was an 'administrator of one of the British Medical Units mainly subscribed for by British Trade Unionists'. In the same letter, dated October 1939, he wrote about his abandonment of any affinity he might have had with communism, although some commentators would maintain that his difference was with Stalinism. In any case, he demonstrated prescience about the fate of fascism and an astute analysis of the power of Stalinist Russia:

> I was able to see from the inside the lengths to which Communist sabotage of everything the Communist Party was unable to dominate was carried. I have no hesitation in saying that this intensive sabotage and domination by intrigue on the part of Moscow-

directed Communism, with the great leverage given to it by control of the distribution of Russian supplies of arms and food, broke the Revolutionary unity of Spain from within in more deadly fashion that Franco's armies from without; I say this in spite of my free admission of Communist organizing power as exemplified in the International Brigade. I saw then that the complete affinity between Fascist and Communist principles and practice was only modified by the superior power of the latter to obtain the assent of the mind to its own mechanical enslavement. In ruthlessness to heretics, in glorification of a hide bound scholasticism supplying ready made arguments whose repetition is the only safeguard from the Inquisition, in docile obedience to its high priests and slavish support of their changes of policy however unprincipled, Communism is a mature and sophisticated philosophy where Fascism by comparison is a naïve ... [remainder of text missing,][38]

Earlier, in an article in *Spain and the World,* on 5 March 1937, White had declared that 'a Christian Anarchist, which, if I am to have a label at all, and I hate all labels, is the nearest label to fit me'.[39]

Meltzer, who although 'frequently inaccurate' according to Fearghal McGarry,[40] wrote that White was involved in London in an arms-buying enterprise which attempted to obviate the British Non-Intervention Act in Spain by posing as some kind of legitimate business.[41] White felt very strongly about the detached position that the United Kingdom took at that time, so much so that, even as late as 1940, he wrote, probably observing Franco's political manoeuvres, that 'one thing is certain, the judgment to be paid now is a moral one and England will pay to the full for her crime against Spain'.[42]

This might give some background to the fact that he was charged with possessing 'firearms and ammunition without certificates' at Marylebone Court in London in January 1939: 'Summonses alleging that he had transferred the firearms and ammunition to an unauthorised person were not proceeded with.'[43] Charged along with him was 25-year-old Frank Beresford, a friend of the family in Broughshane, employed to look after White's son and deal with his correspondence. Ostensibly, the case appeared to be a simple matter of White bringing a Webley revolver with him from Ireland and Beresford finding it and bringing it to his own room for safekeeping. Detective Inspector Stevenson said that there was nothing against Beresford;

however, 'a bullet hole in a door' and some seemingly wild statements by the young man appeared to have aroused police suspicion. 'That man is an Irish revolutionary', Beresford stated, referring to White, and added: 'White gave me the weapons. There is no good being a scapegoat for him. He is not involved in this bomb business, those people would not trust him.'[44]

Beresford presumably was referring to the bombing campaign by the IRA in England at that time, so he obviously had no idea whatsoever of White's political outlook. White, in his explanation for the arms, told the magistrate, 'I had reasons, and very good reasons, for possessing them but I would not tell them publicly. I will tell you privately if you wish.'[45] Mentioning that he had an estate in Ireland, his mitigating plea appeared to be that this needed protection. His pacifism always seemed to rest on the premise that violence was eminently acceptable in defence. Tony, his eldest son, as mentioned earlier, recollected White threatening that if the Nazis came up the avenue in Whitehall, 'he would take out his shotgun and get a few of them first'.[46]

The magistrate appeared to accept White's explanation but said 'that the weapons which [he] might have innocently possessed could have come into the hands of anybody' and fined him £25 with five guineas costs. The unfortunate Beresford was fined £5.[47]

Second World War

At the outbreak of war White had no doubts about the essence of the conflict. 'This is a war of ideas,' he wrote, 'accurate forecast is impossible without grasp of the spiritual principles in conflict.' He believed that 'Germany and Russia' were 'cementing an ideological union, which involves a threat to humanity in general and to Britain in particular, in so far as Britain's cause is identified with the championship of the deepest human value of individual freedom'.[48] To this end he advocated an all-out effort on the part of the various parties on these islands but believed the motives of the Catholic Church to be suspect. In an alliance with General Hubert Gough, the army officer who initiated the 'Curragh Mutiny', he issued a nationwide appeal under the auspices of an association called the Council for Investigation of Vatican Influence and Censorship (CIVIC):

> Separated in the past, we have come together in this hour of crisis, when all liberty, religious, political, or economic, is equally threatened, to appeal for a free and united country in the most urgent

and vital issue which now concerns all free men, namely, that of self-defence.[49]

It is unlikely that the presentation of General Gough as the man who 'refused to be the instrument for the coercion of Ulster' would have found much favour in any of the factions in the south, but nonetheless it was an unusual juxtaposition of what were practically opposing sides in 1913: White leading the Citizen Army and Gough sympathising with the Ulster Volunteers by refusing to attack them.

White reported that the appeal received little publicity because of resistance on both sides of the political divide, sides which 'in their supposed opposition play straight into each others hands'. He quoted the old saw that 'Irish Protestantism is the strongest bulwark of Rome in Ireland.'[50] White was clear-eyed about the bigotry practised by a considerable element of the majority in the North but, in his commentary on the appeal, he appeared to lose objectivity in his analysis of the opposition to it by the Catholic Church. Although he was probably correct when he stated that it was 'the Protestants [...] who have so far remained united in their common hatred of intellectual tyranny', his invective went too far in his speculation that the Catholic Church's argument could be extended to claiming that it was the 'Protestants and Atheists of Britain, America and Russia who were keeping the world divided against the ordered unity of Hitler.'[51] He did raise embarrassing questions, however, about the

> *Dublin Standard,* Eire's chief Catholic weekly, [which, he wrote] went as far as it dare in praising Nazism as a Champion of Christianity. Its editorial column stated: 'Those who do not want a German victory must now reflect on the social and religious implications of a Russo-British victory.'[52]

White, in his conviction that the outbreak of war required a mustering of every resource, offered his services to Sir Charles Wickham, the Inspector General of the Royal Ulster Constabulary (RUC), and received a reply on 8 June 1940 from a Deputy Inspector C.F. Davies. It said tersely:

> The Inspector General has directed me to reply to your letter of 6th. inst. and to inform you, as you desire a candid reply, that in view of your record he regrets that he would be unable to offer you any employment in the Local Defence Volunteer Section.[53]

It seemed that White's transgressions, at least in Northern Ireland, were of a nature that could never be absolved. He did write to the Northern Prime Minister, J.M. Andrews, at Stormont on 16 December 1940 and pointed out that he was being penalised 'for youthful socialistic enthusiasm, of which I have no cause to be ashamed'. He mentioned the joint appeal with General Gough, pointed out that he 'was <u>Red</u> [...] never Green' and stated that 'I believe I would fight against Eire if it came to the pinch.'[54] There is no record of a reply, but it certainly would not have been a positive one.

The war had the effect of confining White to Broughshane for its duration. There is little trace of any his activities during this period except for the correspondence with his niece Pat English (*née* Napier), daughter of his sister Gladys. During that time two more sons were born, Allan and Derrick. T.J. McElligott, a journalist for the *Ballymena Guardian*, reported that when he came to know him in 1944, White was 'concerned more with religion than politics'. However, it was White's own brand of Presbyterian dissent: 'to him the doctrine of Papal supremacy and Protestant elitism were equally unacceptable'.[55] This is borne out in the letters he wrote to Pat, which, apart from general theories about the war, overall make little reference to his earlier activities. McElligott was invited to dinner by White and there he met Betty Sinclair; she had been a member of the Revolutionary Workers' Group. Although the journalist expressed surprise, there is great accuracy in his succinct account of White's views:

> neither of them spoke of Ireland in terms of a political unit; their concern was to effect a social union between all classes north and south. The living conditions of people were what mattered to Jack White and he looked on politics as providing a means of improving these. In all that he wrote and said there was a clearly discernible note, freedom for the individual was more important than freedom for the nation.[56]

McElligott also gave an account of his gift of oratory, which he experienced when White was contemplating a political campaign in 1945, in the Orange Hall at Broughshane. He said that 'the uncompromising, and at times violent nature of his speech must have shaken some of his listeners' when 'in a voice that never had need of amplification [...] he commanded a rich vocabulary of invective which was aimed at a wide range of targets: Stormont and Westminster, Hitler and the Pope, Brookeborough and de Valera'.[57]

Illness and Death

McElligott was not to know that White was aware, for at least five months, that he was under sentence of death. John Cowper Powys recorded in early January in his diary that he had 'heard from White of White that he has a malignant growth in his prostate and is being cured by pills made of female hormones'.[58] In 1945 treatment of this type was merely to assuage the symptoms. On 19 March Powys further reported that 'White of White has cancer of the Prostate Gland. White of White believes that his revelation from God will cure it.'[59] Powys, one of England's best-known novelists at that time, had an enormous regard for White, describing him as one of his two 'most exciting correspondents', this from a man who wrote a vast amount of letters.[60] Powys's partner, whom he referred to as T.T., 'summed him up and his writings wondrously, giving him her greatest praise comparing him to Dostoevsky and Gogol'.[61] His comments about White's writing and thinking are worth quoting in his own idiosyncratic epistolary style:

> I confined myself to posting my letter to old 'White of White' that War-Sex-Macro-Micro of White-hall (County Antrim) who either 'kicked' (or wanted to kick) 'the ARSE' of Lawrence of 'Sons and Lovers' and I expect if he ever gets displeased with me will 'Kick my arse' too! but who got that Greatest Prig and most Conceited Prig of all our writers and of all our men of action, Laurence of Arabia, to 'midwife' his first book called 'Misfit' and is now getting me to 'midwife' his second book containing bolder prophetic utterances than any Lawrence whether of Derbyshire or of Arabia has ever dared to publish! [...] I gave up my walk yesterday afternoon and only posted my Letter to Mr White of White about his Book of Revelation.[62]

Powys's diary includes a number of references to White's last days; they seemed to have remained in close communication. He notes the 'mental and physical pain and fear endured by old White of White' on 22 December 1945 when, a week later:

> A Tragic letter from White of White saying that half a bottle of whiskey made his Cancer of the Prostate worse and he was due

for that operation when you 'excrete' through tubes on your front bowels. He asks my advice about suicide [...] on principle I defend Suicide but I would be too cowardly to kill myself.[63]

Then finally, the inevitable entry:

DEATH OF White of White may he rise to Immortality and Intense Happiness. O it is such a relief to me that he is out of it and I can only say may he be clear of the 'Bad Macro' and its Holy Terrors! He died on Candlemas. A letter from Mrs White of White has been answered by me – Aye! aye! but she says he smoked a CIGARETTE half an hour before he Died. May he rise from Death!!!! I shall tell my son to say a MASS for him.[64]

The *Ballymena Observer* carried the news:

The death took place on Sunday [3 February 1946] in a Belfast Nursing Home of Captain James Robert White DSO [...] For the past few years, Captain White has been living at the family residence at Broughshane. He is survived by his wife and two [sic] sons. The funeral took place from Wilson's Funeral Parlour to Broughshane Burying Ground. [...] The chief mourners were Mrs White (widow) and Mr T. White (son).[65]

There were three clergymen officiating, and the newspaper makes reference twice to his 'chequered career'. It could hardly have been a greater contrast to his father's funeral in 1912, when the king and queen paid their respects as Sir George's remains left London to arrive in Larne, and when the eventual route to the same grave took many hours passing closed shops along the way.[66] A substantial obituary with a detailed analysis of Sir George's career featured in *The Times*.[67] Jack White's passing was commented on in the 'Irishman's Diary' in *The Irish Times*. Although an affectionate portrayal, it was quite inaccurate, maintaining that White had won his DSO in the Great War, but it did comment that after that war he never 'achieved his former prominence':

he was a gay creature, always looking for some crusade in which he might take part, and constantly in revolt against authority of every kind. There could be no more charming man than Jack White when he liked! He could also be exceedingly obstinate. But he was always interesting, and that is more than most of us can say.[68]

The entire extent of White's estate came to £81 19s. 5d.[69] Alan, his son, recalled that he had sold his home-grown vegetables in the market in Broughshane in the latter years: 'I remember the mare that pulled the trap that was loaded with lettuce and other veg for sale in Broughshane. Much later on it occurred to me that no villager would have dared reject the offer.'[70] White himself recounted overcoming three recent financial crises in a letter in 1943, and said 'the next cannot be long delayed'.[71] Although not unusual for a country place like Broughshane at that time, his eldest son Tony wrote that 'we also had no electricity in Whitehall and led a fairly Spartan life. But it didn't do any of us any harm'.[72]

And, so, James Robert White, First Commandant of the Irish Citizen Army, follower of Tolstoy, and advocate of Connolly, had run his course. The man who had espoused unpopular causes all his life had found them a lonely place. But for all his reputation as a contrarian, even in radical activism, his correspondence with his niece shows a man more concerned with scripture than matters mundane. It was a religion however that had an interpretation that was distinctly his own, more Jungian than conventionally Christian. He was a man assailed by unfathomable forces who had the potential to make a mark on the great political movements in this world and singularly failed. But, failed from the conventional criteria of fame and worldly accomplishments; on another level, to another drumbeat, he maintained an integrity that, as Lady Amy said, was nobler than most people would even aspire to.

It is appropriate, I think, to leave the final valediction to his widow Noreen who wrote about him a few weeks after his death, in a letter to Pat English (his niece).

> You see, you knew Jack; so did your mother [White's sister, Gladys, Lady Napier] to a very great extent — a far greater extent than he ever gave her credit for, I knew him; and strange to say, my mother, once his bitter enemy, had an amazing understanding of that bundle of complexities, contradictions and inconsistencies that made up JRW. Just a handful of us; and the rest of the world interpreted him according to its respective taste. One has only to read the different articles on Jack which have appeared since his death, to realize how

little they understood him. The 'Northern Star' (Sinn Féin) presents him as an Irish Republican; the respectable *Irish Times* makes him out a British officer with Socialist convictions; 'Unity' (Communist) hails him as a comrade; the 'Irish News' (Catholic) speaks of him kindly as of a friend to the Church; and I have little doubt that if any anti-R.C. organ has written about him, they will laud him as a fearless opponent of Romish superstition.

The fact is they are all right; but they have only seized on a facet of this many-sided and most brilliant diamond and that one dazzling flash has blinded them to the size of the stone itself.

Jack used everyone, every organisation to further his own ends. Quite shamelessly he made use of his friends, their brains, their money, their social standing, with all the conscienceless acquisitiveness of a child. He had also the child's faith in God and the unshakeable conviction that whatever enterprise he was embarking on, was in fact not merely the work of JRW, but of JRW as divinely-inspired vehicle of the Almighty. Even if one calls it mad, there is no doubt it was a superb madness . . . [73]

Notes

INTRODUCTION
1. Randall McDonnell, *Cushendun in the Glens of Antrim* (Antrim: McDonnell, 1995), p.30.
2. Ward, Colin, *Anarchy in Action* (Freedom Press, London, 2001).
3. Peter Kropotkin, *Anarchism: A Collection of Revolutionary Writings,* Roger Baldwin (ed.), (New York: Dover, 2002), p.284, reprinted from *Encyclopaedia Britannica,* Eleventh Edition, 1905.
4. Saul Newman, *From Bakunin to Lacan: Anti–Authoritarianism and the Dislocation of Power* (Plymouth: Lexington, 2001), p.6.
5. J.R. White, *Misfit: An Autobiography* (London: Jonathan Cape, 1930), p.13.

CHAPTER 1
1. Arthur Mitchell, 'James Robert White', *Oxford Dictionary of National Biography* (ODNB) (Oxford: Oxford University Press, 2004).
2. Katy English Papers (hereafter KE), 527.
3. Sujit Bose, *Essays on Anglo–Indian Literature* (New Delhi: Northern Books, 2004), p.56.
4. J.R. White, *Misfit: An Autobiography* (London: Jonathan Cape, 1930), p.14.
5. KE, 1020–1.
6. Ibid., 391–2.
7. Ibid., 1002.
8. Sir Mortimer Durand, *The Life of Sir George White* 2 vols (London: Wm Blackwood, 1915). His only acknowledgment of Rose is in the introduction where he thanks 'Miss White for arranging some papers'.
9. KE, 1006 Rose White.
10. Mitchell, ODNB.
11. KE, 235–8. Excerpt from White's letter to his niece Pat English, *née* Napier, 11 June 1945.
12. Ibid., 1007. Rose White.
13. Ibid., 471–2.
14. *Belfast Morning Telegraph,* 15 February 1881.
15. KE, 1013.
16. KE, 1017–9.
17. D.H. Lawrence, *Aaron's Rod,* Mara Kalnins (ed.), (Cambridge: Cambridge University Press, 1988), pp.73ff.
18. Durand, vol. 1, p.37.

19. *London Gazette*, 3 June 1881.
20. KE, 496.
21. *The Times*, 25 June 1912.
22. KE, 496.
23. Dr Tony Redmond of Broughshane has a collection of memorabilia that include dishes, tins and playing cards with images of Sir George dated around that time.
24. *The Irish Times*, 1 July 1912.
25. *The Times*, 25 June 1912.
26. Durand, vol. 2, p.221.
27. Royal Collection. www.royalcollection.org.uk/eGallery/image no. 404852.jpg.
28. Durand, vol. 2, p.221.
29. KE, 410–426. Governor's Visitors' Book consisting of the autographs of those who visited the Rock.

CHAPTER 2

1. J.R. White, *Misfit: An Autobiography* (London: Jonathan Cape, 1930), p.13.
2. Ibid., p.14.
3. Ibid., pp.16–17.
4. Ibid.
5. Ibid.
6. Ibid.
7. Derrick White, review of *Misfit*.
8. Copies of Winchester School journals kindly provided by archivist Suzanne Foster. *The Wykehamist*, Number 311, April, 1895; 312, May, 1895; 316, October, 1895; 318, December, 1895.
9. *The Times*, 25 June 1912.
10. A.P. Thornton, *The Imperial Idea and Its Enemies* (London: Macmillan, 1959), p.125.
11. White, *Misfit*, p.26.
12. Ibid., p.28.
13. KE, 79–105.
14. Correspondence with Mr Alan White, second son of Jack White.
15. KE, 276.
16. Ibid., 181.
17. Ibid., 396, Diary of Lady Amy White, 21 February 1935.
18. White, *Misfit*, p.34.
19. Ibid.
20. Ibid., p.35.
21. Pakenham, Thomas, *The Boer War* (London: Abacus), p.xv.
22. Conan Doyle, Arthur, *The Great Boer War* (London: Smith, Elder and Company, 1900), p.2.
23. Hobson, J. A., *Imperialism: A Study* (Gordon Press, e–books, 1975), p.46.
24. See David Cannadine, *History in our Time*, Robert Young, *Postcolonialism: An Historical Introduction* – also note Lenin's 'extensive use' of Hobson.
25. Thomas Pakenham, *The Boer War* (New York: Perennial, 2001), pp.208–14.
26. White, *Misfit*, p.42.
27. Ibid., p.39.
28. Ibid., p.38.
29. Ibid., p.45.

30. Pakenham, p.339.
31. White, *Misfit*, p.41.
32. Ibid., p.42.
33. Pakenham, p.425.
34. Ibid.
35. Cited in ibid., p.427.
36. White, *Misfit*, pp.42–3.
37. Ibid., p.44.
38. Ibid., p.45.
39. Ibid., p.46.
40. Pakenham, pp.252–3.
41. White, *Misfit*, p.47.
42. Ibid., pp.50–61.
43. http://www.mod.uk/DefenceInternet/DefenceFor/Veterans/Medals/HonoursAndGallantryAwards.htm.
44. White, *Misfit*, p.61.
45. Ibid., p.61.
46. Ibid., p.48.
47. Ibid., p.47.
48. Copy of letter in Dr Tony Redmond's collection in Broughshane.

CHAPTER 3

1. White, *Misfit,*, p.62.
2. KE, 410–26, Governor General's Visitors Book 1900–1905.
3. KE, 51, Rose's letter to her uncle John White.
4. White, *Misfit*, pp.68, 70–1.
5. Ibid., p.66.
6. Ibid., p.69.
7. V.W. Baddeley, 'Charles Beresford', revised Paul G.Halpern, *Oxford Dictionary of National Biography* (ODNB).
8. KE, 410–26.
9. Ibid., 411.
10. V.W. Baddeley, revised Roger T. Stearn, 'Hedworth Lambert', ODNB.
11. KE, 419.
12. J. Slinn, 'Horace Farquhar', ODNB.
13. Sir Mortimer Durand, *The Life of Sir George White*, vol. 2 (London: Wm. Blackwood, 1915) p.244.
14. J.R. White, 'A Ride in Andalusia', *Irish Review* 3.26 (April 1913).
15. Durand, vol. 2, p.252.
16. White, *Misfit*. p.70.
17. KE, 511, Rose's letter to her Uncle John.
18. White, *Misfit*, p.70.
19. KE, 507, Rose's letter to her Uncle John.
20. White, *Misfit*, p.105.
21. R.B. McDowell, *Alice Stopford Green: A Passionate Historian* (Dublin: Figgis, 1967), p.94.
22. KE, 229–32, John Cowper Powys, letter to Pat English, 23 June 1943.
23. White, *Misfit*, p.88.
24. *Observer*, 6 July 1930, Review entitled 'The Heart of a Rebel' by John Still.

25. White, *Misfit,* p.64.
26. Ibid., p.65.
27. Ibid., pp.82–3.
28. Ibid., p.137.
29. Alan Watts, *In My Own Way: An Autobiography 1915–1965* (New York: Pantheon, 1972), p.17.
30. KE, 189–201.
31. Ibid.
32. From conversation with the White family at the memorial service in Edinburgh for Derrick, White's youngest son, in November 2007.
33. White, *Misfit,* p.63.
34. KE, 338–9.
35. Ibid., 79.
36. Ibid., 91.
37. Ibid., 88.
38. Ibid., 101.
39. Ibid., 85.
40. Ibid., 339.
41. Ibid.
42. White, *Misfit,* p.84.
43. Ibid., pp.92–3.
44. KE, 80–1.
45. Ibid., 82–3.
46. Ibid., 92.
47. Ibid., 95–6.
48. Ibid., 97–8.
49. Ibid., 100.
50. White, *Misfit,* p.93.
51. Ibid., p.94.
52. Ibid., p.95.
53. Ibid.
54. Ibid., p.103.
55. Ibid., p.104.
56. Ibid., p.106.
57. Katy English papers (KE), 441.
58. Ibid., 439.
59. Ibid.
60. White, *Misfit,* pp.105–6.
61. Ibid., p.107.
62. KE, 448.
63. White, *Misfit,* p.107. Alan, White's son, told me this letter was sold at Sotheby's in the 1970s. A copy of the letter made at the time has been misplaced.
64. Stephen Paget, rev. Caroline Overy, 'Victor Horsley', ODNB.

CHAPTER 4
1. White, *Misfit,* p.118.
2. Ibid., p.129.
3. Ibid., p.112.

4. Wallenstein Family. http://worldroots.com/foundation/personages/wallensteindesc.htm
5. White, *Misfit*, p.111.
6. Ibid., p.115.
7. Ibid., p.116.
8. *T.E. Lawrence Studies*, http://www.telawrence.net/telawrencenet/letters/1930/301018_rothenstein.htm.
9. Henry Summerfield (ed.), *Selections from the Contributions to the* 'Irish Homestead' *by G. W. Russell – Æ* (Gerrards Cross: Colin Smythe, 1978), vol. 2, pp.989–90.
10. White, *Misfit*, p.115.
11. Ibid.
12. Ibid., p.116.
13. ibid., p.119.
14. Ibid., p.130.
15. http://www.nationalarchives.gov.uk/A2A/records.aspx?cat=040–d5574&cid=–1#–1. The Croydon Brotherhood Church had been started by Nellie Shaw and friends along with a number of associated businesses. See Judy Greenway, 'No Place for Women? Anti-Utopianism and the Utopian Politics of the 1890s', *Geografiska Annaler, Series B, Human Geography* 84.3/4, Special Issue: *The Dialectics of Utopia and Dystopia* (2002), p.206.
16. Ibid., p.207
17. White, *Misfit*, p.146.
18. Ibid.
19. http://www.nationalarchives.gov.uk/A2A/records.aspx?cat=040–d5574&cid=–1~–1.
20. White, *Misfit*, p.146.
21. Sharon Butler, Bert Bundy, Peggy Bundy, 'Fact and Fiction: George Egerton and Nellie Shaw', *Feminist Review* 30 (Autumn, 1988), pp.25–35.
22. Ibid.
23. White, *Misfit*, p.149.
24. Greenway, p.206, citing Nellie Shaw, *Whiteway: A Colony on the Cotswolds* (London: Daniel, 1933), p.61.
25. White, *Misfit*, p.147.
26. Ibid., p.149.
27. Ibid., p.153.
28. Ibid., p.151.
29. Ibid., p.150.
30. Durand, vol. 2, pp.313–14.
31. White, *Misfit*, p.176.
32. Ibid., p.177.
33. Durand, vol. 2, p.312.
34. Ibid., p.254.
35. White, *Misfit*, p.142.
36. Ibid.
37. Ibid., p.143.
38. Ibid., p.138.
39. Ibid., p.143.
40. Ibid., p.160.
41. Ibid.
42. *The Times*, 7 December 1912.
43. Ibid.

44. Donal Nevin, *James Connolly: A Full Life* (Dublin: Gill and Macmillan, 2006), p.489.
45. Albert Meltzer, *I Couldn't Paint Golden Angels* (Edinburgh: AK Press, 1996), p.57.
46. White *Misfit*, p.169. This speech is also published in *The Irish Review* 2.23 (January 1913) pp.562ff.
47. Ibid., p.169.
48. Ibid., p.165.
49. Ibid., p.166.
50. Ibid., p.167.
51. Ibid., p.169.
52. Ibid., p.178.
53. Ibid., p.177.
54. Copy of letter to The Rt Hon. J.M.Andrews, PM of Northern Ireland, 16 December 1940, in possession of Dr Tony Redmond, Broughshane, Co. Antrim.
55. White, *Misfit,* p.181.
56. Emmet O'Connor, *Syndicalism in Ireland, 1917–23* (Cork: Cork University Press, 1988), p.6.
57. White, *Misfit,* p.182.
58. Connolly cited by White in *A Protestant Protest—lámh dearg abú,* privately printed pamphlet on Ballymoney dated 24 October 1913, p.14. Copy kindly lent by Dr Angus Mitchell.
59. J.R.B. McMinn, *Against the Tide* (Belfast: PRONI, 1985), p.130.
60. White, *Misfit,* p.183.
61. Ibid., p.184.
62. Ibid., p.183.
63. Ibid., p.185.
64. Ibid., p.184.
65. Ibid.
66. Ibid., p.185.
67. McMinn, p.131.
68. Ibid.
69. McDowell, pp.93–4.
70. Brian Inglis, *Roger Casement* (London: Hodder Stoughton, 1973), p.240.
71. McDowell, p.94.
72. McDowell, p.94.
73. Ibid.
74. McMinn, pp.133–4.
75. Ibid., p.133.
76. Ibid., p.xxvii.

CHAPTER 5

1. White, *Misfit,* p.186.
2. McMinn, p.132.
3. Ibid., p.135.
4. Ibid.
5. *The Irish Times,* 25 October 1913.
6. Ibid.
7. *A Protestant Protest,* p.20.
8. Ibid., p.23.
9. Ibid., pp.24–5.

10. Ibid., pp.26–7.
11. Ibid., pp.26–9.
12. *Where Casement would have stood To–day,* www.geocities.com/irelandscw/scw/jwhite2.htm.
13. Roger Casement, Letter to the Editor, *The Nation,* 11 October 1913.
14. *A Protestant Protest,* pp.29–33.
15. Ibid., p.34.
16. Ibid., p.35.
17. Letter to Alice Stopford Green, 1 November 1913. NLI Ms 10,464 (7).
18. *A Protestant Protest,* pp.37–8.
19. Ibid., p.39.
20. P.H. Pearse, 'From A Hermitage, November 1913', *Collected Works of Padraig Pearse: Political Writings and Speeches* (Dublin, Phoenix, n.d.), p.187.
21. White, *Misfit,* p.192. Quoting from *The Times,* 25 October 1913.
22. *A Protestant Protest,* pp.40–9.
23. Ibid., pp.51–2.
24. McMinn, p.131.
25. Ibid.
26. *A Protestant Protest,* p.16.
27. Ibid., p.10.
28. White, *Misfit,* pp.197–8.
29. *A Protestant Protest,* p.16.
30. Ibid., p.17.
31. McMinn, p.132.
32. White, *Misfit,* p.201.
33. Ibid., p.195.
34. *The Times,* 25 October 1913.
35. Ibid.
36. *Sunday Independent,* 26 October 1913.
37. *The Times,* 25 October 1913.
38. Cornelius O'Leary and Patrick Maume, *Controversial Issues in Anglo–Irish Relations 1910–1921* (Dublin: Four Courts Press, 2004), p.20.
39. *The Times,* 27 October 1913.
40. Ibid.
41. Ibid., 31 October 1913.
42. White, *Misfit,* p.196.
43. McMinn, p.132.
44. A.P. Thornton, *The Imperial Idea and Its Enemies* (London: Macmillan, 1959), p.135.
45. J.R. White, *Misfit: An Autobiography* (London: Jonathan Cape, 1930), p.202.
46. KE, 145–6.
47. White, *Misfit: An Autobiography,* p.202.
48. *The Irish Times,* 7 November 1913.
49. White, *Misfit: An Autobiography,* p.206. White describes this as a report of his speech but does not provide any details of who reported it. It differs slightly in tone from *The Irish Times* account.
50. *The Irish Times,* 7 November 1913.
51. White, *Misfit: An Autobiography,* p.205.

52. *The Irish Times,* 7 November 1913.
53. Ibid.
54. Ibid.
55. Ibid.
56. White, *Misfit: An Autobiography,* p.208.
57. Ibid.
58. White, *Misfit: An Autobiography,* p.209.
59. *The Irish Times,* 7 November 1913.
60. White, *Misfit: An Autobiography,* pp.209–10.
61. Ibid., p.207.
62. Ibid., p.213.

CHAPTER 6
1. Ibid., p.210.
2. Thomas Morrissey, *William Martin Murphy* (Dundalk: Historical Association of Ireland, Dundalgan Press, 1997), p.3.
3. Andy Bielenberg, 'Entrepreneurship, Power and Public Opinion In Ireland: The Career of William Martin Murphy', *Chronicon 2* 6 (1998): 1–35. www.ucc.ie/chronicon/bielen.htm.
4. Fergus A. D'Arcy, 'Larkin and the Dublin Lock–out', in Donal Nevin (ed.), *James Larkin: Lion of the Fold* (Dublin: Gill and Macmillan, 2006), p.39.
5. Ibid.
6. Dermot Keogh quoted in Bielenberg.
7. Letter to *The Irish Times,* 1 September 1913.
8. *The Irish Times,* 1 September 1913.
9. All quotations in this paragraph are from *The Irish Times,* 30 August 1913.
10. Ibid., 2 September 1913.
11. Ibid.
12. *The Times,* 4 September 1913.
13. Ibid., 17 October 1913.
14. Padraig Yeates, *Lockout, Dublin 1913* (Dublin: Gill and Macmillan, 2000), p.xxi. Yeates quotes from Arnold Wright, *Disturbed Dublin* (London: Longman Green, 1914). Cf. Yeates's references, same page, regarding Wright's report, which was reviewed by Connolly.
15. Nevin, p.217.
16. *The Times,* 22 October 1913.
17. Ibid.
18. Ibid.
19. Ibid.
20. Ibid.
21. C.J. Woods, 'David Alfred Chart' *Dictionary of Irish Biography,* vol 2 (Cambridge: Cambridge University Press, 2009).
22. *The Irish Times,* 7 March 1914.
23. Ibid.
24. Ibid.
25. Ibid.
26. Ibid.
27. Ibid., 7 March 1914.
28. Ibid.

29. James Connolly, *Collected Works* (Dublin: New Books Publications, 1987), vol. 1, p.256.
30. Donal Nevin, *James Connolly: A Full Life* (Dublin: Gill and Macmillan, 2006), p.129.
31. White, *Misfit*, p.215.
32. Ibid., p.217.
33. Ibid., p.218.
34. *The Times*, 22 October 1913.
35. Ibid.
36. *The Irish Times*, 23 October 1913.
37. Ibid.
38. Ibid.
39. Ibid., 24 October 1913.
40. *The Times*, 25 October 1913.
41. White, *Misfit*, p.219.
42. Ibid., p.218.
43. R.F. Foster, *W.B. Yeats: The Apprentice Mage* (Oxford: Oxford University Press, 1997), p.500.
44. *The Irish Times*, 23 October 1913.
45. Yeates, p.259.
46. *The Irish Times*, 23 October 1913.
47. Ibid., 27 October 1913.
48. *The Times*, 25 October 1913.
49. White, *Misfit*, p.215.
50. Ibid., p.214.
51. Robert J.C. Young, *Postcolonialism: An Historical Introduction* (Oxford: Blackwell, 2001), p.107. The quotation is from Marx and Engels, *Ireland and the Irish Question*.

CHAPTER 7

1. White, *Misfit*, p.220. Carl Jung, the Swiss psychologist and putative mystic, wrote about 'amazing coincidences which seemed to suggest the idea of an acausal parallelism (a synchronicity, as I later called it)', in *Memories, Dreams and Reflections* (London: Fontana, 1995), p.407. White's autobiography uses Jungian terminology in a number of places.
2. Ibid., p.221.
3. *The Irish Times*, 5 September 1913.
4. Letter written by White, *Irish Worker*, 27 December 1913.
5. *The Irish Times*, 8 November 1913.
6. Ibid.
7. Ibid.
8. *Irish Independent*, 10 November 1913.
9. Ibid.
10. Ibid., 12 November 1913.
11. Ibid.
12. Ibid., 14 November 1913.
13. Report on the Royal Commission on the Rebellion in Ireland 1916 (CD8311), p.110.
14. White, *Misfit*, p.262.
15. Ibid., p.261.
16. White, *Misfit*. p.311.
17. J.R. White, *Where Casement would have stood To–day*. http://spanishcivilwar.tripod.com/jwhite2.htm.
18. White, *Misfit*, p.215.
19. KE, 146.

20. White, *Misfit*, p.226.
21. Ibid., pp.226–7.
22. Andrew Boyd, *Jack White: First Commander, Irish Citizen Army* (Oxford: Parchment, Donaldson Archives, 2001), p.18.
23. Ibid., p.241.
24. See later discussion of his ambulance driving in 1914–1915, also conversations and correspondence with his sons Tony and Alan. White's letter to the press 3 September 1943, KE, 127–8.
25. Boyd, pp.18–19.
26. White, *Misfit*, p.267.
27. *The Irish Times*, 13 January 1914.
28. White, *Misfit*, p.274.
29. Flann Campbell, *The Dissenting Voice* (Belfast: Blackstaff, 1991), p.420.
30. J.R. White, *A Revolutionary Life*, p.240, citing CNT–AIT Boletin de Informacion. no.15, 11 November 1936.
31. Ibid., p.241.
32. Young, p.306.
33. Eric Hobsbawm, *The Age of Empire: 1875–1914* (London: Abacus, 2002), p.143.
34. White letter for publication to press, 3 September 1943, KE, 127–8.
35. Emmet O'Connor, *A Labour History of Ireland 1824–2000* (Dublin: University College Dublin Press, 2011), p.100.
36. R.M. Fox, *History of the Irish Citizen Army* (Dublin: Duffy, 1943), p.68.
37. Boyd, p.23.
38. Ibid., p.70.
39. P.Ó Cathasaigh [Sean O'Casey], *The Story of the Irish Citizen Army* (Dublin: Talbot, 1971), p.69.
40. Ibid., p.55.
41. Ibid., p.52.
42. White, *Misfit*, p.249.
43. Ibid.
44. George Woodcock, *Anarchism* (Ontario: Broadview Press, 2004), p.185.
45. Leo Tolstoy, *The Kingdom of God Is Within You* (New York: Dover, 2006), p.151.
46. White, *Misfit*, pp.275–6.
47. *The Irish Times*, 2 December 1913.
48. White, *Misfit*, p.276.
49. Nevin, *Connolly*, p.96.
50. Ibid., p.279.
51. Ibid., p.278.
52. Ibid., pp.286–7.
53. White, *Misfit*, p.256.
54. James Joll, *The Anarchists* (Cambridge, Massachusetts: Harvard University Press, 1980), p.133, citing anonymous introduction to Leo Tolstoy, *La guerre et le service obligatoire* (Brussels, 1896).

CHAPTER 8

1. Helga Woggan, 'Interpreting James Connolly 1916–23', in Fintan Lane and Donal O'Driscoll (eds), *Politics and the Irish Working Class 1830–1945* (Basingstoke: Palgrave, 2005), p.173.

2. Sorel, Georges *Reflection on Violence*, (Cambridge University Press, Cambridge, 2002), p.107.
3. Graham, p.203.
4. George Woodcock, 'Syndicalism Defined', in George Woodcock (ed.), *The Anarchist Reader* (Glasgow, Fontana, 1980). p.208.
5. Emmet O'Connor, *Syndicalism in Ireland 1917–1923* (Cork: Cork University Press, 1988), p.4.
6. Woodcock, *The Anarchist Reader*, p.208.
7. Ibid., p.6.
8. Bernard Ransom, *Connolly's Marxism* (London: Pluto Press, 1980), p.41.
9. O'Connor, p.5.
10. Ó Cathasaigh, p.22.
11. *The Irish Times*, 14 October 1910. Citing article from *Daily Mail*.
12. James Connolly, *Labour in Irish History* (Dublin: Irish Transport and General Workers Union, 1934), pp.214–15.
13. Ibid., p.xvi.
14. Connolly, *Labour*, pp.3–4.
15. C. Desmond Greaves, *The Life and Times of James Connolly*, (London: Lawrence and Wishart, 1961), p.167.
16. W.K. Anderson, *James Connolly and the Irish Left* (Dublin: Irish Academic Press,1994), p. 37.
17. Albert Meltzer, *I Couldn't Paint Golden Angels* (Edinburgh: AK Press, 1996), p.57.
18. http://libcom.org/history/kavanagh-mat-1876-1954#comment-338235.
19. http://flag.blackened.net/revolt/anarchists/jackwhite.html.
20. Anderson, p.39.
21. Peter Marshall , *Demanding the Impossible: A History of Anarchism* (London: Fontana, 1993), pp.417, 480.
22. Anderson, p.138.
23. Greaves, p.139.
24. Keith Laybourn, *A History of British Trade Unionism* (Stroud: Sutton Publishing, 1997), p.104.
25. J.R. White, *Misfit: An Autobiography* (London: Jonathan Cape, 1930), p.241.
26. *The Irish Times*, 19 November 1913.
27. William O'Brien Papers, National Library of Ireland (NLI), MS15673, no. 40.
28. White, *Misfit*, p.242.
29. Ibid.
30. George Dangerfield, *The Damnable Question: A Study in Anglo–Irish Relations* (London: Constable, 1977), pp.335–8.
31. White, *Misfit*, p.242.
32. *The Irish Times*, 19 November 1913.
33. Ibid., 8 November 1913.
34. White, *Misfit*, p.254.
35. Bertram Collingwood, Professor of Mathematics, Trinity College Dublin, nephew of Charles Dodgson author of *Alice in Wonderland*. http://www.tcd.ie/Communications/news/news.php?headerID=486&vs_date=2006-12-1.
36. Ibid., p.256.
37. *The Irish Times*, 28 August 1943.
38. Ibid., 20 November 1913.
39. White, *Misfit*, p.227.

40. *The Irish Times*, 28 August 1943.
41. Ibid.
42. R.M. Fox, *The History of the Irish Citizen Army* (Dublin: Duffy, 1943), pp.109–10.
43. Donal Nevin, *James Connolly: A Full Life* (Dublin: Gill and Macmillan, 2006), pp.578–9.
44. Dangerfield, p.154.
45. *The Royal Commission on the Rebellion in Ireland* 1916, Government White Paper – ref. cd8311, Minutes of Evidence pp.110–11.
46. Fox, p.45.
47. White, *Misfit*, p.250.
48. Ibid., p.258.

CHAPTER 9

1. P.Ó Cathasaigh [Sean O'Casey], *The Story of the Irish Citizen Army* (Dublin: The Talbot Press, 1971), p.4.
2. Ibid., pp.1–2.
3. Ibid., pp.5–6.
4. White, *Misfit*, pp.262–3.
5. See examples like the 'runaway army'. Frank Robbins, *Under the Starry Plough: Recollections of the Irish Citizen Army* (Dublin: Academy Press, 1977), p.36.
6. Ó Cathasaigh, p.9. This date should be 1913.
7. White, *Misfit*, p.264.
8. White, *Misfit*, p.100. White uses terms like 'extravert' and 'introvert' here seeing them, as Jung did, as a correcting balance by the unconscious. Jung was the first to use these terms.
9. R.B. McDowell, *Alice Stopford Green: A Passionate Historian* (Dublin: Figgis, 1967), p.94.
10. KE, 535 – Letter from Tony White to Linda Simpson, 25 January 1992. Dr Tony Redmond Collection.
11. Alan White, White's surviving son, states that a letter from Tolstoy was auctioned in the 1970s. There was a copy of the letter but at the time of writing it has not come to light.
12. White, *Misfit*, p.265.
13. Ibid.
14. Ibid.
15. Ibid., p.266.
16. *The Irish Times*, 28 November 1913.
17. Ibid., 1 December 1913.
18. Ibid.
19. Ibid.
20. Ibid.
21. Ibid.
22. Ibid.
23. White, *Misfit*, p.226.
24. Nevin, *Connolly*, p.489.
25. *The Irish Times*, 1 December 1913.
26. Ibid.
27. White, *Misfit*, p.256.
28. *The Irish Times*, 2 December 1913.
29. Ibid., 8 December 1913.
30. *Southern Star*, 6 December 1913.
31. Ibid.

32. *The Irish Times*, 23 December 1913.
33. Ibid.
34. *The Irish Worker*, 27 December 1913.
35. Ibid.
36. *The Irish Times*, 12 January 1914.
37. Ibid.
38. Ibid.
39. Ibid.
40. White, *Misfit*, p.272.
41. *The Irish Times*, 13 January 1914.
42. White, *Misfit*, p.273.
43. *The Irish Times*, 13 January 1914.
44. Ibid., 15 January 1914.
45. Padraig Yeates, *Lockout: Dublin 1913* (Dublin: Gill and Macmillan, 2000), pp.434–5.
46. White, *Misfit*, p.275.
47. Ibid., p.276.
48. KE, 536, Letter from Tony White to Linda Simpson, 25 January 1992.
49. George M. Ll. Davies Collection, no. 169. National Library of Wales, from a pamphlet by Davies entitled *Ireland and Peace Politics*, pp.9–10.
50. White, *Misfit*, p.277.
51. Ibid.
52. Ibid., p.306.
53. *The Irish Times*, 26 January 1914.
54. Ibid., 24 January 1914.
55. White, *Misfit*, p.281.
56. Yeates, p.521.

CHAPTER 10

1. White, *Misfit*, pp.259–60.
2. Ibid.
3. Ibid., p.259.
4. Todd May, *The Political Philosophy of Poststructuralist Anarchism* (University Park, Pennsylvania: Pennsylvania University Press, 1994), pp.5–13, passim.
5. White, *Misfit*, p.141. Although there is no evidence available that White was aware of Gurdjieff, it would be very surprising if he had not heard of him considering his interest in the philosopher Henri Bergson and much lesser figures like Hoené Wronski mentioned in his chapter on Mental Evolution.
6. Ibid., p.260.
7. *The Irish Times*, 17 February 1914.
8. Ibid., 14 March 1914.
9. White, *Misfit*, p.288.
10. Ibid., pp.288–92.
11. Robbins, p.36.
12. *The Irish Times*, 14 March 1914.
13. George M.Ll. Davies Collection, no.169, National Library of Wales. Reference courtesy of Dr Jen Llwelyn.
14. *The Irish Times*, 14 March 1914.
15. White, *Misfit*, p.290.

16. Andrew Boyd, *Jack White: First Commander Irish Citizen Army* (Oxford: Donaldson Archives, 2001), p.27.
17. Fox, p.50.
18. White, *Misfit*, p.296.
19. Ibid., pp.298–9.
20. Ibid., p.303.
21. Ibid.
22. Ibid., p.264.
23. Ibid., p.303.
24. Ibid., p.301.
25. Ibid., pp.302–3.
26. Ibid., p.300.
27. *The Irish Times*, 9 April 1914.
28. White, *Misfit*, p.302.
29. *The Irish Times*, 9 April 1914.
30. *The Irish Times*, 17 September 1963.
31. Thomas Johnson Papers, National Library of Ireland, MS 17237–8.
32. Emmet Larkin, *James Larkin 1876 –1947: Irish Labour Leader* (London: Routledge and Kegan Paul, 1977), p.126, citing 'Report of the Committee of Inquiry on the Royal Irish Constabulary and the Dublin Metropolitan Police', *Parliamentary Papers*, 1914, XLIV (Cd. 7421).
33. *Freeman's Journal*, 21 April 1914.
34. Ibid.
35. Ó Cathasaigh, p.11.
36. White, *Misfit*, p.304.
37. Ibid., pp.304–5.
38. Ibid., p.306.
39. Ó Cathasaigh, p.11.
40. Ibid., p.12.
41. White, *Misfit*, pp.250–1.
42. Ibid., p.14.
43. Ibid., p.15.
44. Boyd, p.22.
45. Ibid.
46. Ibid., p.23.
47. William O'Brien Papers, NLI, MS15673, no. 40.
48. Ó Cathasaigh, pp.17–18.
49. Emmet O'Connor, *Syndicalism in Ireland, 1917–23* (Cork: Cork University Press, 1988), p.x. O'Connor states regarding the origin of the name: 'the Irish Trade Union Congress was formed in 1894 and decided to add the words "and Labour Party" to its title in 1912. In 1918 it again changed its name to the Irish Labour Party and Trade Union Congress, until in 1930 it reverted to its original title'.
50. William O'Brien papers, NLI, MS15673, no. 39.
51. Ibid., pp.20–1.
52. Fintan Lane, *The Origins of Modern Irish Socialism 1881–96* (Cork: Cork University Press, 1997), p.1.
53. Conor Kostick, *Revolution in Ireland: Popular Militancy 1917–1923*, Second Edition. (Cork: Cork University Press, 2009), p.118.

54. Lane, p.231.
55. Boyd, p.23.
56. David Krause (ed.), *The Letters of Sean O'Casey* (London: Cassell, 1975), p.47: The letter was published in the *Irish Worker* on 7 March 1914.
57. Fox, pp.65–6.
58. Ibid., p.67.
59. See *The Irish Times*, 10 May 1912, for the detailed arguments. It summarised the judgment: 'In passing sentence, the judge expressed the hope that the trial would have the effect of bringing home to the prisoner the fact that the law on this subject was not what he had suggested it to be and that he would refrain from bringing himself within the statute in future. The incitement of which he had been found guilty was one of which would bring grave punishment on those who followed it. His conduct was mischievous in the highest degree.'

CHAPTER 11

1. White, *Misfit*, p.208.
2. Larkin, Emmet. *James Larkin: 1876–1947, Irish Labour Leader* (Routledge and Kegan Paul, London, 1977). p.xvi. Larkin left for New York in early November 1914 'planning to stay for only a short time, but he remained nearly eight and a half years'.
3. Ó Cathasaigh, p.19.
4. Ibid., p.23.
5. Ibid., p.25.
6. Ibid., p.26.
7. Ibid.
8. *The Irish Times*, 4 May 1914.
9. Jack White, letter to the editor, *The Irish Times*, 5 May 1914.
10. White, *Misfit*, p.306.
11. Ó Cathasaigh, pp.41–2.
12. White, letter to unknown paper reviewing Fox, 3 September 1943, original in possession of Dr Tony Redmond, Broughshane, Co. Antrim.
13. George Woodcock, *Anarchism* (Ontario: Broadview Press, 2004), p.270.
14. White, letter, 3 September 1943.
15. Ibid.
16. Ibid.
17. *The Irish Times*, 15 May 1914. This work will follow the convention of using 'National' to distinguish the Volunteers up to the split and thereafter for the Redmondites. 'Irish' refers to the rebels who took part in the Rising.
18. Note of the Statements in Captain White's Case Marked X, Brixton Jail, 25 May 1916, National Library of Ireland (NLI) MS 13,088 (4/iv) .
19. Cork City and County Archives. Ref.IECCCA/PR12, p.3.
20. Bureau of Military History, Doc. No. WS 971 p.22
21. Ibid., pp.22–4.
22. *Irish Independent*, 27 May 1914.
23. Ibid.
24. *Irish Independent*, 30 May 1914.
25. Ibid., 1 June 1914.
26. *Freeman's Journal*, 8 June 1914.
27. *Southern Star*, 13 June 1914.

28. J.R. White, *Misfit: An Autobiography* (London: Jonathan Cape, 1930), p.307.
29. George Dangerfield, *The Damnable Question: A Study in Anglo–Irish Relations* (London: Constable, 1977), p.133.
30. Ibid., p.135.
31. *Freeman's Journal*, 2 February 1914.
32. White, *Misfit*, p.307.
33. P.Ó Cathasaigh [Sean O'Casey], *The Story of the Irish Citizen Army* (Dublin: The Talbot Press, 1971), p.42.
34. *Manchester Guardian*, 18 May 1914.
35. White, *Misfit*, p.307.
36. *Manchester Guardian*, 6 July 1914.
37. *Freeman's Journal*, 4 July 1914.
38. White, *Misfit*, pp.308–9.
39. Ibid., p.308.
40. *Manchester Guardian*, 6 July 1914.
41. White, *Misfit*, p.309.
42. Ibid., p.310.
43. *Irish Independent*, 9 July 1914.
44. *Freeman's Journal*, 27 July 1914.
45. White, *Misfit*, p.316.
46. Ibid.
47. Ibid., pp.322–4.
48. Ibid., p.321.
49. *The Irish Times*, 9 September 1914.
50. Dangerfield, p.121.

CHAPTER 12

1. White, *Misfit*, pp.316–19.
2. Ibid., p.320.
3. *The Irish Times*, 9 September 1914.
4. White, *Misfit*, p.319.
5. *Leitrim Observer*, 12 September 1914.
6. White, *Misfit*, pp.319, 322.
7. Ibid., p.329.
8. Ibid., p.331.
9. Ibid., p.332.
10. Ibid., pp.333, 335.
11. Ibid., p.334.
12. The Royal Commission on the Rebellion in Ireland,1916.cd8311, p.112.
13. *The Irish Times*, 2 October 1914.
14. Ibid.
15. Joseph P. Finnan, *John Redmond and Irish Unity 1912–1918* (Syracuse: Syracuse University Press, 2008), p.11.
16. Ibid., p.129.
17. Casement–Green Letters, MS 10,464, 31 January 1914, NLI.
18. Finnan, p.132
19. Ibid.
20. Ibid.

21. White, *Misfit*, pp.321, 329.
22. Ibid., p.332.
23. Dangerfield, pp.122–3.
24. Ibid., p.131.
25. Ibid., pp.133–4.
26. Finnan, p.88.
27. White, *Misfit*, p.335.
28. Ibid., p.336.
29. Ibid., p.340.
30. Ibid., p.331.
31. Ibid., p.340.
32. Robert C. J. Young, *Postcolonialism: An Historical Introduction* (London: Blackwell, 2001), p.306.
33. Finnan, p.86.
34. Ibid., p.85.
35. *Irish Independent,* 11 August 1914.
36. White, *Misfit*, p.338.
37. Ibid., p.339, citing Freud's *Thoughts on War and Death*.
38. Ibid., p.340.
39. Ibid., p.251.
40. Ibid., p.341.
41. Ibid., pp.340–2.
42. Ibid., p.343.
43. Ibid., p.345.
44. George M. Ll. Davies Collection, no. 169, National Library of Wales, from a pamphlet by Davies entitled *Ireland and Peace Politics,* pp.9–10.

CHAPTER 13

1. White, *Misfit*, p.345.
2. *Manchester Guardian,* 25 May 1916.
3. Ibid.
4. White, *Misfit*, p.345.
5. *Manchester Guardian,* 25 May 1916.
6. Ibid.
7. White, *Misfit*, p.345.
8. George M. Ll. Davies Collection, no. 169.
9. *Manchester Guardian,* 2 June 1916.
10. *Irish Independent,* 7 September 1916.
11. Andrew Boyd, *Jack White: First Commander Irish Citizen Army* (Oxford: Donaldson Archives, 2001), p.32.
12. *Irish Independent,* 11 July 1917.
13. Ibid.
14. Ibid.
15. Anne Marreco, *The Rebel Countess: The Life and Times of Constance Markievicz* (Philadelphia: Chilton Books, 1962), p.224,
16. Ibid., pp.224, 233.
17. Thomas Johnson Papers, NLI, MS 17238.
18. Ibid.

19. Boyd, p.33.
20. Thomas Johnson papers, NLI, MS 17238. The attempt at conscription related by *Irish Independent* on 6 September 1916, see above, may have been one such incident.
21. Ibid., MS 17237.
22. Excerpts from Powys's Diary, 21 March 1942. Kindly provided by Morin Krissdotir, his biographer.
23. Powys's Diary.
24. Lawrence, D.H.,*Aaron's Rod*, Kalnins Mara (ed.), Cambridge University Press, Cambridge 1988.
25. DHL pp73ff.
26. p.201 Aldington, Richard, *Portrait of a Genius, But* ... London 1950.
27. P.242 ibid.
28. Ed. Kinkead Weekes, *Lawrence –Vol.2*. Cambridge University Press: Cambridge.
29. Manning, Mary, *Mount Venus*. Houghton Mifflin Company, The Riverside Press, Cambridge, Massachusetts, 1938.
30. MM Op.cit. p.359.
31. There are too many references about White that could not be described as coincidental. For example, in a passage relating Considine's family history, much obfuscated to mislead the litigious minded, Simla is mentioned as the place where Mabel, Bob's first wife came from(p.158). Although Dollie, White's wife came from Gibraltar, this little known location in India was where Sir George had his headquarters. Cockeye mentions (also p.158) beating his wife 'with a cricket stump one night when she started examining me in the Thirty Nine Articles'. White had revealed slapping his wife when first married in an argument over Christ. Certainly Ms Manning had gone to the trouble of reading some of *Misfit*.
32. MM Op.cit. pp.62–4.
33. A small cache of documents consisting of correspondence between Jonathan Cape, publishers and H. Rubinstein & Co. Solicitors and containing legal opinion by Denis Johnston were discovered by Ms Jean Rose, Chief Librarian, Random House Group, owners of Jonathan Cape. I am so grateful to her for both her helpfulness and initiative and to Ms F. Howe, Ms Manning's daughter for her kind permission to use these papers.
34. *Manchester Guardian,* 14 December 1918.
35. J.R. White, *The Significance of Sinn Féin: Psychological, Political, and Economic* (Dublin: Martin Lester, 1919).
36. *Irish Independent,* 30 June 1919. The article is signed S. O'C., that is, Sean O'Casey.
37. Joseph J. Lee *Ireland 1912–1985* (Cambridge: Cambridge University Press, 1989), p.41.
38. *The Irish Times,* 9 November 1918.
39. Ibid.
40. Lee, p.41.
41. White *Sinn Féin.*
42. Ibid.
43. *Irish Independent,* 30 June 1919.
44. White, *Sinn Féin,* p.4.
45. Ibid.
46. Ibid.
47. Dangerfield, p.309.
48. White, *Sinn Féin,* p.5.
49. Ibid.
50. Ibid.

CHAPTER 14

1. Tolstoy, Leo *The Kingdom of God is Within You* (Dover, New York, 2006) p.61.
2. Ibid. p.150.
3. *Connaught Tribune,* 3 April 1920.
4. Emmet O'Connor, *A Labour History of Ireland 1824–1960* (Dublin: Gill and Macmillan, 1992), p.107.
5. Ibid.
6. Ibid., p.102.
7. Ibid.
8. Conor Kostick, *Revolution in Ireland: Popular Militancy 1917–1923* (Cork: Cork University Press, 2009), p.151.from *ILPTUC Reports,* 1918, pp.15–16.
9. *The Irish Times,* 4 November 1918.
10. Ibid.
11. Ibid.
12. *Connaught Tribune,* 3 April 1920, as are the previous quotations.
13. Notes written in Brixton Prison, Roger Casement Papers, National Library of Ireland, MS 13,088 (4/iv). Francis Joseph Bigger, a friend of Casement's, was a Belfast solicitor and noted Ulster antiquarian.
14. *Connaught Tribune,* 3 April 1920.
15. Ibid.
16. Ibid.
17. Ibid.
18. *Manchester Guardian,* 13 April 1920.
19. Ibid.
20. Ibid.
21. Ibid.
22. F.S.L. Lyons, *Ireland since the Famine* (London: Fontana, 1973), p.394.
23. *Manchester Guardian,* 17 April 1920.
24. Ibid.,18 April 1920.
25. Ibid.
26. *The Watchword of Labour,* 19 June 1920.
27. This could also be suggested to be a forerunner of the later poststructuralist notion of meta–narrative.
28. Ibid.
29. Andrew Boyd, *Jack White: First Commander Irish Citizen Army* (Oxford: Donaldson Archives, 2001), p.37.
30. *Nenagh Guardian,* 11 December 1920.
31. *Freeman's Journal,* 28 April 1921.
32. Ibid.
33. *Manchester Guardian,* 30 April 1921.
34. Fanning, Ronan. *Fatal Path: British Government and Irish Revolution 1910–1922.* (Faber & Faber, London, 2013) Chaps 1,2 and 3.
35. Public Record Office of Northern Ireland (PRONI). PM/2/23/131.
36. *The Irish Times,* 21 January 1922.
37. Boyd, p.37.
38. *The Irish Times,* 26 June 1922.
39. Letter JRW to Sir James Craig. 22 July 1922. PRONI . PM/2/23/131.
40. Letter from Col G. Moore–Irvine to Lt Col W.B. Spender, Secretary to the Cabinet of Northern Ireland. 26 July 1922. PRONI. PM/2/23/131.

41. Letter, JRW to Lt Col W. B. Spender, 4 August 1922. PRONI.PM/2/23/131.
42. Lee, J.J., *Ireland 1912–1985: Politics and Society.* (Cambridge University Press, Cambridge, 1990). pp.3 –4.
43. Ibid.

CHAPTER 15
1. *The Irish Times,* 16 September 1922.
2. Ibid.
3. Ibid.
4. *The Irish Times,* 28 November 1922.
5. Letters, White to Spender and replies, 20 to 31 October, 1922. PRONI. PM/2/23/131/
6. *Freeman's Journal,* 4 June 1923.
7. Anton McCabe, 'Captain Jack White in Donegal', *Labour History News* 8 (Autumn 1992) http://irelandscw.com/ibvol-JWhite4.htm
8. J.R. White, *Misfit: An Autobiography* (London: Jonathan Cape, 1930), p.311.
9. *The Irish Times,* 14 June 1923.
10. White, *Misfit,* p.311.
11. Ibid.
12. *The Irish Times,* 16 September 1922.
13. White, *Misfit,* p.311.
14. *Freeman's Journal,* 26 June 1923.
15. Ibid.
16. Boyd, p.37.
17. McCabe.
18. Ibid.
19. *The Irish Times,* 19 October 1923.
20. Ibid., 30 September 1978.
21. Ibid.
22. PRONI PM/2/23/131.
23. PRONI letters PM2/23/131 – I presume the reference to De Valera's action refers to his anti–Treaty stance rather than any later position he adopted. At the writing of this letter, he had only been released from Arbour Hill prison a couple of months before where he had spent the previous twelve months. Prior to that deValera had been on the run during what is now termed the Civil War.
24. Boyd, p.38.
25. Emmet O'Connor, *Syndicalism in Ireland 1917–1923* (Cork: Cork University Press, 1988), p.132.
26. Ibid., p.129
27. Georges Sorel, *Reflections on Violence,* Jeremy Jennings (ed.), (Cambridge: Cambridge University Press, 2002), pp.10–11.
28. Robert J.C. Young, *Postcolonialism: An Historical Introduction* (Oxford: Blackwell, 2001), p.303.
29. J.R. White, *The Meaning of Anarchism* (London: Freedom Group, 1937), p.3. Reproduced in http://struggle.ws/anarchists/jackwhite/texts/anarchism.html. White says 'spontaneous voluntarism […] elemental vitality [are] indispensible features in a revolution'.
30. O'Connor, *Syndicalism,* p.129.
31. Ibid.,p.135.
32. Ibid.

33. *Manchester Guardian,* 16 October 1924.
34. Arthur Mitchell, *Labour in Irish Politics 1890–1930: The Irish Labour Movement in an Age of Revolution* (New York: Barnes, 1974), p.234.
35. *The Irish Times,* 8 September 1930.
36. KE (img) 2297–2302.
37. *The Irish Times,* 30 October 1925.
38. *Manchester Guardian,* 30 October 1925.
39. *The Irish Times,* 30 October 1925.
40. James Kelly, *Bonfires on the Hillsides* (Belfast: Fountain, 1995), p.68.
41. *Manchester Guardian,* 19 September 1931.
42. Ibid.
43. *The Irish Times,* 19 September 1931.
44. Ibid.
45. Ibid.
46. Ibid.
47. *Irish News,* 19 September 1931.
48. PRONI HA/32/1/608 – Secret Report by RUC 13 Oct 1931.
49. Kelly, p.68.
50. PRONI HA/32/1/608 – Secret Report by RUC 13 Oct 1931.

CHAPTER 16

1. PRONI HA/32/1/608 – 6 October 1931.
2. Ibid – JRW letter to Dawson Bates, 16 October 1931.
3. *NI Hansard,* 15 May 1934, volume 16, p.1607.
4. PRONI HA/32/1/608 – Minute Sheet to Minister, handwritten, 23 Feb 1934.
5. Ibid – Ministry of Home Affairs to Sam Kyle, 12 March 1934.
6. PRONI HA/32/1/608 – JRW to Dawson Bates, 29 April 1935.
7. PRONI HA/32/1/608 – Minute Sheet, 23 Feb. 1934.
8. Ibid.
9. Kate O'Malley, *Ireland, India and Empire: Indo–Irish Radical Connections, 1919–1964* (Manchester: Manchester University Press, 2008), p.40.
10. PRONI HA/32/1/608.
11. Arthur Mitchell, 'James Robert White (1879–1946)', *Oxford Dictionary of National Biography* (Oxford: Oxford University Press, 2004).
12. Patricia Wheeler, email to author, 4 July 2007.
13. Ibid.
14. Derrick White, 'Review of Misfit', June 2005. Sent to author by Derrick in August 2006.
15. KE, 313. Letter from White to Pat Napier, 6 October 1939.
16. *Ballymena Guardian,* 3 August 1989.
17. KE, 539. Letter from Tony White to Linda Simpson.
18. Alan White, email to author, 28 December 2007.
19. Alan White, email to author, February 2008.
20. KE, 539. Letter from Tony White to Linda Simpson.
21. A conversation with author, November 2007.
22. A conversation with author, June 2007.
23. Alan White, email to author February 2008.
24. NLI – EC Reeves papers, box 3. Thank you to Luke Kirwan, UCC.
25. KE, 253 –4. Letter from White to Pat Napier, 20 July 1942.

26. Derrick White, 'Review of *Misfit*', June 2005.
27. Ibid.
28. Boyd, p.40.
29. Alan Mac Simóin, *Jack White: Irish Anarchist Who Organised Irish Citizens Army*. http://flag.blackened.net/ws/ws50_jack.html
30. Ibid.
31. Jack White, 'A Rebel in Barcelona: Jack White's First Spanish Impressions', *CNT–AIT Boletin de Informacion* 15 (11 November 1936). http://www.katesharpleylibrary.net/tb2sdz.
32. Albert Meltzer, *I Couldn't Paint Golden Angels: Sixty Years of Commonplace Life* (Edinburgh: AK Press, 1996), p.79.
33. Ibid.
34. Ibid., pp.57–8.
35. *Manchester Guardian*, 12 October 1936.
36. Mac Simóin, *White*.
37. Emmet O'Connor, NUI, Galway, 31 January 2011.
38. KE, 242. Fragment of letter by White to the press, or at least for public consumption, October 1939.
39. White, *Misfit*, p.256.
40. McGarry, p.71.
41. Meltzer, p.57.
42. KE, 317. Letter from White to Pat Napier, 10 April 1940.
43. *The Irish Times*, 28 January 1939.
44. Ibid.
45. *The Irish Times*, 28 January 1939.
46. KE, 536. Letter from Tony White to Linda Simpson, 1992.
47. *The Irish Times*, 28 January 1939.
48. KE, 317. Letter from White to Pat Napier, 10 April 1940.
49. KE, 333–7. *Bulletin of CIVIC* 1.8 (15 October 1941), p.6.
50. Ibid., p.5.
51. Ibid., p.8.
52. Ibid., p.9.
53. Copy of letter from Inspector–General's Office, RUC, Belfast to Captain White, Broughshane, their reference number N/W/3, 8 June 1940. Collection of Dr Tony Redmond of Broughshane.
54. Copy of letter Grand Central Hotel, Belfast headed note paper, from J.R. White to the Prime Minister of Northern Ireland, 16 December 1940. Collection of Dr Tony Redmond of Broughshane.
55. *Ballymena Guardian*, 3 August 1989. I would like to express my grateful appreciation to 'Ireland and the Spanish Civil War' web site http://irelandscw.com/docs–NewBiblio.htm who kept this article along with others in the public domain.
56. Ibid.
57. Ibid.
58. Extract from John Cowper Powys's diary, 10 January 1945, kindly provided by Powys's biographer Morine Krissdotir.
59. Ibid., 19 March 1945.
60. Ibid., 6 October 1942.
61. Ibid., 14 September 1941.

62. Ibid., 17 November 1941.
63. Ibid., 28 and 29 December 1945. (Two days' journal entries together).
64. Ibid., 7 and 9 February 1946. (Two days' journal entries together).
65. *Ballymena Observer,* 8 February 1946.
66. *The Irish Times,* 1 July 1912.
67. *The Times,* 25 June 1912.
68. *The Irish Times,* 9 February 1946.
69. Mitchell, ' James Robert White'.
70. Alan White, email to author, 28 December 2007.
71. KE, 147–54. White letter to Pat English, 23 August 1943.
72. KE, 542. Letter from Tony White to Linda Simpson, 25 January 1992.
73. KE,145–6. Letter from Noreen White, *née* Shanahan, to Pat Napier, 25 February 1946.

Bibliography

Archives
National Library of Ireland (NLI)
>*Roger Casement Papers.* MS 13088.
>*Casement Green Letters.* MS10464.
>*Thomas Johnson Papers.* MS 17237–8.
>*William O'Brien Papers.* MS155673.

National Library of Wales
>*George M.Ll. Davies Collection,* No.169.

Public Record Office Northern Ireland (PRONI)
>*Reference NCCL, Special Powers Act. Report of a Commission of 1936 Inquiry. p.35.*

MS in Private Collections
>Jonathan Cape Archives, London and Reading.
>Katy English Collection, Cushendun, Co. Antrim.
>Dr Tony Redmond Collection, Broughshane, Co. Antrim.
>Winchester Public School Journals, 1895.

Government Publications
The Royal Commission on the Rebellion in Ireland 1916, Government White Paper. Ref. cd8311.

Newspapers
Belfast Morning Telegraph.
Connacht Tribune.
Cork Examiner.
Daily Mail.
Freeman's Journal.
Irish Independent.
The Irish Times.
London Gazette.
Longford Leader.
Manchester Guardian.

Nenagh Guardian.
Sunday Independent.
Southern Star.
Times (London).
The Nation.

Allen, Kieran, *The Politics of James Connolly* (London: Pluto Press, 1990).
Anderson, Benedict, *Imagined Communities* (London: Verso, 1991).
Anderson, William K, *James Connolly and the Irish Left* (Dublin: Irish Academic Press, 1994).
Armaline, William, 'Anarchist Pedagogy and Epistemology', Randall Amster, et al. (eds). *Contemporary Anarchist Studies: An Introductory Anthology of Anarchy in the Academy* (Abingdon: Routledge, 2009).
Bakunin, Mikhail, *The Basic Bakunin Writings: 1869–1871,* Trans. and ed. Robert M. Cutler (New York: Prometheus Books, 1992).
——. *Marxism, Freedom and the State.* Trans. K.J. Kenafick (London: Freedom Press, 1950).
Barclay, Harold, *Culture and Anarchism* (London: Freedom Press, 1997).
Beevor, Antony, *The Battle for Spain: The Spanish Civil War, 1936–1939* (London: Weidenfeld, 2006
Bence–Jones, Mark, *Twilight of the Ascendancy* (London: Constable, 1993).
Beresford Ellis, Peter (ed.), *James Connolly: Selected Writing* (Harmondsworth: Pelican, 1973).
Berkman, Alexander, *The ABC of Anarchism* (New York: Dover, 2005).
Bey, Hakim, *Immediatism: Essays by Hakim Bey* (Edinburgh: AK Press, 1994).
Bielenberg, Andy, 'Entrepreneurship, Power and Public Opinion in Ireland: The Career of William Martin Murphy'. *Chronicon* 2. 6.1–35 (1998). www.ucc.ie/chronicon/bielen.htm.
Bose, Sujit, *Essays on Anglo–Indian Literature* (New Delhi: Northern Books, 2004).
Boyd, Andrew, *Jack White: First Commander, Irish Citizen Army* (Oxford: Parchment, Donaldson Archives, 2001).
Butler, Sharon, Bert Bundy and Peggy Bundy, 'Fact and Fiction: George Egerton and Nellie Shaw', *Feminist Review* 30 (Autumn, 1988).
Call, Lewis, *Postmodern Anarchism* (Maryland: Lexington, 2002).
Campbell, Flann, *The Dissenting Voice* (Belfast: Blackstaff, 1991).
Carroll, Clare, and Patricia King (eds), *Ireland and Postcolonial Theory* (Cork: Cork University Press, 2003).
Clark, John P., *Max Stirner's Egoism* (London: Freedom Press, 1976).
Clausewitz, Carl von, *On War* (Oxford: Oxford University Press, 2008).
Cleary, Joe, *Outrageous Fortune: Capital and Culture in Modern Ireland* (Dublin: Field Day, 2007).
Cleary, Joe and Claire Connolly (eds), *The Cambridge Companion to Modern Irish Culture* (Cambridge: Cambridge University Press, 2004).
Collins, Peter (ed.), *Nationalism and Unionism: Conflict in Ireland, 1885–1921* (Belfast: Institute of Irish Studies, 1994).
Comerford, Richard Vincent, *Inventing the Nation: Ireland* (London: Hodder Arnold, 2003).
Connolly, Claire (ed.), *Theorizing Ireland* (Basingstoke: Palgrave, 2003).
Connolly, James, *Collected Works.* Vols. 1 and 2 (Dublin: New Books, 1988).
——. *Labour in Irish History.* Dublin: Irish Transport and General Workers Union, 1934.
——. *The Re–Conquest of Ireland* (Dublin: New Books, 1983).
Connolly, Michael, 'James Connolly, Socialist and Patriot', *Irish Quarterly Review* 41.163–4 (September–December, 1952).

Cruise O'Brien, Conor, *Ancestral Voices: Religion and Nationalism in Ireland* (Dublin: Poolbeg, 1994).
Dangerfield, George, *The Damnable Question: A Study in Anglo–Irish Relations* (London: Constable, 1977).
D'Arcy, Fergus A, 'Larkin and the Dublin Lock–out', Donal Nevin (ed.), *James Larkin, Lion of the Fold* (Dublin: Gill and Macmillan, 2006).
Doherty, Gabriel, and Dermot Keogh (eds), *1916: The Long Revolution* (Dublin: Mercier Press, 2007).
Doyle, A. Conan, *The Great Boer War* (London: Smith, Elder, 1900).
Dunphy, Richard, *The Making of Fianna Fáil Power in Ireland, 1923–1948* (Oxford: Clarendon Press, 1995).
Durand, Mortimer, *The Life of Sir George White*. 2 vols. (London: Wm. Blackwood and Sons, 1915).
Eagleton, Terry, *Heathcliff and the Great Hunger: Studies in Irish Culture* (London: Verso, 1996).
Ealham, Chris, *Class, Culture and Conflict in Barcelona, 1898–1937* (Abingdon: Routledge, 2005).
Edwards, Owen Dudley, *The Mind of an Activist* (Dublin: Gill and Macmillan, 1971).
Engels, Friedrich, *The Conditions of the Working Class in England*, Victor Kiernan (ed.), (London: Penguin, 1987).
English, Richard, *Armed Struggle: A History of the IRA* (London: Macmillan, 2003).
——. *Irish Freedom: The History of Nationalism in Ireland* (London: Macmillan, 2006).
Fanon, Franz, *The Wretched of the Earth* (Suffolk: Penguin, 1985).
Featherstone, Simon, *Postcolonial Culture* (Edinburgh: Edinburgh University Press, 2005).
Finnan, Joseph P, *John Redmond and Irish Unity 1912–1918* (Syracuse: Syracuse University Press, 2008).
Flannery, Eóin, and Angus Mitchell (eds), *Enemies of Empire* (Dublin: Four Courts Press, 2007).
Foster, Roy F., *Modern Ireland 1600–1972* (London: Penguin, 1989).
——. *W.B. Yeats: The Apprentice Mage* (Oxford: Oxford University Press, 1997).
Foucault, Michel, *Archaeology of Knowledge,* Trans. A.M. Sheridan Smith (London: Routledge, 2007).
——. *Madness and Civilization: A History of Insanity in the Age of Reason,* Trans, Richard Howard (London: Routledge, 1993).
——. *The Will to Power: The History of Sexuality,* vol.1. Trans, Robert Hurley (London: Penguin, 1978).
Fox, R.M, *History of the Irish Citizen Army* (Dublin: Duffy, 1943).
——. *Green Banners: The Story of the Irish Struggle* (London: Secker and Warburg, 1938).
——. *James Connolly: The Forerunner* (Tralee: The Kerryman, 1946).
Garvin, Tom, *Origins of Modern Irish Socialism: 1881–96* (Cork: Cork University Press, 1997).
Gibbons, Luke, *Transformations in Irish Culture* (Cork: Cork University Press, 1996).
Goldman, Emma, *Anarchism and Other Essays,* Introduction Richard Drinnon (New York: Dover, 1969).
Gordon, Uri, *Anarchy Alive: Anti–Authoritarian Politics from Practise to Theory* (London: Pluto, 2008).
Graeber, David, *Possibilities: Essays on Hierarchy, Rebellion, and Desire* (Edinburgh: AK Press, 2007).
Graham, Robert (ed.), *Anarchism: A Documentary History of Libertarian Ideas. Volume One: From Anarchy to Anarchism* (Montreal: Black Rose Books, 2005).
——, ed. *Anarchism: A Documentary History of Libertarian Ideas. Volume Two: The Emergence of The New Anarchism (1939–1977.* (Montreal: Black Rose Books, 2005).

Greaves, C. Desmond, *The Life and Times of James Connolly* (London: Lawrence and Wishart, 1961).
Greenway, Judy, 'No Place for Women? Anti–Utopianism and the Utopian Politics of the 1890s', *Geografiska Annaler, Series B, Human Geography* 84. 3/4. Special Issue: *The Dialectics of Utopia and Dystopia* (Blackwell, Swedish Society for Anthropology and Geography 2002).
Guérin, Daniel, *Anarchism: From Theory to Practice,* Trans. Mary Klopper (New York: Monthly Review Press, 1970).
Hart, Peter, *The IRA at War 1916–1923* (Oxford University Press, 2005).
Hassed, Mark (ed.), *The Prosperity Paradox: The Economic Wisdom of Henry George – Rediscovered* (Canterbury, Australia: Chatsworth, 2000).
Hobsbawm, Eric, *The Age of Empire: 1875–1914* (London: Abacus, 2002).
Hopkinson, Michael, *Green against Green: The Irish Civil War* (Dublin: Gill and Macmillan, 2004).
———. *The Irish War of Independence* (Dublin: Gill and Macmillan, 2004).
Howe, Stephen, *Ireland and Empire: Colonial Legacies in Irish History and Culture* (Oxford: Oxford University Press, 2005).
Howell, David, *A Lost Left: Three Studies in Socialism and Nationalism* (Manchester: Manchester University Press, 1986).
Inglis, Brian, *Roger Casement* (London: Hodder Stoughton, 1973).
Johnston, Andy, James Larragy and Edward McWilliams, *Connolly: A Marxist Analysis* (Dublin: Irish Workers Group, O'Brien Press, 1990).
Joll, James, *The Anarchists* (Cambridge, Massachusetts: Harvard University Press, 1980).
Jung, Carl G, *Memories, Dreams and Reflections* (London: Fontana, 1995).
Kelly, Fergus, *A Guide to Early Irish Law* (Dublin Institute for Advanced Studies, Dublin: Dundalgan Press, 2005).
Kelly, James, *Bonfires on the Hillsides* (Belfast: Fountain, 1995).
Kennedy, Dane, *Britain and Empire, 1880–1945* (London: Longman, 2002).
Kenny, Kevin (ed.) *Ireland and the British Empire* (The Oxford History of the British Empire, Companion Series, Oxford: Oxford University Press, 2004).
Keogh, Dermot, with Andrew McCarthy, *Twentieth–Century Ireland* (Dublin: Gill and Macmillan, 2005).
Kiberd, Declan, *Inventing Ireland* (London: Jonathan Cape, 1995).
Kinkead–Weekes, Mark, *D.H. Lawrence: Triumph to Exile 1912–1922* (The Cambridge Biography. Vol. 2. Cambridge: Cambridge University Press, 1996).
Kissane, Bill, *Explaining Irish Democracy.* (Dublin: University College Dublin Press, 2002).
Kolakowski, Leszek, *Main Currents of Marxism.* Trans. Paul S. Falla. (New York: Norton, 2005).
Kostick, Conor, *Revolution in Ireland: Popular Militancy 1917–1923* (Cork: Cork University Press, 2009).
Krause, David (ed.), *The Letters of Sean O'Casey* (London: Cassell, 1975).
Kropotkin, Peter, *Anarchism: A Collection of Revolutionary Writings*, Roger Baldwin (ed.), (New York: Dover, 2002).
———. *Mutual Aid: A Factor of Evolution* (U.S.A.: Forgotten Books, 2009).
Laffan, Michael, *The Resurrection of Ireland : The Sinn Féin Party, 1916–1923* (Cambridge: Cambridge University Press, 1999).
Laird, Heather, *Subversive Law in Ireland, 1879–1920* (Dublin: Four Courts Press, 2005).
Lane, Fintan, *The Origins of Modern Irish Socialism 1881–96* (Cork: Cork University Press, 1997).
Lane, Fintan, and Donal O'Driscoll (eds), *Politics and The Irish Working Class 1830–1945* (Basingstoke: Palgrave Macmillan, 2005).

Larkin, Emmet, *James Larkin: 1876–1947: Irish Labour Leader* (London: Routledge, 1965).
Lawrence, D.H., *Aaron's Rod*, Mara Kalnins (ed.), (Cambridge: Cambridge University Press, 1988).
Laybourn, Keith, *A History of British Trade Unionism* (Stroud: Sutton Publishing, 1997).
Lee, Joseph, *Ireland 1912–1985* (Cambridge: Cambridge University Press, 1989).
——. *The Modernisation of Irish Society: 1848–1918* (Dublin: Gill and Macmillan, 2008).
Lloyd, David, *Ireland after History* (Cork: Cork University Press, 1999).
——. *Irish Times: Temporalities of Modernity* (Dublin: Field Day, 2008).
Lyons, F.S.L., *Culture and Anarchy in Ireland: 1890–1930* (Oxford: Oxford University Press, 1979).
McBride, Ian (ed.), *History and Memory in Modern Ireland* (Cambridge: Cambridge University Press, 2001).
McCabe, Anton, 'Captain Jack White in Donegal', *Labour History News* 8 (Autumn 1992).
McCavitt, John. *The Flight of the Earls* (Dublin: Gill and Macmillan, 2005).
McCracken, Donal P., *MacBride's Brigade: Irish Commandos in the Anglo–Boer War* (Dublin: Four Courts Press, 1999).
McDonnell, Randall, *Cushendun in the Glens of Antrim* (Antrim: McDonnell, 1995).
McDonough, Terrence (ed.), *Was Ireland a Colony?* (Dublin: Irish Academic Press, 2005).
McDowell, R.B., *Alice Stopford Green: A Passionate Historian* (Dublin: Figgis, 1967).
McElligott, T.J. 'Jack White of Ballymena', *Ballymena Guardian,* 3 August 1989. http://irelandscw.com/docs–NewBiblio.htm.
McGarry, Fearghal, *Eoin O'Duffy: A Self–Made Hero* (Oxford: Oxford University Press, 2007).
——. *Irish Politics and the Spanish Civil War* (Cork: Cork University Press, 1999).
McKenna, Lambert, *The Social Teachings of James Connolly* (Dublin: Veritas, 1991).
McMinn, J.R.B., *Against the Tide* (Belfast: PRONI, 1985).
Mackey, Herbert O. (ed.), *The Crime against Europe: Writings and Poems of Roger Casement* (Dublin: Fallon, 1958).
Macmurray, John, *Reason and Emotion* (London: Faber and Faber, 1966).
MacSimóin, Alan, *Jack White, Irish Anarchist Who Organised Irish Citizens Army.* http://flag.blackened.net/ws/ws50_jack.html.
Malatesta, Errico, *At the Café: Conversations on Anarchism,* Trans. Paul Nursey–Bray (London: Freedom Press, 2005).
Manning, Mary, *Mount Venus* (Cambridge, Massachusetts: Houghton Mifflin, 1938).
Marreco, Anne, *The Rebel Countess: The Life and Times of Constance Markievicz* (Philadelphia: Chilton Books, 1962).
Marshall, Peter, *Demanding the Impossible: A History of Anarchism* (London: Fontana, 1993).
Marx, Karl, *Capital: A New Abridgement*, David McLellan (ed.), (Oxford: Oxford University Press, 2008).
Marx, Karl, and Friedrich Engels, *The Communist Manifesto* (Oxford: Oxford University Press, 1998).
Mauss, Marcel, *The Gift: The Form and Reason for Exchange in Archaic Societies.* Trans. W.D. Halls (London: Norton, 2000).
May, Todd, *The Political Philosophy of Poststructuralist Anarchism* (Philadelphia: Pennsylvania University Press, 1994).
Meltzer, Albert, *I Couldn't Paint Golden Angels* (Edinburgh: AK Press, 1996).
Mitchell, Angus, *Casement* (London: Haus Publishing, 2003).
Mitchell, Arthur, *Labour in Irish Politics 1890–1930: The Irish Labour Movement in an Age of Revolution* (New York: Barnes and Noble, 1974).

——. 'White, James Robert (1879–1946)', *Oxford Dictionary of National Biography (ODNB)*, (Oxford: Oxford University Press, 2004).
Morrissey, Thomas, *William Martin Murphy* (Dundalk: Historical Association of Ireland, Dundalgan Press, 1997).
Nevin, Donal, (ed.) *Between Comrades: James Connolly, Letters and Correspondence, 1889–1916* (Dublin: Gill and Macmillan, 2007).
—— *James Connolly: A Full Life* (Dublin: Gill and Macmillan, 2006).
——, (ed.) *James Larkin: Lion of the Fold* (Dublin: Gill and Macmillan, 2006).
Newman, Saul, *From Bakunin to Lacan: Anti–Authoritarianism and the Dislocation of Power* (Plymouth: Lexington, 2001).
O'Brien, Conor Cruise, *Ancestral Voices: Religion and Nationalism in Ireland* (Dublin: Poolbeg, 1994).
Ó Broin, Léon, *Dublin Castle and the 1916 Rising* (Dublin: Helicon, 1966).
Ó Cathasaigh, Aindrias, (ed.), *The Lost Writings of James Connolly*, (London: Pluto, 1997).
Ó Cathasaigh, P. [Sean O'Casey], *The Story of the Irish Citizen Army*, (Dublin: Talbot, 1971).
O'Connor, Emmet, *Syndicalism in Ireland 1917–1923* (Cork: Cork University Press, 1988).
——. *A Labour History of Ireland 1824–1960* (Dublin: Gill and Macmillan, 1992).
——. *James Larkin* (Cork: Cork University Press, 2002).
O'Connor, Gary, *Sean O Casey: A Life* (New York: Athenaeum, 1988).
O'Donnell, Ruán, (ed.), *The Impact of The 1916 Rising: Among the Nations* (Dublin: Irish Academic Press, 2008).
O'Grady, Standish James, *To the Leaders of Our Working People* (Dublin: University College Dublin Press, 2002).
O'Leary, Cornelius, and Patrick Maume, *Controversial Issues in Anglo–Irish Relations 1910–1921* (Dublin: Four Courts Press, 2004).
Ó Longaigh, Seamus, *Emergency Law in Independent Ireland* (Dublin: Four Courts Press, 2006).
O'Malley, Ernie, *On Another Man's Wound* (Dublin: Anvil Books, 1994).
O'Malley, Kate, *Ireland, India and Empire: Indo–Irish Radical Connections, 1919–1964* (Manchester: Manchester University Press, 2008).
Orwell, George, *Homage to Catalonia* (London: Penguin Classics, 2000).
Orwin, Donna Tussing, *The Cambridge Companion to Tolstoy* (Cambridge: Cambridge University Press, 2002).
Pakenham, Thomas, *The Boer War* (New York: Perennial, 2001).
Pearse, Padraic, *Collected Works of Padraic Pearse: Political Writings and Speeches.* (Dublin: Phoenix, n.d.).
Pouget, Emile, *Direct Action* (London: Kate Sharpley Library, 2003).
Protestant Protest: lámh dearg abú. Privately printed pamphlet on Ballymoney. n.p. 24 Oct. 1913.
Proudhon, Pierre–Joseph, *What Is Property?*, Donald R. Kelley and Bonnie G. Smith (eds), (Cambridge: Cambridge University Press, 2007).
Ransom, Bernard, *Connolly's Marxism* (London: Pluto Press, 1980).
Robbins, Frank, *Under the Starry Plough: Recollections of the Irish Citizen Army* (Dublin: Academy Press, 1977).
Russell, Bertrand, *Proposed Roads to Freedom: Socialism, Anarchism and Syndicalism* (St Petersburg, Florida: Red and Black, 2009).
Russell, George William, *Selections from the Contributions to the 'Irish Homestead' by G.W. Russell – AE*, Henry Summerfield (ed.), Vol. 2. Gerrards Cross: Colin Smythe, 1978.
Said, Edward, *Culture and Imperialism* (London: Vintage, 1994).

Shaw, Nellie, *Whiteway: A Colony on the Cotswolds* (London: Daniel, 1933).
Sorel, Georges, *Reflections on Violence*, Jeremy Jennings (ed.), (Cambridge: Cambridge University Press, Cambridge, 2002).
Synge, J.M., *The Aran Islands* (London: Penguin, 1992).
Thompson, E.P., *The Making of the English Working Class* (Harmondsworth: Pelican, 1968).
Thornton, A.P., *The Imperial Idea and Its Enemies* (London: Macmillan, 1959).
Tolstoy, Leo, *The Kingdom of God Is Within You* (New York: Dover, 2006).
Tribe, Keith, Review of *Finance Capital*, *The Economic Journal* 91.364 (December 1981).
Ward, Colin, *Anarchy in Action* (London: Freedom Press, 2001).
Weber, Max. *Essays in Sociology*, H.H. Gerth and C. Wright Mills (eds), (London: Routledge, 1997).
White, Jack, 'Anarchism – A Philosophy of Action', *Spain and the World*. 5 February 1937. http://struggle.ws/anarchists/jackwhite/texts/action.html.
———. 'The Church: Fascism's Ally, An Interpretation of Christianity', *Spain and The World*, 5 March 1937. http://struggle.ws/anarchists/jackwhite/texts/christian.html.
———. 'The Meaning of Anarchism'. *London Freedom Group*. 1937, Belfast:*Organise!*, 1998. http://flag.blackened.net/revolt/anarchists/jackwhite/texts/anarchism.html.
———. *Misfit:An Autobiography*, (London: Jonathan Cape, 1930).
———. *Misfit: A Revolutionary Life,* (Dublin: Livewire, 2005).
———. 'A Rebel in A Rebel in Barcelona'. http://www.katesharpleylibrary.net/tb2sdz.
———. 'A Ride in Andalusia', *Irish Review* 3.26 (April 1913).
———. *The Significance of Sinn Fein: Psychological, Political, and Economic.* Dublin: Martin Lester, 1919.
———. 'Where Casement would have stood To–day'. 1936. http://irelandscw.com/docs–NewBiblio.htm.
Woggan, Helga, 'Interpreting James Connolly 1916–23', Fintan Lane and Donal O'Driscoll (eds), *Politics and the Irish Working Class 1830–1945* (Basingstoke: Palgrave, 2005).
Woodcock, George, *Anarchism* (Ontario: Broadview Press, 2004).
Woodcock, George, 'Syndicalism Defined', *The Anarchist Reader,* George Woodcock (ed.), (Glasgow: Fontana, 1980).
Yeates, Padraig, *Lockout, Dublin 1913* (Dublin: Gill and Macmillan, 2000).
Young, Robert J.C., *Postcolonialism: An Historical Introduction* (Oxford: Blackwell, 2001).

Index

1798 Rebellion, the, 68, 70
1913 Lockout, the, 78, 80, 81–2, 104, 106, 107–8, 171, 173–4; placing of children in English homes, 89–93, 123
1918 General Election, 189, 196, 215
1922 Civil Authorities (Special Powers) Act, 229

Aaron's Rod (novel), 186–7
Acton, Lord, 5
ADC *(aide-de-camp)* to his father, 34
ADU (Irish Automobile Drivers and Mechanics' Union), 198
agricultural programs to avoid conscription, 184–5
ambulance duties in the Great War, 178–9
American syndicalism, 112
anarchism, 4–6, 53, 99, 111–12, 113, 114–15, 136, 140, 223
anarchists at the outbreak of war, 155
anarcho-syndicalism, 110, 114, 116
Andrews, J.M., 33
Anglo-Irish Treaty, the, 117
Armour, Rev. J.B., 61, 62–3, 64, 67, 73, 74
arms shipments to Howth and Larne, 160, 166
arrest and imprisonment by the Provisional Government, 212–13
arrest and imprisonment for possession of anti-army documents, 182–3
arrest outside Mountjoy jail, 202–3
article in the Confederacíon Nacional del Trabajao, 102–3
Ashbourne, Lord, 172
Asquith, H.H., 72, 170
ASU (Anarcho-Syndicalist Union), the, 114, 236
attempt to get Welsh coal miners to strike, 181–2
attitude to Catholic nationalism, 55, 98–9, 206–7, 210
attitude to war, 31–3; pacifism of, 163, 178, 180, 232, 238
attitude to work, 50
authority of Catholic clergy, 99
awarding of a DSO, 32

Bakunin, Mikhail, 111, 115
Ballymoney meeting, 59–64, 65–72, 73, 74
Baly, Joseph, 10
Bates, Sir Dawson, 218, 227, 229, 231–2
Battle of Johannesburg, the, 8–9
Battle of Paardeburg, the, 28–9, 163
Beaumont, Sean, 212
Belfast Volunteers, the, 66–7
belief that the Citizen Army drove the 1916 Rising, 191–2
Bennett, Louie, 185

Beresford, Admiral Charles, 36
Beresford, Frank, 237–8
Berkeley, George, 157
Birrell, Augustine, 145–6
Bloody Sunday, 140
'Bloody Sunday,' August 1913, 82, 94; police inquiry into, 131, 140
Bodenstown marches, 235
Boer War, the, 8–9, 22, 25–31, 163, 170
border and division of the country, the, 220–1
Boundary Commission, the, 220
Boyd, Andrew, 2
Brennan, John (aka Sydney Gifford Czira), 145
British army, size of the, 48
British interests in Ireland during the war, 176–7
Bucke, Richard, 40
Buller, General Sir Redvers, 31
Butcher, John G., MP, 145–6
Butt Bridge incident, 141–3, 147

cadetship at Sandhurst, 21–2, 23
call for strike to support prisoners on hunger strike, 202–4
Cameron, Sir Charles, 85, 92
capitalism, 191, 228; exploitation of workers' labour, 139, 146–7; need to overthrow, 102, 110, 116, 127, 128, 136, 195, 202
Carpenter, Edward, 40
Carson, Sir Edward, 77, 101, 152, 169–70; Unionist opposition to, 59, 60, 61–4, 66–7, 69, 70–1, 98, 129, 164
Casement, Sir Roger, 98–9, 119, 156–7, 158, 173, 179, 200–1; at the Ballymoney meeting, 60, 61–4, 65, 67–9, 72, 73, 74
Catholic Church, the, 57, 74, 77, 99; attitude to, 29, 46, 197, 206–7, 210, 233–4, 238, 239; involvement in placing of children in England, 90, 92, 93
Catholic teaching on mixed marriages, 46
CGT (Confederation Generale du Travail), the, 113
charges of possessing firearms and ammunition, 237–8
Charnwood, Lord, 73
Chart, David A., 87–8
childhood and education, 18–22
Christianity in Ireland, 9
Churchill, Winston, 28, 31, 59
Citizen Army, the, 3, 100–2, 113, 116–22, 147–8, 155–6; drilling and training of, 98, 124, 126, 130, 131–2, 133, 135, 137; and social class, 104, 153–4, 155 (see also Connolly, James)
CIVIC (Council for Investigation of Vatican Influence and Censorhsip), the, 238–9
Civic League, the, 100, 119, 120, 131, 133–4
Clancy, John Joseph, 233
class resentment in the Citizen Army, 153–4
class struggle and national struggle, 103–5, 113–14, 133, 146–7, 150, 154, 190, 193–4, 196, 201–2, 215, 240 (see also syndicalism)
co-operation between Catholics and Protestants, 58, 66–9, 70, 76–7
Cogswell, A.M., 51
colonial wrangling over Morocco, 34–5
communism, 52–3, 110, 207, 236–7; and capitalism, 201–2, 204; and Christianity, 217, 230
Conan Doyle, Sir Arthur, 25, 57
concern for social injustices, 78–9, 155–6, 223; inner city slums of Dublin, 85–8, 90 (see also 1913 Lockout, the)

condemns use of physical force, 214, 215
confinement to Broughshane during Second World War, 240
confinement to England as conscientious objector, 183–4
Connolly, James, 57, 66, 82, 100, 105–6, 121, 128–9, 155, 181; on need to form the Citizen Army, 101–2, 104; perception of as a thinker, 3, 108, 222–3; relationship and influence on White, 102–4, 106–7, 108, 109, 136–7, 186; on socialism and class struggle, 89, 95, 101–2; and syndicalism and anarchism, 112, 113–16, 136–7, 156
Connolly, Roddy, 207, 208, 224
Conradh na Gaeilge letter to the Citizen Army, 152–3
conscription, 156, 167, 176, 184, 185, 189, 203
cost of living in Dublin slums, 87–8
council of the Irish Citizen Army, 147–8
CPI (Communist Party of Ireland), the, 205, 208, 218, 222
Craig, Sir James, 209, 211
Croydon Park assembly and march, 127–8, 129, 137
Curragh Mutiny, the, 150–1

Dangerfield, George, 60, 117, 120
Davies, George M.Ll., 179–80, 182
de Rohan, Prince Raoul, 50
de Valera, Eamon, 190
Democratic Programme of Dail Eireann, 190; pamphlet in response to, 189, 190–6
departure from the army, 47–8
desire to stand for election, 185–6
Dillon, John, 75–6, 77, 173–4
disillusionment with Citizen Army, 146, 147

disillusionment with the National Volunteers, 165–6
DMP (Dublin Metropolitan Police), 82, 83–5; treatment of strikers and marchers, 94–5, 128, 133–4, 141–3, 145, 226–8
Doyle, Kevin, 2, 114
drilling of Citizen Army and National Volunteers, 124, 126, 130, 132, 133, 135, 137, 158–60, 165, 168
Duke, Henry E., 183, 184
Duke of Marlborough, the, 31
Dunraven, Lord, 61
Durand, Sir Mortimer, 11, 37

Easter 1916 Rising, the, 102, 103, 104, 108, 181–2, 191–2, 200
economic analysis of national and class struggle, 193–4 (*see also* class struggle and national struggle)
Edward VII, King, 34, 35, 36
efforts to prevent conscription, 156, 167, 176, 184–5, 189, 203
Elliott, Rowley, 230
Emerson, Ralph Waldo, 40
English, Katy, 2–3
English, Pat (née Napier), 240
entry into politics, 56–7, 58, 59–61
equivocation in the face of strikes and the Easter rising, 97–8
Ermitage and the Curate (book), 51
evolution of political ideas, 204–5, 207, 223, 235–7; formation of political philosophy, 94, 97–8; influence of Connolly, 59, 102; radicalisation of, 108, 138–9, 201, 208, 215, 222, 232
experiences in the Great War, 51–2, 178–9
explanation for aberrant behaviour, 39–40

Fanon, Frantz, 222
Fellowship of Reconciliation, the, 179–80
Finlay, Fr, SJ, 88–9
Fisher, Adm Jackie, 22
Free State, the, 210, 215, 216
French, Sir John, 28

Gaelic League, the, 152–3, 172
Gallacher, Willie, MP, 204
Geehan, Thomas, 227
gold mines of Doornkop, 25, 26
Goldman, Emma, 110
Gompers, Samuel, 112
Gonne, Maud, 91–2
Gordon Highlanders, the, 8, 24, 26–7, 29
Gough, Gen. Hubert, 238–9
government authority, 197–8
Gralton, Jimmy, 230
Gramsci, Antonio, 138
Green, Alice Stopford, 63, 64, 65, 66–7, 72
Griffith, Arthur, 117, 190
Gunawardena, Phillip Rupasangha, 232
Gurdjieff, G.I., 140
Gwynn, Stephen, 184

Hamilton, General Sir Ian, 28, 29, 169, 170
Heywood, 'Big' Bill, 128
hierarchical arms of the modern state, 138–9
hiring of a boat in Kingstown, 225–6
Hobsbawm, Eric, 103
Home Rule, 59, 61, 66, 67, 70–2, 73, 76, 87, 150, 169, 173, 177, 206 (*see also* Irish question, the)
honesty and certainty in biographical writings, 38–9
Horgan, J.J., 63
Horsley, Sir Victor, 49

'hunger march' in Belfast, 226–8

ideas for training the National Volunteers, 167–71
illness and death, 241–4
ILPTUC (Irish Labour party and Trade Union Congress), 199, 203, 222
imperialism, 25–6
Imperialism: A Study (book), 25–6
imprisonment, 182, 205, 227, 232
imprisonment for uttering sedition, 205
incident at Cushendall, June 1922, 208–9, 211
individual, the, and Catholicism and Protestantism, 78
inheritance of the family home, 218–20, 233
instability in the North, 160–1
invitation from East Tirconaill to stand for election, 214, 215, 217
involvement in the Boer War, 27–30
Irish Agricultural Organisation Society, the, 89, 126
Irish Independent, 96, 158, 183, 184, 189
Irish National Unemployed Movement, the, 226
Irish Protestant Home Rule Committee, the, 57
Irish question, the, 56, 57, 58–62, 69, 71–3, 98–9 (*see also* Home Rule)
Irish Revolutionary Workers Party, the, 226, 228, 230
Irish Times, The, 66, 75, 91, 101, 135, 153; coverage of strikes and riots, 82, 83–4, 142; portrayal of White, 106, 168, 242
Irish Volunteers, the, 28, 105, 119, 125, 130–1, 147, 152–3; involvement of White, 156–60, 161–2, 163–6, 167–70; offer by Redmond for role in the war, 174–6, 177; split, 133, 172, 174, 175; suspicions of by

labour movement and Citizen Army, 103–4, 146, 150, 153–4 (*see also* National Volunteers, the; Redmond, John)
Irish Workers Voice (newspaper), 225
ITGWU (Irish Transport and General Workers Union), the, 80, 85, 150
IWL (Irish Workers League), 222
IWW (Industrial Workers of the World), the, 114, 115

James Connolly Centuria, the, 236
Jameson Raid, the, 25, 28
Johnson, Thomas, 184–5, 198, 200, 203, 204, 223
Johnston, Denis, 188
Joint Industrial Councils (Whitley Councils), 194–5
Jonathan Cape Publishers, 188
Joyce, James, 230
Jung, C.G., 125

Katy English papers, the, 2–3
Kelly, James, 226
Kettle, Tom, 77, 78, 100
Kitchener, Lord, 28, 31, 32, 170
Kropokin, Pieter, 5
Kyle, Sam, 230, 231

Labour in Irish History (book), 113–14, 115, 201
Labour Party, the, 189–90, 192, 198, 199–200, 204, 223–4 (*see also* Connolly, James)
labour riots in Dublin, 82–4
Lambert, Hedworth, 36
land acts, the, 70
Lao Tse, 5
Larkin, James, 100, 107, 108, 123, 142, 144, 145, 146, 152; and the 1913 Lockout, 80, 81, 82, 90, 92–3; relationship with White, 101, 134–5

Larne gunrunning, the, 160, 166
Lassalle, Ferdinand, 115
Lawrence, D.H., 15, 186, 241
Lawrence, T.E., 51, 186, 241
legacy of estate, 243
Lenin, 177, 207
letter to Sir Ian Hamilton, 169–70, 174–5
letters in *Irish Independent* over trans-Liffey Art gallery scheme, 96–7
libel risk from character portrayals in novels, 188
Liberty Hall speech before founding of Citizen Army, 95–6
'liqueur sensation' as justification for aberrant behaviour, 39–40, 55–6
Lloyd George, David, 117, 190, 195

Mac Simóin, Alan, 235
MacLean, John, 183
MacNeill, Eoin, 172
Manchester Guardian, 57, 65, 160–1, 162–3, 189, 203, 223–4, 225, 226
Mann, Tom, 116, 151
Manning, Mary, 187
manoeuvres in Derry, 161–2
Markievicz, Casimir Dunin, 82–3
Markievicz, Constance, 131, 134, 142, 147, 152, 184
marriage, 46–7, 55, 56, 233–4; disapproval of marital intentions, 42–4, 45
Marx, Karl, 92, 111, 191, 192, 216 (*see also* class struggle and national struggle; social conditions needed for a revolution)
Marxist attitudes, 102, 103
Maude, Aylmer, 53
May, Todd, 3
McAlpine, Eamon, 207, 208
McElligott, T.J., 233, 240

media portrayal, 81, 106, 129, 168, 183, 184; on his death, 242, 243–4
Meltzer, Albert, 235–6, 237
Methuen, Lord, 26, 27
Misfit (autobiography), 2, 6, 10, 18, 39, 186
Moore, Col. Maurice, 157, 168, 189
mooting of a general strike, 222, 223
Mosley, Alexander, 43, 44, 45
Mount Venus (novel), 187–8
Murphy, William Martin, 80–1, 96, 121, 171
Murray, Sean, 218

Napier, Lady Gladys (née White), 13, 244
Nathan, Sir Matthew, 120
National University meeting, 74–8
National Volunteers, the, 106, 125, 130–1, 149, 150, 153, 156–60, 161–5, 175; organisational weaknesses of, 165–6, 168 (*see also* Irish Volunteers, the)
nationalist attitudes to Ulster Protestants, 76–8

Oath of Allegiance, the, 217
O'Brien, William, 116–17, 148, 149, 198, 205, 223
OBU (One Big Union) concept, 112, 128, 150
O'Casey, Sean, 104, 105, 123, 124–5, 154–5, 190–1; and the Citizen Army, 113, 147, 148, 189; suspicions of the Volunteers, 150, 152, 153
O'Connor, Emmet, 110–11
offer by Redmond of role for Volunteers in the War, 174–6, 177
O'Kelly, Sean T., 192
opposition to organised religion, 197–8 (*see also* Catholic Church, the)

organise assemblies of crowds, need to, 123–5

pamphlet in response to the 'Democratic Programme of Dail Eireann,' 189, 190–6
Parliamentarianism, 190–1, 195
Peace Committee, the, 100, 117, 119, 152
Pearse, Patrick, 191
perception of aristocrats and nobility, 35–7, 150–1
perception of English trade unionists, 90–1
perception of White as a politician, 206
pessimism and syndicalism, 222–3
placing of 1913 strikers' children in English homes, 89–93, 123
Plunkett, Horace, 126
police inquiry into 'Bloody Sunday,' 131, 140
police treatment of strikers and marchers, 94–5, 128, 133–4, 141–3, 145, 226–8
political analysis of national and class struggle, 190–3 (*see also* class struggle and national struggle)
political involvement, 73–4, 75
portrayal in novels, 186–8
poststructuralism, 6
poststructuralist anarchism, 140
power and corruption, 5–6
Powys, John Cowper, 1, 38, 186, 241
prison terms, 232
problem of 'Scotch Protestants and Celtic nationalists,' 192–3, 196
prohibition on entering Northern Ireland under the Civil (Special Powers) Authorities Act, 229–32
Protestant Home Rulers, 73
Proudhon, Pierre-Joseph, 115
Provisional Government and *habeas corpus* application, the, 212–13, 215

purpose of strikes, 132

qualities of drilling, 140

race and stereotyping, 210–11
reasons for the British to train the Volunteers, 172–3, 176
received wisdom, need to question, 6
recommendations on courses of action for Ulster, 207, 210, 220, 221
recruitment to the Citizen Army, 149
Redmond, John, 72, 165, 173–7 (*see also* Irish Volunteers, the; National Volunteers, the)
Redmondite faction of the Volunteers, 169, 174, 175
representation of Northern refugees, 217–18
Republican Congress, the, 235
request for employment in Local Defence Volunteer Section rejected, 239–40
request of employment from Spender, 213–14
requests British Army to train the Volunteers, 169–70, 172–3
resistance to authority, 2, 6–7, 8–9, 12, 18, 20–1, 24, 30–1, 38, 54–5, 214, 217, 232, 242–3
restructuring of the Citizen Army, 147–8
Roberts, Lord 'Bobs,' 176
Rotunda Rink meeting, 130–1
Royal Commission on the 1916 Rising, 121, 163
Russell, George, 51, 86, 89, 96–7, 100, 118, 126, 129
Russell, T.W., 73

Second World War, the, 238
sectarianism in Ulster, 69–70, 163–4
Sedlak, Francis, 53–4
selective stoppage by dockers and railwaymen in 1920, 198

sexual attitudes, 53
Shanahan, George, 233
Shaw, George Bernard, 57, 129
Shaw, Nellie, 53
Sheehy Skeffington, Francis, 121, 129, 140–1, 147–8, 178, 232
siging of the Treaty and the new Free State, 206–7
significance in Irish history, 3, 243–4
Significance of Sinn Féin: Psychological, Political and Economic, The (pamphlet), 189–96
Sinclair, Betty, 240
Sinn Féin, 103, 201, 204–5, 206; pamphlet on, 189–96
Slemish mountain, 9
social conditions needed for a revolution, 136–7, 140, 149–50
socialism and the Hegelian dialectic, 216
socialist need to overthrow capitalism, 193–5, 196, 202, 204, 207–8
socialist view of conditions required for an Irish rebellion, 177, 191, 197, 200–1, 222 (*see also* syndicalism)
socialist view of the international order after the war, 192
Sorel, George, 110, 118, 222, 223
Spanish Civil War, the, 24, 102, 236–7
Spanish Medical Aid Committee, the, 236
speech at the Memorial Hall, London, 56–7, 58
speech at Trinity College, Dublin, 116–17
Spender, William B., 209–10, 211, 212, 213, 218–19, 221–2
split in the Volunteers, 133, 172, 174, 175
St. Patrick, 9–10
Stalinist Russia, 236–7
strategic philosophy, 140
strike by the ADU, 198
strike picket at North Wall, November 1915, 120–1

suffragettes, the, 75–6, 133
Sunday Independent, 72
syndicalism, 60, 109–16, 132, 151, 199–200, 201, 222; of James Connolly, 108, 121, 124, 136–7, 200

tactical philosophy, 140
Thompson, E.P., 3, 25
Times, The, 71–3, 74, 85, 86–7, 90, 93, 141, 242
Tolstoy, Leo, 6, 49, 52, 53, 54, 106, 108, 197, 198
trade union strength, 203
trade unions, role of, 127 (*see also* syndicalism)
training strikers for the Citizen Army, 124
tramway strike, 94, 97
treatment of the Citizen Army by other nationalist organisations, 152–3
trial for Butt Bridge incident, 142–6
Trinity College Historical Society, 130

Ulster Farmers' and Labourers Association, 73
Ulster Liberals, 73
Ulster Protestantism and race, 192, 196, 210–11
Ulster Volunteer Force, the, 160–1
Ulster's Opportunity (pamphlet), 206–7, 216
unification and civil war, 220
uniforms, 148
Unionist opposition to Edward Carson, 59, 60, 61–4, 66–7, 70–1, 129, 164
Unionist opposition to Home Rule, 76–7
use of military experience to train Citizen Army, 98, 100, 118, 124, 126, 135
use of the Volunteers as a home defence unit, 167

Victoria, Queen, 17
Victoria Cross citation for Sir George White, 15–16
view of Protestantism and Catholicism, 58
vision for society, 215–17

Ward, Colin, 4
Watchword of Labour, The, 204–5
Watson, Edward, 120
Watts, Alan, 40
Webb, Sydney, 200
Wells, H.G., 51
Wheeler, Patricia, 233, 234
White, Alan (son), 22, 243
White, Derrick (son), 233, 235
White, Dolores (Dollie, née Mosley), 37, 39, 42–3, 44–7, 50, 52, 56, 65, 145, 157–8, 164, 179, 182, 235, 236
White, Field Marshall Sir George, 3, 10, 11, 13–17, 22–3, 34, 37, 42–4, 47–8, 55, 242; insulted by Larkin, 134, 137
White, Georgina (sister), 224
White, Jack: alienation from elite circles, 130, 179; anarchist ties, 1, 3–4, 6, 53–4, 60, 105–6, 108, 114, 116, 178, 236; through Spanish Civil War, 24, 102–3; birth and background, 1, 10–13, 17; conflicts in loyalties, 29, 33, 97–8, 159; desire for self-fulfilment, 54–6, 74; independence of thought, 128–9, 131, 171, 172–3; leaves the Citizen Army, 153–6; leaves the Volunteers, 177–8; oratorical skills, 57–8, 64, 70, 76, 77, 78, 132, 240; and pacifism, 98, 155–6, 163, 178, 180, 232, 238; perceptions of, 206, 243–4; relationship with Connolly, 106–7, 108, 109, 136–7, 186; relationship with Larkin,

133, 134–5; religious and spiritual convictions, 40–1, 44–5, 51, 58, 101, 179, 197–8, 216, 234–5, 239, 240, 243, 244; unworldiness, 38, 99, 125–6, 217

White, Lady Amy (mother), 23, 34, 37, 45–6, 142, 176, 182, 218–20, 224, 233

White, Noreen (née Shanahan), 12, 99, 233–5, 243–4

White, Rose (sister), 10–12, 14, 34, 37

White, Tony (son), 233, 243

Whiteway Colony, 52–4

Whitman, Walt, 40

Wickham, Sir Charles, 239

Wilde, Oscar, 5

William II, Kaiser, 35–6

Wilson, Alec, 69

Winchester school, 19–21

Wobblies, the (*see* IWW (Industrial Workers of the World), the)

Woodcock, George, 110, 111

Workers Party of Ireland, the, 224

writings and resources available, 2–3

Yeats, W.B., 81